HOUDINI'S
ESCAPES and MAGIC

PREPARED FROM HOUDINI'S PRIVATE NOTEBOOKS AND
MEMORANDA WITH THE ASSISTANCE OF BEATRICE HOUDINI,
WIDOW OF HOUDINI, AND BERNARD M. L. ERNST, PRESIDENT
OF THE PARENT ASSEMBLY OF THE SOCIETY OF
AMERICAN MAGICIANS

by Walter B. Gibson

Introduction by Milbourne Christopher

Funk & Wagnalls   NEW YORK

Manufactured in the United States of America

3   4   5   6   7   8   9   10

Library of Congress Cataloging in Publication Data

Gibson, Walter Brown, date.
  Houdini's escapes and magic.

  Reprint of the 1932 ed. published by Blue Ribbon Books, New York.
    CONTENTS: Houdini's escapes.—Houdini's magic.
    1. Houdini, Harry, 1874-1926. 2. Conjuring.
I. Gibson, Walter Brown, date. Houdini's magic. 1976. II. Title.
GV1547.G52 1976   793.8'092'4 [B]   75-30523
ISBN 0-308-10220-7
ISBN 0-308-10235-5 (pbk.)

INTRODUCTION
by Milbourne Christopher

A new generation, caught up in the biggest magic boom since the heyday of vaudeville, is enthralled by the incredible exploits of Houdini. Books, films, television and radio documentaries, and magazine and newspaper features have presented thrilling, if frequently fanciful, accounts of his feats. This dynamic showman, a critic noted, could get out of manacles quicker than most people get out of bed. No restraining device could hold him; Houdini released himself from welded cylinders, government jails, and submerged iron-banded boxes—without leaving a clue to his methods.

How did "the Elusive American" do it? Sir Arthur Conan Doyle thought he knew. The creator of Sherlock Holmes stated unequivocally that his friend was a powerful medium. How else could he free himself, wrists shackled four feet apart in a position that made it impossible for him to reach a duplicate key, or a lock pick? Conan Doyle also insisted there was no "normal way" for Houdini to penetrate a paper bag or a "sealed glass tank" without ripping the first or smashing the second.

Earlier, J. Hewat MacKenzie, president of the British College of Psychic Science, had been on a London stage when Houdini was locked in an airtight, water-filled container, then enclosed in a curtained cabinet. Moments before the drenched escapologist burst through the drapes, MacKenzie felt a draft. This, he stated, was positive proof that Houdini had dematerialized his body and oozed out.

An explanation for Houdini's escape from a challenge packing crate was advanced by a woman who saw him during a record-breaking nine-month run at Keith's Theatre in Boston. She said Mrs. Houdini, concealed in the cabinet that covered the box, freed him by extracting the nails with a magnet. Another spectator disagreed. In her opinion, the man who came forward to accept the applause was a double. Houdini, she continued, stayed in the crate until his assistants released him after the show.

So much for conjectures. Practical instructions for the box-escapes and the feats Conan Doyle and MacKenzie said were done with psychic aid are to be found in the pages that follow.

Houdini died at the age of fifty-two in Detroit on October 31, 1926. Later, his widow and his lawyer sent stacks of the notes he had made through the years to his friend, Walter B. Gibson. Houdini had written three manuals—*Handcuff Secrets*, *Magical Rope Ties and Escapes*, and *Paper Magic*; he had hoped to produce more.

It was not an easy task for Gibson, a facile writer and a clever conjurer, to prepare this material for publication. Houdini jotted down not only his own methods, but those of his rivals. Some descriptions were brief and required amplification, others were more extensive and sometimes repetitive. Occasionally a sketch would explain more than pages of text. It is fortunate this work is in print. Some of Houdini's notes, all of which Gibson returned, have since disappeared.

It will soon become apparent to the reader that, though Houdini was daring, he never took an uncalculated risk. He would not accept a challenge unless he was sure he could meet it. He was physically fit, an athlete, and a strong swimmer. Yet his assistants were poised to rescue him if he didn't surface on schedule from an underwater box. A dozen less careful performers have been drowned, or seriously injured, because they attempted this feat without sufficient knowledge, or without taking precautions.

Houdini experimented constantly, striving to make his escapes and his magic more effective. This sustained effort, plus his marvelous showmanship, enabled him to become a legend during his lifetime. Fifty years after his last performance, Houdini still is the world's most famous mystifier.

PREFACE

by Bernard M. L. Ernst

HAD Houdini lived he would have written this book. He planned to write a number of books other than those which were published during his lifetime. Among them was to be the first-hand story of his unusual and remarkable career and accomplishments. A volume on the lives of famous magicians was to follow. A work on plagiarism was contemplated and an authoritative exposure of the methods and devices of fraudulent mediums. A number of books on controversial subjects were also planned as well as a series of essays and treatises on magic and finally an encyclopedia of magic and kindred art.

He had gathered a mass of material for all of these contemplated publications and in some cases had prepared parts of his manuscript. In *M.U.M.*, the official journal of the Society of American Magicians of which he was the president, and elsewhere, he had published serially much of his material dealing with the lives of famous magicians; and he also had dictated many chapters of his autobiography. These, un

fortunately, were lost during his life, to his great re-
gret and discomfiture.

During the summer of 1926, only a few months
before his death he sent me a mass of material including rough notes, drawings, blue prints, and manuscripts, with the request that it be arranged, edited
and published in a series of books on magic and
escapes with which his name should be connected.
Much of the material in this book is taken from this
source.

More than a year before, while staying with Mrs.
Houdini at my home at Sea Cliff, L. I., he had begged
me to examine a trunkful of his material and write
one or more of the books which he was eager to publish and which he never found time to write himself.
He described what he had gathered together and insisted that many of his ideas and inventions had never
been thought of or made public. As late as October
9, 1926, the last day he was in New York, before his
death at Detroit, Mich., on October 31, 1926, he
again spoke to me at my home about the projected
books, and referred to additional material he had for
such use. After his death, Mrs. Beatrice Houdini, his
widow, knowing of his plans and familiar with his
collections, sent this additional material, a part of
which also appears in Mr. Gibson's work. Indeed
during Houdini's life Mr. Gibson had practically com-

pleted two volumes of a proposed series of books on "small magic" along lines projected by Houdini; but because of the latter's untimely death the publication of these works was abandoned.

Houdini made it plain that certain of his greatest and most distinctive escapes were never to be made public. Among these was his escape from the so-called Chinese Water Torture Cell, which he used in vaudeville for many years and which he referred to as his "upside down." Other methods and escapes now used by professional magicians are also withheld from publication in justice and fairness to conjurers generally. The contents of this book have been referred to the Committee on Exposures of the Society of American Magicians and to Hardeen, Houdini's brother, who is using many of Houdini's effects upon the stage, and deletions have been made as suggested by them. Magic exposed is deprived of mystery and ceases to be magic—at least for entertainment purposes and use in the theater. Thus the vanishing of an elephant from a cabinet on a full lighted stage as done by Houdini and many similar illusions of the professional performer are omitted here.

Many releases from restraints, however, at one time or another used by Houdini or devised by him, are published, it is believed, for the first time, and many of the creations of his ingenious mind now find their way into print as he intended. The reader will be amazed at the simplicity in some cases and at the complexity in others of the devices and methods employed or originated by the master of escapes, the "handcuff king," the man whose power of releasing himself has been described by Sir Arthur Conan Doyle and others as being super-normal and super-natural. In his book entitled *Spirit Intercourse*, J. Hewat McKenzie, president of the British College of Psychic Science, writes: "The force necessary to shoot a bolt within a lock is drawn from Houdini, the medium, but it must not be thought that this is the only means by which he can escape from his prison, for at times his body has been dematerialized and withdrawn." Houdini's reply was in part as follows: "I do not claim to free myself from the restraint of fetters and confinement, but positively state that I accomplish my purpose purely by physical, not psychical, means. My methods are perfectly natural, resting on natural laws of physics. I do not *dematerialize* or *materialize* anything: I simply control and manipulate material things in a manner perfectly well understood by myself, and thoroughly accountable for and equally understandable (if not duplicable) by any person to whom I may elect to divulge my secrets."

Some of the secrets of Houdini as communicated

to me and as put in the writings which he gave to me are found in the pages which follow. Many of his effects were so hazardous and nerve-racking that no one, even if familiar with the *modus operandi,* would have the courage, physical ability, or temerity to attempt to duplicate them.

There has been only one Houdini and he is gone.

CONTENTS OF BOOK ONE

CONTENTS

CONTENTS

PART FIVE. UNDER-WATER ESCAPES

PART SIX. TRUNKS—BARRELS—COFFINS

PART SEVEN. MISCELLANEOUS ESCAPES

PART EIGHT. SPECTACULAR MYSTERIES AND ESCAPES

HOUDINI'S ESCAPES

PART ONE.

INTRODUCTORY

THIS section tells of Houdini's notes—their purpose and their extent—and surveys the material that was used for this book. It also gives certain general information concerning escapes, with brief references to Houdini's writings on the subject.

HOUDINI'S NOTES

THE notes left by Houdini form a remarkable collection of material on methods of escape, magical tricks and illusions, and spiritualistic effects. Of these, the methods of escape constitute a large and interesting portion. Houdini was famous as a magician and as an exposer of fraudulent spiritualistic phenomena, but it is an undeniable fact that he gained his great reputation through his sensational escape tricks, which he performed during the early years of the present century. Millions of people remember Houdini as the man who "could get out of anything," and public interest finds a natural center in this particular branch of his work.

The notes which Houdini left are of great variety. Some of his most important escapes are not covered by them. The reason is that these notes were intended primarily for his own reference. Methods that were already built or in operation did not require written descriptions; in fact, Houdini made it a practice not to set them down in writing. The system he employed—so far as his note-making had a system—was to put down any idea that occurred to him as suitable for an escape. In some of these notations he offered no solution whatever; in others, he gave a rough idea of how the escape might be accomplished. Some ended at this point; on other escapes, he made additional notes, or new notes which gave more definite ideas of working methods. Occasionally he mentioned when and where he had employed the escape in the manner described; with others, there is no definite evidence that he actually used the escape or that it proved entirely practicable as explained.

The best of Houdini's notes were found in a loose-leaf book. Records of the methods were typewritten and illustrated with pen or pencil sketches. Other notes were typewritten on separate sheets of paper, some written in ink in longhand, and others penciled on steamship and hotel paper. Houdini was an active enthusiast; whenever he heard of or saw a new form of restraint, his mind began to work on it, and he made his notes accordingly. Some of his notes are ideas; others are plans; others are finished effects. All of them, in the final analysis, are Houdini's methods. In the present volume, the plan has been to adhere as closely as possible to the notes themselves, supplying certain statements that are obviously to be understood, and endeavoring to make plain Houdini's methods from the information that he himself supplied. Elaborate working diagrams are not included, for they did not appear in the explanations, which should not be misrepresented. The "revelations" that have been made by certain writers who have advanced questionable claims to knowledge of Houdini's secrets are notoriously inaccurate and are not in accord with his actual notes.

It should be remembered that there is a vast difference between the description of a trick or an escape and its actual presentation. Properly exhibited on the stage, a very simple device becomes a seeming miracle. The artfulness of any deception lies in introducing simplicity where people look for complexity, and this is evident in many of Houdini's methods. Some of the escapes included in the notes are the outgrowth of suggestions given to Houdini; others are improvements or additions to older methods. These are presented in this book.

There are definite indications that Houdini intended to publish his notes, or a considerable portion of them. One trick carries, instead of an explanation, the statement that he did not wish the secret to become known. A few of the tricks were typed ready for publication, but there is very little evidence of any definite arrangement. The chief difficulty encountered in the legible notes consists in references to other methods that are missing from the records, or that were never set down. When two escapes depended upon a similar mechanical device, Houdini has said that the one works like the other; but without a description of the first escape, the second is incomplete.

Had Houdini undertaken the writing of a book from this available material, he would necessarily have prepared preliminary chapters dealing with escape methods, following these with the secrets in the notes, clearing up obscure points, and adding further material from memory. Remarks of a preliminary nature were lacking, but this material has been supplied as a résumé of Houdini's little books on *Handcuff Secrets* and *Rope Ties and Escapes* and from other sources. The actual notes cover all types of escapes and give an excellent insight into working methods employed by Houdini. Further material that he may have intended to publish cannot, of course, be supplied.

Only those escapes of which some explanation is given are included. Some of them are not in the final state of development that Houdini would have demanded prior to presenting them in public. But in each instance, the fundamental principle of operation is described; and it was upon such fundamental principles that Houdini based all his finished escapes.

HOUDINI'S METHODS

D ESPITE the fact that a prominent spiritualist once declared that Houdini was a medium who made his escapes by dematerializing himself and then resuming his material form, the average person is aware that Houdini was a normal individual who accomplished his escapes by physical methods. There are, however, two popular misconceptions regarding Houdini: one that he was a veritable contortionist who could slip his hands through the tightest handcuffs and accomplish acts that seemed physically impossible; the other that he relied entirely upon mysterious, phenomenal secrets that were almost beyond human understanding, and that these secrets died with him. As a matter of fact, Houdini did possess great physical strength and agility that enabled him to accomplish escapes impossible or too difficult for the great majority of people. He also had secret methods which he kept to himself and of which he left no trace. But both of these were merely adjuncts to his work.

The greatest factor in Houdini's success was his showmanship. He knew how to present his escapes so that they were both amazing and spectacular; and with his ability as a showman he also possessed a thorough knowledge of every form or type of escape. He was familiar with every type of lock and every make of handcuff. He was constantly experimenting and inventing new tools and appliances. His natural ingenuity and his long experience gave him full confidence in his ability to meet any challenge or to attempt any form of escape. Houdini could employ a regular escape, using a method well known among escape artists, and present it with the same effectiveness that marked the other items of his program. On the contrary, there were escapes in Houdini's repertoire that could not have been successfully accomplished by his imitators even if he had given them the instructions.

Furthermore, if both Houdini and another performer had presented a similar escape under similar conditions, the average audience would have received Houdini's work with much more enthusiasm and wonderment than that accorded the other performer. This was because Houdini had the personality and the showmanship to exhibit a type of performance that offered numerous obstacles to effective presentation. Consider one of Houdini's challenge performances from the standpoint of a spectator. Attracted to the theater by large advertisements, the spectator watched a committee bind Houdini or secure him in some form of restraint. Then, while the orchestra played, the audience waited during a period that might vary from ten minutes to an hour, while Houdini was out of sight in his cabinet. At the conclusion of this period, Houdini made his appearance, free.

The spectator came to see Houdini make a sensational escape; he saw him bound; he saw him free; he did not see the actual escape. Yet he was highly pleased with the performance! Why? Because Houdini was a showman to the nth power. His greatest secret was his own showmanship. He possessed the ability to rouse the interest of his audiences to such a pitch that it would not decrease while he was out of sight. No one left the theater during his prolonged escapes. People were held there by an irresistible desire to await Houdini's accomplishment of his task.

To Houdini belongs the credit of bringing the escape act into popularity and using it to build up a lasting fame. There was only one Houdini, and there will never be another. He was a genius who could apply all his effort to practical purposes, and who relied on research and hard work as much as on inspiration. There were other performers who sought fame as escape artists, and some of them used methods in certain escapes that were similar to those employed by Houdini. But their knowledge was superficial when compared to his, and most of them made the mistake of imitating his work. The escape act is recognized as a type of magic or mystery that is dependent on certain useful and fundamental principles. Houdini was the originator of many new methods; some became known to the profession; others were copied very closely. Houdini was not radical in his work; it is evident from his notes that he relied on accepted methods, but increased their effectiveness by improving or disguising them. He possessed the three qualities essential to a great mystifier: inventive genius, mechanical ability, and showmanship.

The very difficulty that Houdini so splendidly overcame in the presentation of his work, namely, the holding of interest while he was out of sight of the audience, served him well in the protection of his methods and secrets. When a trick or an illusion is performed in full view, it is seen through all stages of its operation. An escape from a device concealed in a cabinet is not seen during its most important stage. Therefore it may perplex the best-trained observer, who can only attempt to invent a way in which the trick could be done, and trust to luck that he has found the method actually used.

Houdini had a very practical mind. His notes show

that in devising escapes he frequently chose the simplest and most direct way to obtain the results he desired, then depended on his showmanship and his ability as a performer to make the escape effective. He constantly made improvements; his ideas were limitless, and he was never satisfied with an escape until he knew that it could be done effectively. The brief summaries of escape work that follow this introduction may therefore be regarded as a partial explanation of Houdini's methods. It may be said that Houdini made use of these principles whenever necessary, but discarded them when he invented newer or better methods. For Houdini was an escape artist extraordinary, a master in his chosen field, and the fact that his work so completely mystified the public stands as a proof of his remarkable capabilities.

THE ESCAPE ACT

Houdini set the standard for the escape act; his work received great popular acclamation, and he surpassed all rivals in that field. His escapes were of various types, and they come under two distinct groups: challenges and straight escapes. In the former, Houdini allowed his challengers to bring their own appliances and lock him in; in the latter, he was confined in specially built apparatus of his own construction, subject to thorough examination by a committee from the audience.

The advantage of challenges lay in the fact that they offered opportunities for advertising and also proved a special attraction that led to capacity audiences. Their disadvantage lay in the fact that they were not routine work, and therefore presented problems that must be solved quickly. There was also the element of uncertainty in a new challenge, and for this reason Houdini preferred challenges that had been used before and that had proven effective and interesting to the audiences that witnessed them.

New challenges sometimes came unexpectedly. The old ones were usually arranged in whatever city Houdini was playing. A local concern supplied a packing box, a brewery supplied a barrel, or other devices were employed. All such challenges were bona fide, the stipulations being that the apparatus should be built a few days in advance, and that certain specifications as to size and construction be followed.

In straight escape work, Houdini used contrivances that were very convincingly built, and gave every one a good opportunity to satisfy himself that the apparatus was strong and secure. With his own escapes, Houdini could present a regular act that would, except in unexpected circumstances, run through on a fairly regular schedule. In handcuff escapes, challenges were accepted; but in dealing with the usual handcuffs, these performances were very close to routine work. In most of his escapes, Houdini used a cabinet, executing the escape out of sight. In others, such as the straitjacket escape, he performed the feat in full view of the audience. This type of work was desirable and practical whenever the escape depended entirely on effort and strenuous exertion. Where mechanical means were employed, the cabinet was usually essential in order to protect the secret.

In escaping from contrivances built by challengers,

Houdini required tools with which to work his way out. These are mentioned in his notes; the means of their concealment is not always explained. It was not a difficult matter for him to hide the required tools on his person, especially as very few were required for most of the escapes. Inasmuch as the possession of tools would afford no explanation of the average escape, it was an easy matter for him to avoid a thorough search by committee-men. In some cases, however, bulky implements were required; and in such instances special precautions must have been used to conceal the appliances. Some of the large escapes explained in Houdini's notes were designed to operate without the aid of any appliances; this was a desirable factor.

It is a known fact that Houdini was thoroughly searched on various occasions, and effected his escape from jails and prisons with no apparent means of obtaining any tools or keys to assist him. It is obvious that the more formidable the escape, the less interested is the committee in searching the performer for hidden appliances. Boxes, trunks, and other apparatus locked on the outside seem secure in themselves. In jail-breaking, where instruments seemed specially desirable, an escape would not have been effective without a thorough search. Whenever Houdini escaped from a prison cell, he emphasized the fact that he had no keys or lock-picking devices on his person.

The jail escape may be classed as a challenge. None of Houdini's notes refer to it. Included with the notes was a pamphlet published in England that covers the subject of jail-breaking but does not satisfactorily explain the majority of Houdini's spectacular escapes of this type. The presence of this pamphlet with the notes indicates that Houdini might have included prison escapes in the contemplated book; the absence of notes on the subject does not point to the contrary, as Houdini was so thoroughly familiar with this type of escape work that he could have supplied all necessary information from memory. Most of his celebrated prison escapes were performed early in his career; Houdini did not include them among his future plans, and it is noticeable that in the notebooks he avoided descriptions of secrets which did not have a definite bearing on contemplated escapes.

The methods of imitators who sought to perform the jail escape could not have survived the severe tests to which Houdini submitted. Any one can get out of a prison cell by "fixing" it with the police, and it is a known fact that self-styled "escape kings" have resorted to this practice. Houdini made bona fide escapes from prisons; and the police certificates that he received are permanent proof of that fact. He spared no effort to show the world that his escapes were genuine and that they were made in spite of every possible measure to prevent them.

Houdini sought new challenges, but in his later career he limited his work to those which had proven most effective. Similarly he looked for spectacular effects in his straight escape work and, during his final years, the only escape that he regularly performed was the Chinese Water Torture Cell, which was quick, spectacular, and effective.

HANDCUFF ESCAPES

H OUDINI explained the methods of escaping from handcuffs in his book entitled *Handcuff Secrets,* and certain of his introductory notes in that volume are of interest.

They are quoted here in part:

"In writing this book on handcuff tricks, and allied mysteries, I simply do so as a great many people imagine you must have exceptionally rare talent to become a handcuff king, but such is not the case. The primary lesson is, to learn to use both hands with equal facility, as—if I may use a proverbial expression—one hand washes the other, but in this case one hand releases the other. The method adopted by me to acquire this end was, when at table I practiced to use the left hand persistently, until I could use it almost as easily as the right.

"You will notice that some of these tricks are very simple—but remember it is not the trick that is to be considered, but the style and manner in which it is presented.

"I do not *deliberately say* that the following methods given are precisely the same as I have used on opening the handcuffs or in performing the various other sundry acts, but I speak with absolute confidence when I assert that these are the methods that can be, and have been, used to imitate my performances without much outlay and with little practice."

The third paragraph quoted supports the assumption that Houdini depended on presentation as much as method. The italics in the third paragraph carry the impression that Houdini actually used the methods he described in the book; and it is highly probable that he used other methods which he did not explain.

Regular handcuffs are made alike; that is, all of one pattern may be unlocked by the standard key. The performer insists that all handcuffs brought upon the stage be of a regulation pattern. He is provided with keys of all makes and is thus enabled to unlock the cuffs when in the cabinet. The locks of all handcuffs are not reachable when the hands are bound; therefore special keys have been designed, fitted with extension rods so that they can be manipulated by the hand. Others may be opened by holding the key in the teeth. Certain forms of regulation handcuffs may be opened without keys. Houdini stated that "you can open the majority of the old-time cuffs with a shoestring. By simply making a loop in the string, you can lasso the end of the screw in the lock and yank the bolt back, and so open the cuff in as clean a manner as if opened with the original key." He also explained that cuffs can be opened by striking them against a plate of lead fastened underneath the trousers at the knee or by striking them upon a block of metal.

The greatest problem in opening regulation cuffs is the concealment of the keys. They may be hidden in a bag strapped around the knee, or somewhere else on the performer's person. They may also be hidden in the cabinet where the performer retires to make his escape; details of the cabinet appear later in this book. Or they may be smuggled to the performer by an assistant, this last method requiring only the keys that are needed for the particular cuffs that have been brought up by the committee.

There are also various forms of trick handcuffs— that is, regular cuffs that have been faked in some ingenious manner. These can stand inspection; when locked on a person who does not know the secret, escape is impossible; but the performer can open such cuffs automatically. The escape artist who uses such handcuffs usually has them brought on the stage by a confederate, who hands them in with others brought by genuine committee-men.

Among various instruction sheets that were with

Houdini's notes is an ingenious idea for coping with strange handcuffs of which the performer is doubtful. The performer has keys of all descriptions, and in examining the challenger's handcuffs he or his assistant notes the key that unlocks the challenger's cuffs. This is "switched" for a key that resembles it; the performer thus gains possession of the genuine key and uses it, making another exchange after the escape, while the challenger is looking over the cuffs that the performer has opened.

The performer who attempts handcuff escapes must be familiar with all patterns of cuffs, must be provided with the necessary keys and implements, must hide these instruments effectively, and must be ready for any emergency. There are various artifices whereby difficult or doubtful cuffs may be avoided. A cuff that cannot be opened may be put on the wrists after several other handcuffs have been placed there; being high up on the forearm, it can be slipped over the wrists after the other cuffs are removed. It is readily seen that there are limitations according to the performer's knowledge and ability, and the information given here simply reveals a few of the fundamental methods.

Houdini's knowledge of this subject was tremendous. He studied all types of handcuffs and was so experienced in opening them that he could accept any challenge that was offered. His book on *Handcuff Escapes* contains enough useful information to enable a capable person to become a good escape artist, but it is only a partial exposé of Houdini's total knowledge of this subject.

Opening padlocks with special keys or picks is another phase of escape work that comes under the heading of handcuff escapes, and Houdini also revealed many essential methods of lock-picking. Houdini devised a split master key that was patented in England and that could open the different styles of regular handcuffs used in the British Isles. None of Houdini's imitators possessed more than a fraction of his knowledge of locks; hence they relied upon faked handcuffs and were limited in their work. They used methods similar to those employed by Houdini on certain forms of standard cuffs, but Houdini's knowledge was so much greater that his work really began where others' ended.

ROPE TIES

IN HIS book, *Magical Rope Ties and Escapes,* Houdini reveals the fundamental methods of this type of escape work. Apart from actual tricks with ropes, there are many effective ways of handling ropes so that escapes from them are less difficult. In contrast to handcuffs, which are rigid and are placed on a performer in one single, direct operation, ropes may be placed in many ways and tied with a multitude of knots. It is an old saying that "you can't beat a man at his own game," and this applies directly to rope ties. The man who is experienced in getting out of ropes—and Houdini was the master of this art—invariably "knows the ropes" better than the persons who seek to bind him.

The average person plays easily into the performer's hands. There are various positions in which a man may be tied that look very difficult, yet that are easy for purposes of release. Slack, slip-knots, pliable rope that is easily untied—all these are advantages to the performer. Even sailors, with their knowledge of intricate knots, are not ordinarily accustomed to tying persons; and the skillful performer can usually master any situation they create. Houdini could untie the most intricate knots with his hands, ordinary knots with his teeth, and some knots with his feet. He was always ready to accept any challenge in which ropes were involved, but there were occasions on which he encountered unexpected difficulties. Here he depended largely on his strength and endurance. He evidently worked on the theory that the release from any arrangement of ropes was merely a matter of time, and he always kept on until he was free.

Rope ties depend considerably on the limitations of the performer. The man of slight physical strength and small skill in untying knots can escape from some rope ties, but he must depend on favorable positions and certain types of knots. These factors were useful to Houdini also, and he never neglected them; but he was virtually without limitations in this work; his ability was so far above the average that he could attempt escapes that others would have found impossible. There is one other factor in rope ties that is of tremendous advantage to the escape artist; that is, ropes can be cut. With a knife available—especially when the performer is hidden in a cabinet—there is one way out of virtually every emergency.

A few paragraphs from Houdini's book on *Rope Ties* will prove illuminating. They refer to the Clothes Line Tie, in which the performer is bound with about sixty feet of sash cord.

"The whole secret lies in the fact that it is quite impossible to tie a man while in a standing position, with such a length of rope, so that he cannot squirm out of it with comparative ease, if the tying BEGINS AT ONE END OF THE ROPE and finishes at the other. . . .

"It is the experience of all who have used this tie, that the first few knots are carefully tied, but after a time it will be found that the rope is being used up very slowly, and they will begin winding it around the body and making very few knots. . . .

"If the committee . . . begin to make more knots than suits you, it will be well to swell the muscles, expand the chest, slightly hunch the shoulders, and hold the arm a little away from the sides. After a little practice you will find that such artifices will enable you to balk the most knowing ones. You should always wear a coat when submitting to this tie, as that will be found to be an added help in obtaining slack. . . .

"A sharp knife with a hook-shaped blade should be concealed somewhere on the person, as it may be found useful in case some of the first, carefully tied knots, prove troublesome. A short piece cut from the end of the rope will never be missed."

Certain qualities of rope are more readily adapted to escapes than others. Houdini mentions this both in his book on *Rope Ties* and in his notes. In all escapes it is preferable for the performer to supply his own rope; in accepting challenges the type of rope used can usually be specified by him.

Rope is rope, so far as the public is concerned, and it is so easily examined that suspicion is seldom attached to it.

The following statement on rope ties was among Houdini's notes:

"There are many types of rope ties and in all of them the secret of escape depends on the ability of the one being secured to gain the necessary slack for a starter. Just as with the straitjacket, it becomes necessary to gain the first slack. It may be done by 'misguiding' the tier or by main muscular strength of the tied. In either case, once secured, the escape can be effectually made."

HOUDINI'S CABINETS

IN THE great majority of his escapes, Houdini used a cabinet, and all other escape artists have invariably followed the same custom. The cabinet must not only be unsuspicious in appearance; it must stand an examination by committee members, who go through it before the escape takes place. Houdini's notes on special cabinets are in the form of reference, listing arrangements for a new scene cabinet; hence they do not give complete details; they show that a cabinet can, if desired, be well equipped with special appliances. In many of his regulation escapes, Houdini utilized an ordinary cabinet which was exactly what it appeared to be: a light framework, suitable for easy packing, with curtains hanging from horizontal rods. The more elaborate cabinets were not part of Houdini's regular act; they were ideas that he evidently considered of possible value in certain forms of escape work.

The notes on a *new scene cabinet* include the following:

"First, a small tube, or opening fitted into the side or back of the cabinet; this to allow an assistant to slide in any special key or device which might be required. Such a system would make it unnecessary to stock the cabinet with small appliances; these could be obtained from off-stage and slipped in after the inspection."

The notes mention "places to hide 'gags'; knife, ropes, cuffs, belt, plug 8 'fakes,' [1] files, extensions, etc." The suitable places for concealment were secret pockets or ornamental trimmings of the curtains, or the top of the cabinet. The horizontal bars at the top of the cabinet afforded an excellent hiding-place for keys. These bars are made of tubing; the upper portion, when cut away, is not visible, and the recess serves as a long container where articles are laid in a regular, orderly row. Where ropes were used, Houdini planned an arrangement to bring out a knife in any position, for the cutting of ropes and straps. This is not described in detail; probably it was fitted into one of the corner posts of the cabinet. A chair was sometimes used in the cabinet, the bottom of one leg fitted with a slot into which keys or fakes could be inserted so that the performer could work on handcuffs without using his hands. This chair is described

---

[1] The "plug 8 'fake'" is a special device required to open a type of handcuff known as the "plug 8," which is invulnerable to the usual keys.

among the notes. The chair also had possibilities as a place for concealing small articles. The cabinet was designed to hide numerous articles up to the size of saws. As its secret was never detected, it is certain that all the places of concealment were ingeniously devised.

Houdini's notes describe two more elaborate cabinets in which a person could be concealed. Such cabinets were designed for contemplated escapes in which it would be impossible for the performer to extricate himself. Houdini's imitators frequently got out of difficult situations by the crude expedient of having a man come up through a trap in the stage, thus entering the cabinet and working on the locks that were on the outside of the container; but his purpose was to avoid anything that would appear so obvious to the committee. He made trapdoors useless by spreading a canvas on the floor, or (in a method to be described) by having the cabinet mounted on a platform.

The simplest method was to have a person concealed in a curtain of the cabinet, all the sides of the cabinet being curtained, and two curtains drawn together at one corner. Houdini's notes mention this, and such a plan has practical effectiveness because of the innocent appearance of the cabinet. It would not do with a large committee on the stage, especially

FIG. 1

FIG. 2.

FIG. 3.

TOP—THE BUILT-UP CABINET
BOTTOM—THE PLATFORM CABINET

when a close examination of the cabinet was under way.

The *built-up cabinet*, described in the notes, is a cabinet to be built on the stage in the presence of a large committee, and yet to serve as a place in which to conceal an assistant. Inasmuch as this cabinet is of simple construction, it seems, more than any other, to preclude the possibility of a hidden person. The cabinet is large, and rather heavy when completed. Hence it is mounted on rollers, and pushed over the object in which the performer is confined. The cabinet is put together while the committee stands around it; people walk inside and out before the escape is begun. The vital point of this cabinet is a door that opens inward, the hinge being a few feet away from one corner. After the cabinet is finished, the performer invites several persons to enter it and to inspect the interior. As soon as they are in, he pulls the door shut and turns the lock. This amuses the audience as a bit of by-play and causes consternation among those in the cabinet. So the performer finally unlocks the door and pushes it inward; the committee members, glad that the prank is ended, come forth in a hurry.

Among the committee on the stage is a confederate. He is one of the group that enter the cabinet. As soon as the performer closes the door, the confederate, in the darkness, quietly takes his position in the extreme corner of the cabinet. When the door is pushed in, it swings toward the side wall and the man is hidden behind it. His absence is not noticed when the others come out. The open door apparently shows the cabinet still empty. It is left open until the performer is confined; then the cabinet is pushed over the container and an assistant in uniform closes the door. The confederate is then free to do the work. After the escape is finished the cabinet is wheeled back and left on the stage with the door still open. Regarding this type of cabinet the notes state:

"This is positively certain, but you must be sure to have a lot of men volunteer or else one may be missed. In making the cabinet door, have it hinge at least 14 inches from the side wall and thus allow a man ample room to hide."

This is probably the most subtle method ever devised for concealing a person in a cabinet. Its simplicity of operation makes it very effective. One or two extra confederates might prove of use in the cabinet to urge the crowd toward the door and thus keep the hidden man well away from the others. The natural tendency of every one is to get out from in back of the door, and leave the cabinet. The confederate stays there with a purpose.

The *platform cabinet* was a very ingenious method of concealment devised by Houdini. The cabinet consisted of four upright posts supporting a solid top, mounted on a wooden platform. The committee was invited to inspect the cabinet; and it would pass all examination. The assistant was concealed in the top, as in an illusion cabinet; but his hiding-place was rendered very effective, first by using a tall, wide cabinet so that the top had a thin appearance; second, by using a very small person who could fit into an unusually compact space. The height of the cabinet was also designed to prevent committee-men from in- specting the top. Their visual examination would prove satisfactory, and the top being unreachable, they would go no further. The only obstacle would be some agile committee member who might concen- trate the attention of the audience on the top by climb- ing up one of the metal rods that supported it. To overcome this in a subtle manner, the notes specify that the rods should be greased or slightly oiled. That would end any attempt of a climb the moment it was begun.

The ingenious method for bringing the assistant into the cabinet after the curtains were closed lay in the construction of the bottom part of the top. A long board served as a trap. This was hinged at one end, the other end being fastened so that the assist- ant could release it with his feet. There were cleats on the upper side of the trap to give it the effectiveness of a ladder. Before the cabinet was brought on the stage, the assistant took his place on the hanging ladder; it was swung up and fastened by an automatic catch. Going up in this position, the assistant required a minimum of space, reducing the necessary thickness of the top to inches. The inside of the top was stocked with tools and keys. As soon as the performer was in the device from which he was to escape and the cabinet was closed, the assistant let the trap swing down so that he could come into the cabinet. Any special tools that he required could be obtained by a trip up the ladder. On releasing the performer, the assistant returned to his hiding-place and was shut in again, with the assistance of the performer. This cabinet is remarkably ingenious, and indicates how Houdini applied all his knowledge of magical principles as possible and useful methods in his work.

The purpose of *assistant cabinets* is very definite. Houdini never intended to use them in ordinary escape work. His regulation cabinet, with its appliances and method for introducing required articles, made it unnecessary for him to carry articles on his person; in a regular type of escape such as the trunk or milk can, he had his own method of concealing necessary instruments. He planned the assistant cabinets for two reasons: one to counteract any unfair method in an open challenge, in which some person might attempt to lock him in cuffs that were "fixed." Such cuffs were ruled out in challenges, but with the assistant in the cabinet, they could be accepted, as the other man could work on them. The second purpose of the assistant cabinet was to make it possible to accept any challenge at any time, without having to devise a method of escape in short order. Houdini planned a milk can that would be entirely unprepared, made of seamless material, or of spun brass. He also considered a glass milk can in which the top could be firmly clamped and locked in place.

From his notes it is clear that he ignored no possible form of restraint. He frequently described a device before evolving a working method that would make a convincing escape. The assistant cabinets offered a plan whereby virtually any type of restraint or container could be conquered when no other solution was available. There is no indication that Houdini ever found it necessary to employ one of these cabinets; but his notes show that he regarded them as both practical and necessary in certain escapes, and because of this they hold an important place among his methods.

PART TWO.

ROPE TIES AND CHAIN RELEASES

HOUDINI's notes revealed certain escapes and challenges which were not included in his book on *Magical Rope Ties and Escapes.*

Among these are escapes that Houdini performed successfully, and they give an excellent idea of his ability to free himself from rope restraints.

Information on chain releases is included in this section.

HOUDINI'S TRICK ROPE

A SPECIAL type of rope was designed by Houdini, and is mentioned in his notes, with the statement "GREAT for tying-up purposes." Its usefulness is based on the fact that an ordinary piece of rope will generally pass inspection. The rope is specially made in two sections. One portion has a screw imbedded in the rope; the other section has a socket. When the two portions are fastened together the joining cannot be noticed if the proper type of rope is used, and the ends of the rope may be pulled with no fear of its coming apart. The rope breaks or unscrews by a simple half turn. When locked it may be handled by any one. The performer is tied with the rope around his wrists, with the joining directly above the wrists. By a simple twist he unlocks the rope and releases his hand. He can do this with the wrists alone, or with the aid of his teeth. He can also replace his hands in the rope afterward. This rope serves many useful purposes; it is good for "spiritualistic" tricks in which a quick release and return are necessary. It can also be used in connection with elaborate ties, where several ropes are involved, for the opening of this single rope will start the performer on the road to freedom.

THE SAILOR CHALLENGE

A N ESCAPE from an eight-foot plank to which he had been tied by a group of sailors was a typical Houdini challenge, and one that required strength and capability.

The notes read as follows:

"I am lashed to an eight-foot plank, with broomstick behind my knees and hands secured at each side.

"Long soft cord or rope is used for fastening the stick to the knees. I get into a sitting position, the stick is placed behind my knees. The rope is in the center of the stick, and is fastened to the knees; then both my hands are placed under the stick and tied firmly to it.

"I am now laid on the plank, which ought to be at least an inch and a quarter thick, and nearly eleven inches wide so that I can rest easily on my back.

"I am lashed to the plank with heavy rope starting under my arms, crossing over my body and coming back to my neck; the neck is fastened with the same rope, tying it off at the end of the board.

"My feet are now tied together with heavy rope and are tied off at the end of the board.

"There are two methods of release.

"One is to be able to pull the feet out. This can be done with a great deal of effort; if the rope is tied around both feet together it is almost impossible to secure my feet closely.

"When my feet are loose, I can get my mouth to the rope that holds my hands, and untie it with my teeth.

"Second method: After working awhile I can push the stick out from my hands; this will make me virtually loose.

"The articles used are an eight-foot plank; a strong broomstick; and three ropes: one for the hands and knees; one for the feet; and one for the body."

Houdini's description and explanation of this challenge illustrate his individual ability to work himself loose from all forms of ties. It is apparent that certain positions were to his advantage, and that when he gained them he could escape no matter how tightly the ropes were lashed and tied.

THE ROPE PILLORY

THIS escape is mentioned by Houdini as a good opening effect for a new routine of escapes. It is not a difficult release, but it is convincing and can be performed in full view of the audience. The apparatus used is a T-shaped device—a large post with arms projecting. Each arm holds a ring and each of the performer's wrists is tied to a ring with a double cord. The exact position of the rings is not quite clear in the description of the trick (dated January, 1905). It appears that the hands are tied alongside of the rings, but it is possible that they pass through the rings before the ropes are tied.

In either method the performer can make his escape, and the exact method of placing the hands is a matter for experiment or individual choice, depending somewhat on the size of the rings used. The secret lies in the fact that the rings are larger than the wrists, and the ropes therefore run from the wrists to the rings in opposite directions. This binds each wrist firmly, and the persons who do the tying can satisfy themselves that the hands cannot be slipped from the posts, for any attempt to move a wrist in one direction will tighten the opposite cord. This is the very effect that the performer endeavors to produce, and he emphasizes the fact as the strong feature of the tying.

But the rings enable the performer to slip the cords along the sides and as the cords come closer together on the ring, slack is gained, which enables the escapist to draw his hands free. If the hands are already through the rings, the position is as desired; if they are not through the rings when tied, they must be pushed through the rings in order to take advantage of the slack. The rings must be large enough to permit this, and the manner in which the wrists are tied depends entirely upon which method appears most effective. With the wrists against the rings and not through them, the rings can be set in either a vertical or a horizontal position. The escape is quick and fairly easy, but it has real effectiveness when used as an opening release as Houdini intended it.

THE SELF-TIE

THIS is an interesting item as it is the opposite of the usual escape trick. It is a rope tie of the type used by fraudulent mediums to prove that they have spirit aid; but in the notes it is listed merely as a trick. The performer enters his cabinet carrying a piece of sash cord about five feet in length. The cabinet is opened a few moments later and the performer is seated on a chair, his wrists and knees tied together so firmly with solid knots that the rope must be cut to release him. This is done with the aid of a duplicate rope, which is already tied. There is a loop at the center—either a single knot or a slip-knot, just large enough to encompass both legs above the knees. Above the slip-knot is a smaller loop just large enough for both wrists, and it is tied with solid knots, which are made tight with short wire nails buried in the rope. These knots may also be glued. As they are impossible of untying, no one will deny their genuineness.

In the cabinet the performer substitutes the original rope for the one that is already tied. The feet are put through the lower loop, with the slip-knot clear up to the solid knots. The large loop is drawn up to the knees; then the small loop is opened and the wrists are inserted. The whole rope is drawn well up above the knees, and becomes tighter the farther it goes. If it does not seem quite tight enough, the knees are moved slightly apart so that the solid knot comes in close contact with the wrists. All this work is accomplished very rapidly. Then the performer calls for the committee, and he is found tied.

This trick is not only interesting and effective in itself; it illustrates a rule that may work both ways. If an escape artist sees to it that his thighs are bound with a slip-knot or single-knot loop, and his wrists tied solidly in a loop above, he can work himself loose, by pushing the cords down over the knees. Outward pressure of the knees is helpful during the tying. This shows the advantage gained by the escape artist who is bound with ropes, whenever he can induce the committee to bind him in a way that appears secure but is really not so secure as it seems.

THE GALLOWS RESTRAINT

As DESCRIBED by Houdini, this is a very formidable restraint, from which release requires special manipulation. It appears from the notes that the first part is performed in the cabinet and the finish is done in full view, the curtains being withdrawn at the performer's call. The performer's feet and neck are incased in straps that have metal rings in them. He takes his position beneath a strong gallows and is secured as follows:

Chains are passed through the rings on the foot straps and are snapped to the posts of the gallows. The chains may be encircled about the feet, the leather straps preventing injury to the performer's ankles. A rope is wound three times about the performer's neck and the ends are secured to the gallows. Here again the strap is important, as it keeps the ropes from choking the performer. A rope is run through the ring in the neck strap and is secured to a ring in the floor. Thus the performer cannot move his head upward. Then the performer's arms are

45

folded and fastened with ropes that are tied in back of his body. Both wrists are against the performer's chest; the notes do not state whether or not straps are used on the wrists; but the ropes holding the arms are fastened at the wrists. There is no possibility of the performer's slipping his hands over his head, as the ropes on the neck would interfere.

This release is quite difficult. The first part of the escape requires a cutter that is close to both wrists. As a knife would be difficult to reach and to use, it is probable that the belt type of cutter is used: namely, a very short knife blade projecting from a belt strapped around the performer's chest. The cutter enables him to release his hands by working the ropes against the blade and cutting as few ropes as are necessary. With his hands free, the performer works on the ropes at the neck. He cannot reach the gallows, and he cannot bend down to release his feet. Therefore he works on the three loops.

As the ropes are not over-tight, because the performer must breathe, he chokes himself temporarily by drawing on one of the loops, thus tightening the other two. This gives sufficient slack to work the single loop over the head. This accomplished, the other loops can be slipped over singly. Freed from above, the performer finds the rest of the escape easy; he works on the rope holding his neck to the floor and releases it; the chains are removed by unsnapping them from the posts of the gallows. Houdini's notes state that the wrists are replaced so as to finish the escape in full view. This indicates that a cut rope must be replaced, or if straps are used on the wrists,

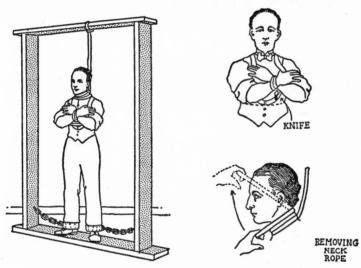

APPEARANCE OF THE GALLOWS RESTRAINT WITH IMPORTANT DETAILS OF THE ESCAPE

one or both are replaced, the straps being cut instead of the ropes.

When doing the final release in full view the performer makes himself appear as secure as possible, so that the spectators will not realize how much work has already been accomplished.

Houdini also provides for a lock on the neck strap.

This can be picked or unlocked; but if a committee-man provides a lock that is unworkable, the neck strap must be cut.

It is then replaced with a duplicate that is prepared so that it can be attached to the lock, to give the appearance of the original strap.

LADDERS AND ROPE CHALLENGE

THE Ladders and Rope was a challenge that Houdini accepted on several occasions, and among his notes is a description of the challenge with some instructions for the escape.

The challenge, which is presumably original with its author and therefore the cause of the escape's coming into Houdini's repertoire, reads as follows:

"Harlesden, N.W.,
"October 11th, 1910.
"HOUDINI (The Hippodrome, Willesden, N.W.)
"DEAR SIR,

"Will you submit yourself to a Test I have to propose as follows:—I will furnish three of my strongest

BUILDING WRECKING LADDERS

about 12 to 18 feet in height and laced together in the form of a Tripod; rope your feet or rather your ankles to an iron staple-ring secured to the floor; encircle your neck with rope, knotted, and tie the long ends securely to the top rungs of the ladders. Even with your hands free, you could not untie your feet or neck, but to make assurance doubly sure, I will secure an

IRON BAR OR STEEL TUBE

3 feet in length, behind your back, your elbows encircling same, bringing your hands in front where I will

TIE YOUR WRISTS

in such a position as to render them absolutely useless to you; and will lash different parts of your body to the ladder rungs so that you will be utterly unable to move in any direction whatsoever.

"If you accept, name your night, and I will come upon the Stage with a number of my Employees and test your abilities to the limit.

"You must make the attempt to escape in full view of the audience.

> "Yours, etc.
> "Signed—HENRY HARVEY
> "183 & 187, High Street,
> "Harlesden, N.W.
> "Wholesale and Retail Building Material Dealer."

Houdini accepted the challenge and made the escape under the conditions imposed, despite the best efforts of the building employees. The trick was so spectacular that he used it on other occasions.

Before we consider his notations on this particular challenge, it should be recalled that the general methods used in rope tie escapes were, of course, used by Houdini in this release. With so much tying, conditions were actually made easier for him; there were sure to be opportunities for obtaining slack.

In his book on *Rope Ties*, Houdini stated: "Strange as it may appear, I have found that the more spectacular the fastening to the eyes of the audience, the less difficult the escape really proves to be."

This applies to the Ladders and Rope Challenge, as the performer has opportunities to shift affairs to his advantage; but the escape presents complications because of the performer's inability to bend his body. Freeing the hands presents difficulties, and with them loose, it is not possible to reach the knots at the feet or above the head.

Houdini made special provision for the release of his feet. His notes read: "Three ladders are used; they are secured together and fastened to the stage so they will not slip. Next my feet are tied with thick rope; this prevents the knots from holding fast, and I can slip from them if required.

"The two ends of the rope are tied into a ring or

staple in the stage; I can eventually untie these with my toes after sliding off my shoes."

Houdini's ability to accomplish the feat last mentioned made it possible for him to dispose of any knots on the ring that kept him from slipping his legs free.

His instructions on the tying of the arms were also important:

"A gas piping forty inches in length is placed behind my back; my elbows encircle it. Sash cord is tied about one hand, then to the other; the pipe is secured to my elbows. Care must be taken to make all the ropes encircle the bar or they will deaden my arms and make me helpless.

"Have the wrists tied as low as possible, so they will not pain, whereas if they are tied as high as possible, it will not only make the escape harder, but will cause unbearable pain."

With this mode of tying, the slipping of the bar became an important part of the escape, as it gave slack. With freedom of body motion gained to some degree by the process of freeing the feet, the slipping of the bar could slowly be accomplished.

"The sash cord," stated Houdini, "is so long that one end is tied to the end of the bar and then to the ladder; another rope is taken and eventually two ropes (sash cord) are tying me from the bar to the ladders, back and front. My legs are tied around the knees and back and front lashed to the ladders. The long rope for the neck is encircled about my neck; tied, encircled twice or thrice and tied; then taken up and tied off away from my hands."

Houdini did not neglect measures for obtaining slack in the ropes that were about his neck. Ordinarily this part of the escape would depend upon freeing the feet so the body could be raised, then freeing the arms so the hands could work upward as far as necessary. But he states that the last time he tried the escape, he managed to get his head out first; then by taking off his shoes he untied the knots that held him to the floor, which allowed him to pull his feet free, and after that it was easy sailing.

Without question, this challenge presented unusual difficulties, and all of Houdini's skill and experience were required in the escape. This is evident from his final notation: "In a test like this, if done behind a curtain, it is best to have a knife to cut ropes if necessary." In such an emergency, it would be necessary to cut only one or two of the ropes. The knife would be concealed on the performer's person, under his belt, reachable with one hand. When depending on this method various short lengths of rope are desirable, so that cut ropes will not be noticed afterward. The performer can also hide any very short piece. The cutting is merely an aid to overcome the difficulties encountered at the start.

As Houdini performed the escape in full view, he never resorted to this expedient. The slipping of the rod from the elbows was the crux of the situation; by forcing it endways, the ropes gradually came free of it and slackened; hence a very formidable obstacle (from the committee's viewpoint) was actually to his advantage.

CHAIN RELEASES

C HAIN releases are a variety of handcuff escapes, and may be placed in the same category. Houdini's notes include some typewritten material which was evidently intended as part of a separate manuscript, possibly for his book on *Handcuff Escapes*. This describes methods used in chain escapes.

The *chain and lock* is a way of escaping from a chain used instead of handcuffs by police in Europe. The method used by most of the police is to lock the hands crosswise, and from this position it is possible to slip the chain. The performer presents one hand to be chained, and as soon as the chain has encircled the wrist, he lays the other hand on the crossing, and allows the second hand to be encircled also. The chain is then drawn tight, and the lock is attached to two links of the chain. This binds very tightly and appears secure, as the hands cannot reach the lock.

It would not be possible to slip the chain from this position, but it will be noticed that the crossing of the chain makes it form a figure 8 around the wrists. To make the escape, the hands are swung together, inward or outward, according to the position of the chain. When the wrists are parallel, one on the other, the chain takes the shape of a circle, and considerable slack is gained—enough to slide one hand free, and then remove the chain from the other wrist. If the wrists are moistened the slipping is accomplished more easily. It should be noted that bringing the hands together in one direction increases the twist and tightens the chain; in the other direction, the result is the gaining of the required slack.

In the *chain challenge act*, the performer invites persons to come on the stage and chain him, bringing their own locks and using chains that are unprepared and that may be examined.

The committee-men are supplied with chains of various lengths; the performer is bound and the chains are locked, with the padlocks out of reach. Then the performer is placed in his cabinet. He escapes from the chains and brings them out with the locks for a final examination. One method of handling such chains is to slip them. Houdini states that he used a strong pair of hooks, attached to a rope fastened to his foot. After securing the hooks to the chains, it was possible to slip them by foot pressure. He describes this process as being painful at first. Its practicability and usefulness are increased if the performer has managed to obtain an amount of slack while being chained. Chains that could not otherwise be slipped yield when this method is employed. Where chains cannot be slipped, cutting is the method used. This is done with a pair of pliers or wire-cutters that have been concealed in the cabinet.

Since the locks are not in a position where they can be reached, the performer must cut the chain at the most accessible link; when the work has been accomplished, the chain will come free. Obviously the broken chain cannot be exhibited; so the performer removes the locks by picking them, and substitutes a duplicate chain which has been concealed in the cabinet. This is why he must use his own chain; if a committee-man brings a chain it must either be ignored or placed in some position from which the performer can slip it. But the conditions call for the challengers to bring their own locks, as the chains are shown to be without preparation. Therefore the performer seeks to create the impression that he escapes by working on the locks, no matter how inaccessible they may be.

Instead of placing a lock on a duplicate chain and bringing the chain out in its original condition, the performer prefers to appear with the locks open, for that diverts attention from the real secret of the trick —namely, the chain. So whether the chain is slipped or cut it is policy to pick the lock and show it open, thus apparently proving that the lock was vulnerable despite its inaccessible position. This introduces the obstacle of the committee-man who brings a special lock that is difficult to pick or that the performer cannot pick. The performer, to be consistent, must create the impression that he actually opened this particular lock. He accomplishes this very ingeniously. In the committee is a confederate who is provided with a lock that appears very formidable, but that can be easily opened by the performer either with or without a pick.

After the performer is chained and the chain is fastened with the unpickable lock, the confederate steps forward with *his* lock and insists that it also be used to make the chain absolutely secure. The performer finally complies with this request; the second lock is attached to the chain, and the escape artist goes into his cabinet. Having cut the original chain, he also cuts the links holding the lock that he cannot pick, thus freeing it from the old chain. He then opens the confederate's lock, links it in the closed lock, and brings both locks out in this condition.

These padlocks are handed to the genuine committee-man, and he must use his key to free his lock from the other. The audience observes this. Inasmuch as each lock held the chain separately at the beginning of the act, the inference is that the performer somehow managed to open both of them, otherwise he could not have escaped; and that he linked them together when he brought them out. As the confederate's lock is more imposing, the bona fide committeeman is quite satisfied that his lock was opened, and he wonders how the performer managed to do it. With two locks on the chain, the performer states that the escape will require more time than with one; this allows for the extra time consumed in cutting the genuine lock from the links that hold it.

The *dog chain escape* is very quick, and the method is extremely simple. Houdini considered it as a possible effect to be used in his new show opening in August, 1905. It appears among notes dated Woolwich, England, January 4, 1905. A long dog chain is examined and wrapped around the performer, binding him securely; then the end links of the chain are padlocked. In full view of the audience, the performer works on the chain and finally frees himself from it.

To the audience it appears that he manages to shake himself free from the chain in some remarkable fashion, and the merit of the trick lies in the fact that it is a quick preliminary to the regular items of the program. The chain is actually faked. One of the end links is insecurely fastened. Houdini's notes state that the chain is examined, but do not specify whether the extra link will pass a quick inspection or whether it is secretly added to the chain after a thorough examination. Either plan is workable. By exerting muscular expansion the performer breaks the faked link, and as the padlock is attached to it, the chain spreads and falls to the floor in a mass. The break in it is not noticeable. Houdini planned to experiment with one chain and with two chains (both faked) to see which mode of presentation was more effective. Chain escapes, as Houdini remarks in his notes, must be worked smartly in order to be convincing.

THE ESCAPE BOARD

THIS is a highly effective escape which is accomplished by a very simple mechanical device. Houdini describes it briefly in a note dated Detroit, January 18, 1918. The performer is tied to a large board which is constructed from about eighteen narrow boards, set vertically and held together by long cross-braces. There are holes between the narrow boards, placed so that the performer may be tied in a standing position, his wrists, neck, and ankles being secured by short ropes. He makes his escape from this difficult position. Houdini specified "match lining boards" and stated that by using the feet or unloosening a bolt, the match linings pull apart and thus permit the ropes to be pulled over the boards.

Elsewhere among the notes were finished drawings showing the construction of the board, but no detailed explanation accompanied them. The idea, however, is clear. The bottom holes are below the lower cross-brace; the upper holes, for neck and wrists, are above the upper brace. The trick lies in the upper cross-brace. This is ingeniously constructed and slides a short distance; from the diagrams the end appears to be within easy reach of the performer's hand. The action of loosening this cross-brace spreads the ver-

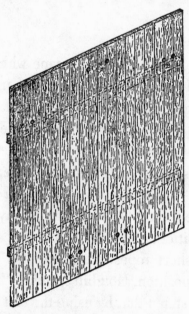

ORIGINAL ILLUSTRATION OF ESCAPE BOARD. B INDICATES THE UPPER CROSS-BRACE WHICH IS RELEASED TO SPREAD THE SECTIONS

tical boards, and the performer is able to push the ropes over the top, for the holes are so arranged that each rope goes around a single board. Once the hands and neck are released, the rest of the escape is easy, for the performer can reach down and unfasten his ankles, or can cut the lower ropes if necessary.

The escape board offers great possibilities for clever mechanical construction. Houdini (from his notes) evidently considered a board that would spread at both top and bottom, thus quickening the escape. With special bolts to hold the board so that it would stand close inspection by a committee, it would be quite practical to have the assistants turn the bolts while placing the board in the cabinet, thus reducing the performer's work to the mere action of spreading the boards. This was a method of release that Houdini employed in other escapes; hence it may be considered in this one.

PART THREE.

SPECIAL CHALLENGES

THIS section deals exclusively with escapes of the challenge type, in which genuine appliances were used, and frequently supplied by the challengers.

These are not all the challenges explained in Houdini's notes; the others are included in different sections of the book according to their classification.

THE STRAITJACKET ESCAPE

PERHAPS the greatest of all Houdini's challenges was the escape from a straitjacket. He performed this spectacular feat before thousands and thousands of people. In the later years of his career, when he did less escape work than before, he still retained the straitjacket, and demonstrated his ability to free himself from the formidable restraint.

The general method of the straitjacket escape is well known, especially as the feat is often performed in full view and the spectators can watch the performer struggle with it. The straitjacket is a device used to bind insane persons who are struggling for freedom, and who try to overcome it by force alone. A sane man, in attempting the escape, can use reason to advantage. In escaping from an ordinary straitjacket, the primary objective is to slip the arms over the head. Both arms are confined in sleeves that terminate in straps, fastened together or to the body of the jacket. If the sleeves are at all loose, the escapist can get his upper arm above his head and finally work himself into a position from which he can undo the buckles of the jacket. But the average performer avoids using a heavy jacket. The difficulty of the escape increases with the efficiency of the jacket, and many who are capable of escaping from some jackets will fail when placed in others.

Houdini, aided by his physical strength, and experienced in this escape, could free himself from regular straitjackets, which were strapped on him by asylum attendants, and in this escape he clearly demonstrated his superiority over those who imitated the feat after he had made it famous. In his most spectacular presentation of the straitjacket escape, Houdini allowed himself to be hung head downward from a building while he effected his release in mid-air. There are a few references to straitjackets in Houdini's notes, and it is quite evident that he considered the possibilities of special jackets for certain escapes. In challenges, regular jackets are usually encountered; but in escapes where the performer supplies his own jacket it is obvious that cleverly concealed preparation is possible, as in other escapes.

Hanging head downward, the sliding of the arms is facilitated rather than handicapped; but reaching all the straps and buckles is a difficult matter. It is claimed that Houdini used a straitjacket in which a hidden bar on the back released the buckles of the straps all together, so that by reaching his back he could free himself. There is good authority for this, but it is not mentioned in the notes. Houdini refers to two special jackets, one with extra long sleeves to help the sliding of the arms when doing the escape in full view. The other is a special release in the end of the sleeve, a strap that can be unhooked by the fingers or cut with a hidden blade. This is for use when the performer is concealed from view, especially when he is straitjacketed in a box or in cramped quarters. The release of the strap is effective, making the remainder of the escape an easy matter; well faked, this device will not be detected, for the straitjacket will stand a close examination, and a careful inspection of the inside end of a sleeve is not an easy matter. Houdini refers to this as the "Bonza" straitjacket in a notation made in Nottingham, on January 12, 1911.

In another note he gives an addition to a straitjacket escape. After the performer is bound in the jacket he is fastened more firmly with heavy sheeting laces so that he cannot move his arms sufficiently to make the escape. The note states that "it is essential to cut the sheeting lace before it can be removed"; hence the escape is made in the cabinet. A special cutter is attached to a post or some part of the cabinet, hidden so that it will not be observed. In the cabinet, the performer leans against the cutter and in this manner severs the laces. This enables him to continue with the escape in the ordinary way; after he is out, the performer can replace the cut laces with new ones. Houdini's note adds that this can be done with two prepared laces, but does not give the details of the arrangement. Prepared laces would eliminate the cutter.

The following description of the release from a regular straitjacket is Houdini's own; it is quoted from his book on *Handcuff Secrets:*

"It [the jacket] is made of strong brown canvas or sail cloth and has a deep leather collar and leather cuffs; these cuffs are sewn up at the ends, making a sort of bag into which each arm is placed; the seams are covered with leather bands, attached to which are leather straps and steel buckles which, when strapped upon a person, fit and buckle up in back. The sleeves of this jacket are made so long that when the arms of the wearer are placed in them and folded across the chest, the leather cuffs of the sleeves, to which are attached straps and buckles, meet at the back of the body, one overlapping the other. The opening of the straitjacket is at the back, where several straps and buckles are sewn which are fastened at the back.

"The first step necessary to free yourself is to place the elbow, which has the continuous hand *under* the opposite elbow, on some solid foundation and by sheer strength exert sufficient force at this elbow so as to force it gradually up towards the head, and by further persistent straining you can eventually force the head under the *lower arm*, which results in bringing both of the encased arms in front of the body.

"Once having freed your arms to such an extent as to get them in front of the body, you can now undo the buckles of the straps of the cuffs with your teeth, after which you open the buckles at the back with your hands, which are still encased in the canvas sleeves, and then you remove the straitjacket from your body."

THE BLANKET RESTRAINT

DURING the period that he specialized in escape work, Houdini was constantly endeavoring to devise some escape that would take the place of the straitjacket. He regarded variety in escapes as essential to his work, and every feat that proved spectacular made him desire another that would match it. The escape from a blanket of the type used in private asylums seemed suitable for this purpose. His notes on the subject are dated Hull, England, February 1, 1911, and he states: "This idea has been in my mind since Circus Busch, when the asylum attendant related to me about the wet sheet restraints, August or September, 1908." Like the straitjacket, the blanket required a partial freeing of an arm to continue the rest of the work; but it had a wonderful advantage in the fact that the performer's body was entirely out of view during the operation, and the audience's first knowledge that he was gaining success came when the entire apparatus was thrown free.

"This," state Houdini's original notes, "is a regular blanket, strapped around the body in such a manner that the head alone is uncovered.

"The hands are strapped to the sides with straps and buckles. This is done in such a manner that I can always get the hands or one hand free, and can then release the neck straps and struggle out.

"The body is strapped into the blanket, first rolled in, and the straps are fitted around the body: one about the neck, one over the shoulders, one over the hips, one over the knees, and one at the ankles.

"When the blanket is placed on the body, it fits way over the head, but after the neck strap is placed, this portion of the blanket is folded over and makes a sort of collar for the blanket.

"I can figure out a great finish for the escape. By turning over, I can kick the restraint way off, so I can make a quick get-up for a bow."

Following this preliminary outline of the escape, we read, in capital letters: "THIS CAN BE MADE A GREAT FINISHING OR OPENING TRICK AND IS WORTHY OF TRIAL. THE BEST THING I HAVE EVER THOUGHT OF TO TAKE THE PLACE OF THE STRAITJACKET."

The first detail that occurred to Houdini as presenting difficulties was the matter of releasing the feet. With a hand free, he could work on the buckles through the blanket, and thus attend to all the straps from the neck to the knees. But the escape would have a rather inglorious finish if he could not kick the blanket free, but would have to sit up and deliberately undo the final strap that bound him. To overcome this, Houdini planned a leather-like bottom for the device; this would make it impossible for his feet to be too tightly strapped to prevent escape, for he could gradually slip them free and withdraw them while working on the other straps. Then, with the final release of the neck-strap, he could gradually kick the entire restraint into the air, stripping it from the body and finally pushing it entirely free with a final kick.

Having thus brought the escape to a workable state, Houdini began to plan its actual presentation, in order to make the trick spectacular. The next day (February 2, 1911) he added these notes: "A novel arrangement would be to have the blanket swung between two jacks, so that I would be swinging whilst working. One jack would be at each side of the stage, like those the wire-walkers use, so that all that has to be done is to hook me up first by my head, then by my feet, and I can start in working. If essential, the blanket can be strapped by a ring at each side of the body, with chains leading down to the stage."

Considering the restraint in this form, Houdini made additional plans to make the release an absolute certainty. One was to have the entire apparatus made of leather, thus making it impossible to strap him too tightly, as in the case of the leather bottom for the feet. More important, however, was his alternate method for handling the wrist straps. These, of course, were the key to the entire escape. Hence his final arrangement calls for a special pocket in his clothing, to contain a knife and a duplicate wrist strap. This pocket, of course, is reachable with one hand. The straps proving too tight to slip either hand, the knife is used to cut one strap; from then on the escape proceeds in the usual way; the knife and the cut strap are pushed into the pocket and the duplicate strap is brought out, to be found by the committee after the escape.

The only point on which the notes on the blanket release are at all obscure is the position of the straps, whether they are inside the blanket or not. No diagram appears to show this; but an analysis of the working method indicates that the wrist straps are inside the blanket, binding the performer tightly at the start; then he is rolled in the blanket and all other straps are secured from the outside. Hence the ankle strap goes outside the leather bottom, while the neck strap is out of view because the upper end of the blanket is folded down over it. All operations on the wrist straps are entirely hidden; the others are unbuckled through the cloth, preferably on the side away from the audience. The neck strap is hidden during this operation; the ankle strap is slipped; thus the trick comes to a startling conclusion before the spectators are aware that it has reached an advanced stage.

Use of the leather bag suggested by Houdini makes the unbuckling a more difficult undertaking, but this is offset by slackness in the straps, which assists the performer in slipping from the restraint.

ESCAPE FROM A CRAZY CRIB

THE escape from a crazy crib is performed in full view of the audience; therefore it serves as a substitute for the straitjacket or the blanket release. The performer is strapped to a common cot, which has been heavily reënforced and provided with loops at the sides through which the straps are passed. Everything may be examined, and committee-men do the strapping. The performer is fastened to the crib as follows: first, a leather belt is placed around his body, buckled, and tied to the sides of the crib with short ropes. Then each ankle is separately strapped to the side of the cot, the performer lying on the crib. Each wrist is placed in a leather cuff, through which a long sash cord is passed; the arms are folded, and the cord is tied firmly to the cot. The performer's neck is fastened down by a leather strap that passes through bars in the end of the crib, and another strap may be secured about his knees. To all appearances he is in a most helpless position; nevertheless he makes his escape.

The full secret, Houdini's notes state, is that the performer is never strapped in a really difficult position. The crazy crib, despite its formidable appearance, is not an unusually strong restraint. The exact procedure of the release is not given; but it depends principally on the position of the arms. As in the straitjacket and certain rope ties, the arms cannot be drawn outward, but the upper arm can slide up toward the neck. This is possible because the wrists are not actually fastened to the sides of the crib; they are attached to cord that is fastened there. With his right arm on top, the performer, by straining to the left, can work his hand close to his head. He cannot slip it over the head because of the neck strap; but it is not difficult for him to reach his neck and work on the strap located there. He then has freedom of motion, which enables him to proceed, once the neck is free. By shifting his body, his hand is enabled to undo the bonds on one side, and from then on the entire escape is merely a matter of continued effort, ending when the performer is in a sitting position, undoing the straps that bind his ankles.

To make the escape more difficult, Houdini suggests that both elbows can be strapped to the body strap by a short strap. This does not interfere with the release of the neck, but it causes difficulty thereafter until the short strap is removed. The performer disposes of the troublesome strap by pushing his arms upward and bending his head forward, so that he can undo the short strap with his teeth. He must do this in order to separate the arms; and unless he is capable of the work, that part of the restraint should be omitted. Any artifice employed by the performer to gain slack while he is being strapped and tied is, of course, to his advantage, and will enable him to make his escape more rapidly.

The release from the crazy crib is highly effective, as the device appears strong and reliable and it looks as though the performer must certainly make very strenuous efforts. Houdini states that the straining at the neck strap makes the test look extraordinarily difficult and that the escape is great for a change—that is, as a substitute for the straitjacket. He adds: "It all depends upon the manner of 'selling.' If it is not 'sold hard,' the test is bad. 'Sold' well, it is great." That is, the escape requires showmanship. Nothing must be neglected to make the performer appear as tightly secured as possible. He must be in a position in which real effort is essential, to convince his audience that the job is not easy.

Therefore the test is only suited to the experienced performer. Houdini could allow the committee-men to strap him to the limit of their ability and to convince themselves as well as the audience that escape was nearly impossible; yet he could also release himself quickly and effectively. An inexperienced performer, on the contrary, would either encounter real difficulties or would perform the test so crudely that it would not excite enthusiasm among the members of the audience. In tests of this nature, Houdini's superiority in showmanship and ability placed him in a class by himself—far above those who sought to imitate his work.

HOT WATER AND WET SHEETS

THIS was a special test introduced by Houdini, and he classes it as one of the best of all challenges. Houdini was first secured with a piece of cloth tied around his body, holding his hands to his sides. For this test he was dressed in a bathing suit and laid on a sheet placed in the center of the stage. The committee rolled him in the sheet, placed him on another sheet and rolled it about him, and finally used a third sheet as an outer wrapping. Then he was placed upon a strong-framed bed, and his body was encircled by cloth bandages at the head, waist, knees, and feet. The ends of the bandages were secured to irons on the sides of the bed.

The notes made by Houdini specify that the upper bandages should be five yards in length, and the lower bandages four yards; the diagram also shows four additional bandages each three yards in length, running from head to foot at the performer's sides. To make escape from the sheets more difficult, buckets of hot water (about 110 degrees Fahrenheit) were thrown over the sheets, and it was up to Houdini to release himself. This test was genuine; it was very difficult, in fact one of the hardest ever undertaken by Houdini. The only special provision lay in the arrangement of the uppermost bandage which fitted around his neck.

The irons on the bed were placed at intervals so that the distance from the bottom irons to the top was almost the length of Houdini's body. Hence, when the bandages were fastened, beginning with the feet, the bandage at the neck was slanting upward in both directions. This gave Houdini some leeway at the top of the bed, and was of aid to him when he worked his way out of the sheets. His object was to release himself without untying his hands; this he did by literally wriggling from the sheets, a very difficult and strenuous procedure. Once clear of the sheets, he rolled from the bed to the floor, with his hands still tied, and there he slipped the long cloth over his feet and undid the knots with his teeth. As each hand was bound separately and the cloth then circled about the body, this was a task much less difficult than the escape from the sheets.

"This test is so hard," Houdini stated in the notes, "that several times I have had barely enough strength to walk off the stage.

"The committee refuses to allow a silk bathing

suit, insisting on cotton, which will not slip as readily as silk."

There is an alternate method of procedure that can be used on occasions when wriggling out seems impossible. The notes read:

"In case the sheets will not allow you to wriggle out, you can, as a last resort, untie your hands, slip them out of the sheets, and undo the knots outside.

"One time I failed to release my hands; so this is a test in which I must actually struggle for freedom with all my strength."

THE MAIL BAG ESCAPE

H OUDINI, in his notes, classed the mail bag escape as the most genuine challenge he had ever been forced to accept. He appends a copy of a challenge given in Los Angeles, when he was appearing at the Orpheum Theater. The challenge states:

"Houdini will be locked into a leather mail pouch by post office officials. This pouch will be secured with the patent Rotary Government Mail Locks used on registered mail pouches. These locks are made by the government for the sole use of the post office department. They are never allowed out of the possession of postal officials, and their possession or use by others is an offense punishable by fine or imprisonment. The keys are never allowed to leave the post office, and should Houdini fail to release himself he must be taken to the central post office to have the lock opened."

The notebook also contains photographs of the mail pouch, and Houdini marked it as the "greatest test possible in the United States of America," but he did not give an explanation of the method which he used in the challenge.

In other notes he tells the secret of the usual type of mail bag escape, in which a bar is put through the holes in the top of the bag to hold it closed. While

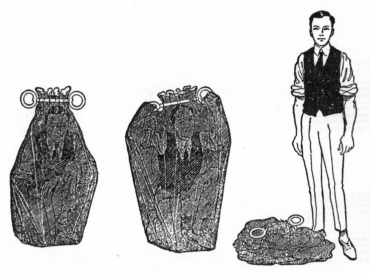

EXPLANATORY DIAGRAMS OF THE MAIL BAG ESCAPE SHOWING HOW THE BAR IS UNSCREWED

this is not Houdini's famous escape, it is a very ingenious trick; for padlocks are placed in holes on the ends of the bar, and the bag is still attached to the bar after the escape. This requires a special bar that screws apart. The construction of the bar is so perfect that it is virtually impossible to find the joint when the bar is screwed together; in fact the bar is smooth on its entire surface and may be handled without worry.

The bar is so tightly screwed together that it cannot be separated by the people who examine it; but when padlocks are placed on the end they act as levers, and by gripping them through the bag, the performer can unscrew the bar. When the sections of the bar are drawn apart the bag opens and the performer steps out; then replaces the bar through the holes in the bag. Any locks may be supplied for the trick, and they may be sealed by the committee. A duplicate bar of solid construction is kept by the performer for exhibition purposes. The bars are exchanged before and after the trick.

THE PASTEBOARD BOX ESCAPE

ESCAPING from a box made of pasteboard would not be at all impressive if the performer merely undertook to break loose from the flimsy cell. But in all regulation escapes, the customary finish is to show the device which held the performer still fastened and secured identically as it was when he was imprisoned. For this reason an escape from a pasteboard box is very convincing, when the committee is allowed to examine everything afterward. In fact such an escape is quite as effective as one from a trunk or packing box, for the audience knows that secret openings or traps are impossible.

In his escapes, Houdini implied that he actually left the device in which he was confined without opening it; this at least was always the indication of the evidence. Hence a flimsy device, which could not apparently be opened without tampering with it, afforded an excellent mystery. It was not a case of strong effort, but of delicate work. The pasteboard box was entirely unprepared; hence it could be made by a challenger, the only condition being that it follow specifications as to size and shape given by the performer. Houdini used this escape, and his explanatory notes are given here.

In presenting this escape, the performer was placed in the box, and a deep cover was put on it. Then the box was bound with ropes like a package, making it impossible for him to reach the knots. Apparently the only way to get out was to demolish the box; but after Houdini made the escape the box was roped as before and stood the closest inspection. Houdini's instructions read:

"The box must be made to your order. My box is generally made about 30 inches high, 24 inches wide, and 37 inches long. The inside is strengthened by a wooden frame. If possible use a dark paper covering, not figured but all black or brown glazed.

"The top must be about 12 inches deep, fitting like a telescope and fitting easily. The bottom of the box has two spaces cut away, each nine inches deep, and curved, looking as though they were there simply for the hands to take hold of in lifting.

"The ropes must be cut, and for this you must carry a very sharp knife that has an extra long handle. The cutting would be very difficult but for the space at the handles, which makes it fairly easy to cut the ropes from inside the box.

"You may cut all the ropes on the sides, but it has happened the longest rope was unreachable and could not be cut from the side. The only way to beat this is to carry with you a sheet of paper with which the box is covered and some photo paste. Feel along the bottom for the rope and deliberately cut a slot on the bottom edge, and cut until you have cut the rope.

"In challenges where I cut this rope, I try to use cheap cord that resembles sash cord; this cuts easily and can be carried wrapped around the body. But it is best to use as heavy a rope or cord as possible, as it makes the trick appear more difficult.

"The object of having a solid color on the box is so that in case you tear it or have to cut it, you can repair same and this will be almost impossible to detect.

"Once I had to do a new job on the arm-holes as the pasteboard was weak and was badly torn; but I had scissors, paste, and brush, and a sheet of the paper used on the box, and thus repaired the damage.

"The box cannot be moved after you once enter, so the best plan is to allow it to remain on the same spot and move the cabinet over the box.

"Always go into these weak challenges as heavily manacled as possible, as this strengthens the trick."

The reason for keeping the box in one spot is the performer's weight, which makes it impossible to lift the box without breaking it. The instructions do not give the details of the work following the escape, except regarding the repairing of the box, if cut or damaged. But the reference to "sash cord wrapped around the body" explains this clearly. The performer has duplicate ropes exactly the same as those

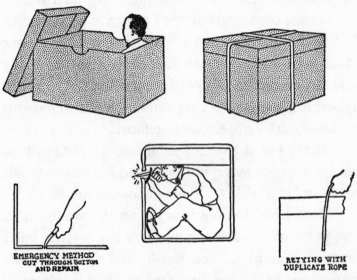

EMERGENCY METHOD
CUT THROUGH BOTTOM
AND REPAIR

RETYING WITH
DUPLICATE ROPE

THE PASTEBOARD BOX OPEN AND CLOSED. DIAGRAMS OF ESCAPE

used on the box. After he is out, he removes the original ropes, and ties up the box with the ropes that he has on his person. The positions of the cut ropes serve as a guide, and the old knots are still there as models when he ties the duplicate ropes. The long rope that may cause trouble is one that has been tied lengthways around the box. This cannot be reached from the sides; to have handles at the ends of the box as well as at the sides would look suspicious. When a single rope is used, as appears to be preferable, it is twisted around the box, going lengthways and sideways. Cutting from the sides, reaching as many ropes as possible, should ordinarily allow the performer to release himself by carefully raising the lid. Additional cutting through the bottom of the box is therefore necessary only in an emergency. Obviously the best type of rope to use is strong rope that is convincing yet easily cut, and that can be carried around the body without bulging. Heavier rope would have to be concealed in the cabinet instead of on the person.

This trick is an excellent challenge, because the performer or his representative can give the specifications for the box and easily obtain a sample of the paper which is to be used in covering it. The sample serves the performer if he needs to make repairs. The type of rope to be used and all other details are decided on before the challenge is made public; this of course is customary.

The escape from the pasteboard box, while simple in method, offers certain complications, and may prove troublesome. The knife must be concealed or smuggled in; also any appliances for undoing handcuffs. The simple procedure of cutting the ropes and supplying others in their place is effective in practice, for no one knows what is going on inside the cabinet, and if the performer removes all evidence and does a good job in replacing the duplicate ropes, no one will even begin to suspect the secret.

THE BASKET ESCAPE

THE basket escape is a corollary to the pasteboard box, but presents some interesting variations. It is stronger than the pasteboard box, but the method of escape is quite similar. Houdini's more complete notes on this escape are as follows:

"The easiest basket to escape from is the so-called 'Laundry Basket' made from split elm. This basket has a wooden top and can only be tied with ropes.

"To get out of this, you have two ropes; one you hand to your challengers, the other you have wound about your body.

"They can tie you in, any old way; but the best way is to rehearse them, getting them to tie the basket the same way that the trick trunk is tied: three ropes one way and one the other; this will enable you to retie the basket quicker than will be possible if you have to study out how to retie it.

"You carry a sharp knife with which you can cut the original ropes from the interior of the basket.

"In getting out of a basket that has a lock, accept

a basket that you can reach out of at the sides and reach the lock, which you can pick or unlock with a duplicate key.

"Be sure and always try the basket first before having it announced as a challenge. Make conditions to suit yourself. When you have the basket in your dressing-room, you can change the locks or cut off the hinges to suit yourself. But make it dead certain of not holding you."

A notation on the basket trick, dated "Liverpool, England, October 26, 1904," is very brief, and states: "The unprepared basket escape is about the best that can be worked, as the basket is not prepared and all you have to do is to have a duplicate rope and cut the one that encircles the basket; then re-tie the basket with the duplicate rope. This is not as good as being nailed up in the box, but will do for a change."

This is an escape that can unquestionably be made convincing, and the fact that Houdini suggested it as an alternate for a packing box escape is proof of this. A well-constructed basket of large size gives an appearance of solidity. Well roped, it appears secure. While it might be possible to work a thin knife through the weaving of the basket if the weaving yields easily, this is not the method intended for regular use.

The performer seizes the basket by the rim, inside

the cover, and draws inward. As the basket is flexible, it bends sufficiently to allow a space between the rim and the inside of the cover. The performer pushes the knife down through the space thus provided and

THE BASKET ESCAPE. NOTE CONCEALMENT OF THE DUPLICATE ROPE

is able to cut the rope without great difficulty. There is no danger of injuring the side of the basket; and, as in the pasteboard box escape, the audience has no knowledge of the subterfuge whereby a duplicate rope is substituted for the cut original. A very subtle procedure is revealed in the instructions to show the com-

mittee-men the best way to tie the basket. Their purpose is to secure the basket as firmly as possible; the
performer's suggestion being practical, they invariably follow it, not realizing that they are making an
important part of his job easier for the escape artist.

As certain baskets have hasps and staples fitted
to them so they may be locked, the consideration of
locks in this trick is important. With the handle-holes,
a duplicate key, fitted if necessary, to an extension
rod, can be used. The reference to fixing the hinges
is useful in a basket where handle-holes are absent.
If the hinges are not already vulnerable, the performer can make them so, and thus open the top
without attempting to work the lock. His procedure
afterward is to open the lock, fix the hinges as they
were, and lock the basket again before encircling it
with the duplicate rope.

The performer is sure of the ropes; the only complication lies in locks. If the opportunity is favorable
for brief but effective preparation of the top of the
basket before the show, any basket may be accepted.
The ropes are the important part of the escape. The
committee puts the greatest confidence in them;
hence the locks are of secondary importance, from
the viewpoint of the challengers.

THE PAPER BAG ESCAPE

L IKE the pasteboard box, the paper bag escape is one that is convincing because the appliance must be handled carefully, and the performer must show it in exactly the same condition after he has made his escape.

Houdini's description reads:

"The bag must be made of stiff, strong paper, and must be large enough to hold you comfortably so that after you are inside you can raise your hands above your head with ease. My bag is generally 7 feet and 6 inches long and about 40 inches in circumference. You can easily find your required measurement by trying one beforehand.

"In presenting this escape, call attention to the fact that you are not going to destroy the bag; to prove that only one bag is used, you take the bag after the committee has brought it on the stage and allow members of the audience to write their names on it, or to make secret marks; but be careful not to have them too near the top of the bag.

"Come back on the stage, allow yourself to be handcuffed, and then enter the bag feet first. The bag is tied with cord, as in the trick trunk bag, and sealed with the challengers' seals. As you cannot move after you are in the bag, they have to pull the cabinet over the bag.

"In from five to ten minutes you escape, and bring out the bag, uninjured and still sealed."

The escape from the paper bag is somewhat similar to the escape from the pasteboard box. The bag is entirely unprepared; but the seal used is a matter of importance. The escape artist must either obtain a duplicate of the seal that the challengers intend to use, or he must see that they are supplied with an ordinary seal. The cord is wrapped around the neck of the bag, and then the seal is applied.

The directions state:

"You make your escape by cutting the cord of the bag with a sharp knife. You must cut through the paper to do this. After you are out, look at the cord and see how many knots have been tied: re-tie the bag; re-seal it with the duplicate seal, using wax that you have taken along.

"As you have furnished the cord for the bag, you have the same length of duplicate cord for re-tying the bag.

"In sealing, use wax matches or tapers that will

light without making a noise. See that your cabinet will not show light from the inside; if it does, line it with black cloth, and when you are re-sealing the bag, place your body so that it will shield the light; that is, toward the front curtain."

In this escape the performer shows the committee-men how to wind the cord around the neck of the bag so he can gauge the number of turns that will be made, and thus be able to duplicate the tie more easily.

The cord fits tightly; and when the bag is re-tied, the duplicate cord covers the hole made in the paper. The cord may be sealed to the bag; the cut is made close to the wax, and the new seal is placed over the old one. This seals the paper at the spot where the cut is made.

PART FOUR.

BOX ESCAPES

THIS type of escape shows such variety of method and presentation that all releases from boxes are included in this separate section.

Boxes of wood, boxes of metal, all were alike to Houdini, either as challenges or as regular escapes.

BOX ESCAPES OF VARIOUS TYPES

HOUDINI was famous for his escapes from boxes; and his notes are filled with descriptions of various forms of box tricks. Some of these were used by Houdini; others were standard or accepted methods of escaping from a box; while others were ideas or suggested improvements and varied developments. No attempt has been made to distinguish these, as the notes on box escapes do not specify which were used and which were not; but under the general heading of boxes and packing cases there are three important groupings that must be considered.

Houdini performed three types of box escapes: first, spectacular escapes, freeing himself from a box dropped in a river; second, challenges, in which he escaped from a box built and supplied by his challengers; third, routine escapes as part of his regular performances. There are conditions governing each type of escape. In the under-water escape it is essential that a quick-working box or packing case be used; for the performer can take no chances of prolonged delay. In a challenge, the box must be of simple construction, or in accordance with definite specifications, depending upon the conditions of the challenge. In a regular escape, the box that is used must be very convincing in appearance and capable of standing close examination. There are also great possibilities for added effectiveness and additions in the construction of the box: the more formidable it appears and the more complications must apparently be overcome, the more important the escape seems.

For the *under-water escape* Houdini describes a type of box very simple and effective in construction. There are four boards in the end of the box. Two of these are fastened together, but they are not nailed to the sides of the box. They make up the lower half of the end, and are held securely in place by two concealed hinges at the bottom, and by two automatic catches that hold fast to the upper half of the end. These two boards thus constitute a trap hinged at the bottom and releasable at the top. The joint between the trap and the board above is not seen, as the catches are in the edges of the board. To operate, the performer requires a thin piece of steel which can be pushed between the trap and the board above, to push back the catches. The notes suggest an improvement in the form of an inner slat or brace that runs horizontally across the end between the solid board and the trap. This board is held in place by two screws, and it hides the opening between the trap and the solid board. Therefore it must be removed to get at the trap. But Houdini's notes explain that the brace itself, if attached to the trap, can be made to operate

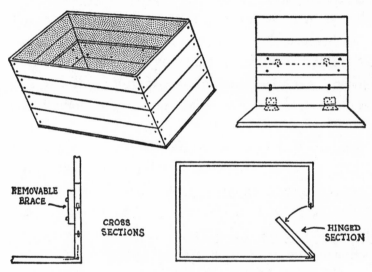

REMOVABLE BRACE

CROSS SECTIONS

HINGED SECTION

APPEARANCE AND CONSTRUCTION OF THE BOX USED IN THE ESCAPE FROM UNDER WATER

the catches, by simply unscrewing one screw and pulling down the end of the brace, using the other screw as a pivot hinge. The notes suggest using screw-head bolts instead of screws for more effective operation.

The trap is provided with air-holes; these enable the man in the box to pull it inward, and after he is out of the box he draws back the trap so that the catches hold it fast. The box may be roped; this does not interfere with the escape, for the trap opens inward and there is sufficient space between the ropes to permit the passage of the performer's body. The box remains under water after the escape, and when it is brought up later it is removed from the scene; hence there is no examination of the interior and the brace can remain loose. But it is important to close the opening so that any one seeing the box after the escape will gain no inkling of the secret. The notes do not state that this was the method regularly used by Houdini in his overboard escape. It is probable that he used different types of boxes, and that this was one of them. It will be noticed that this type of escape requires quick operation and certain release. The escape from a box under water is a hazardous undertaking, and nothing can be left to chance.

The *packing box escape* is very similar to the under-water box escape; the only difference from the viewpoint of the spectator is that one is performed on the stage, the other under water. Working in a cabinet, the performer runs no risk, and can utilize a box that will stand close inspection. The inferior method is to use a packing case that opens outward. Such a box cannot be roped or bound too tightly, and it lacks the advantages of a type of packing box described and explained in Houdini's notes. This box requires preparation, but if the box is built to the performer's specifications (as is done in challenges) he can make the alterations quickly and easily. There is always an opportunity for fixing the box, as very few minutes are required and the box will stand inspection afterward.

Houdini explains this method in his notes; the instructions are given briefly on the back of a letter that was written as a challenge, and these notes show how the trick can be performed with a wire-bound box, as follows:

"Wire or steel-banded box. Have the end work. The band-iron is put on with staples, and the board that is the 'gag' falls in as usual, the staples being faked.

"Screws and nails are used; when out, simply put in long screws. To make it look more complicated have staples driven in one way and then reverse. This box is quickly made, easy to work, and looks good. It makes a quick challenge, with no locks required. The box can be put in a long bag; untie from inside."

This explains the working method as a board in one end, held by screws on both sides. The screws are removed from the outside and short screws are put in their place; thus nothing has to be done to the inside of the box. The inside screws hold the board in place.

The board is near the bottom, and must be wide enough to allow the performer to get through. The nailing of the top does not interfere with the special board, and the performer's assistants see to it that no troublesome nails are driven through the side where they might interfere with the special board.

To escape, the performer takes out the long screws on the inside and puts in short screws; then removes the board and replaces the outside short screws with long ones so the box will be as solid as before. Air-holes can be placed in the ends so as to hold the board in place while inserting the long screws. In banding or wiring the box, genuine staples may be used except on the special board. Any staples placed there must be short ones, hammered in by an assistant or a confederate. A short staple will yield when the performer pulls the board from within. There are not enough wires or bands to interfere with the performer when he comes through the end of the large box.

In his numerous experiments with box escapes, Houdini frequently struck out new ideas. Two of these, applied to the end-working box, are very interesting. One is to have a box tied up in wrapping paper. When the end of the box is opened inward, the end folds of the paper are easily managed so that the performer can feel between and cut or untie the ropes (using the latter method if the box is tied at the end). The other idea is that of a box placed in two bags; both bags are seamless. One bag is slipped over the box and the mouth is tied at the end; the other bag is put on the other way, over the first bag, and is tied at the other end of the box. Getting free from one bag with the knots at the proper end of the box is not difficult, but the second bag appears troublesome. The plan is to use thin bags tied with ordinary knots and to fit the box with panels at both ends. Opening one end, the performer has no trouble with the inner bag. Opening the other end, he unties the knots of the outer bag through the cloth of the inner bag. Then both bags can be manipulated. But even from this point it is a difficult escape, as one bag must be entirely removed from the box to permit the escape through the opening of the other bag.

Special boxes or packing cases, made by the performer or to his order, lend themselves to ingenious methods of manufacture. Various types of boxes are explained in Houdini's notes.

Each corner of the *sliding panel box* consists of upright boards nailed together, forming an angle. The sides of the box are placed within these posts and are nailed or screwed in place. The box stands very close inspection, for all parts are tight-fitting and nothing can be pried loose. No one looking for a trap will find it.

The box opens by a very ingenious arrangement. There are three horizontal boards in each side. One of these boards is attached only to a post at one end. That particular post is attached to no other board or post. The boards above and below the special board have grooves that admit metal slides from the special

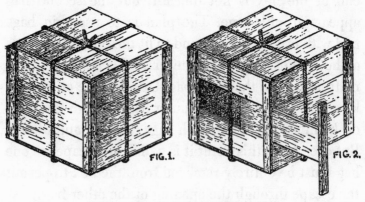

FIG. 1.   FIG. 2.

OPERATION OF SLIDING PANEL BOX

board. Hence the board and the post at the end will slide away and make an opening through which the performer can escape. Short screws or nails give the appearance of security on the parts that are not fastened, and this device is so neatly constructed that it will stand close examination even if unfastened; thus the performer can escape from a box of this type without the use of tools.

When the cover is nailed on, care must be taken to prevent any nails from going directly in the top of the corner post. This can be prevented by having the top no larger than the box exclusive of the posts. Secured from the inside with long screws at the end away from the free post, the slide cannot operate until the performer removes the long screws when inside the box. By replacing them with short screws and putting long screws on the outside, he can fasten the slide as firmly as before.

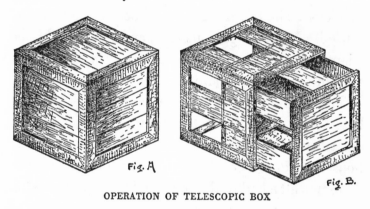

OPERATION OF TELESCOPIC BOX

The *telescopic box* is a further development of the box with the sliding panel. The box opens like a drawer. It is difficult to describe but may be understood from the illustration. The telescopic box is an unfinished idea, as it cannot be used in the form shown. The alternate boards and the ends of the frame slide out of the top and sides, which hold the remaining boards. Finished drawings accompany a very brief description of this idea, and it is probable that the artist had a false impression of the trick. In the form illustrated, getting into it would be the mystery. Attaching the center board to the frame work of the top would make the top a separate portion, but would not solve the problem as the top could be nailed only at the sides and not the ends. A top locking to the sides with staples would be practical, but the lack of attachments on the ends would excite suspicion. The box has been included in the book because it is a very ingenious idea, and can probably be adapted in some practical way. Only a brief typewritten reference accompanied the drawing.

The *slide-up box* is a very useful form of packing box, for it lends itself to adaptations that will be described later. The box is made in two separate sections, one of which slides up from the other. The bottom is attached to the four angle-like posts, which have a framework connecting them. The box itself is made separately, with neither top nor bottom, and slides down into the framework provided for it. The cover is just the size of the inner portion of the box; hence it cannot be nailed to the posts. The performer who is imprisoned in the box merely stands up, and the whole interior section rises with him and may be lifted clear for him to make his escape.

Under certain circumstances it is desirable to have the inner section of the box always loose; being well

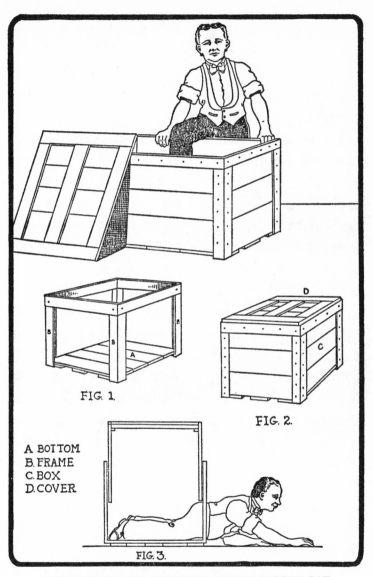

FIG. 1.

FIG. 2.

A. BOTTOM
B. FRAME
C. BOX
D. COVER

FIG. 3.

CONSTRUCTION AND OPERATION OF THE SLIDE-UP BOX

made, it will not reveal its secret, and no one will be able to lift the inner section easily. With the top in place the performer can exert sufficient pressure to lift the box without difficulty; hence a tight fit is desirable.

A few long screws on the inside will make the box absolutely secure. If these are removed and replaced with short ones, the long screws can be transferred to the outside after the escape to make the box positively tight.

It is not necessary for the performer to remove the inner section, as he can make his escape by crawling out between the posts of the frame.

The *metal-rimmed box* is an adaptation of the "slide-up" principle. It is a box constructed without corner posts, made entirely of heavy boards that are bound with angle-shaped strips of metal. The cover is set on the box, and the metal on the upper edge of the box is bent over and nailed in place so that the box is positively secure at the top. The effectiveness of this operation is apparent. The box is made in two separate portions, a top half and a lower half. The metal rim is actually nailed or screwed to the top section, but the lower half is free, provided with dummy heads. Cleats are provided where the metal bands on the sides meet the metal bands of the bottom, and here the bands are separate.

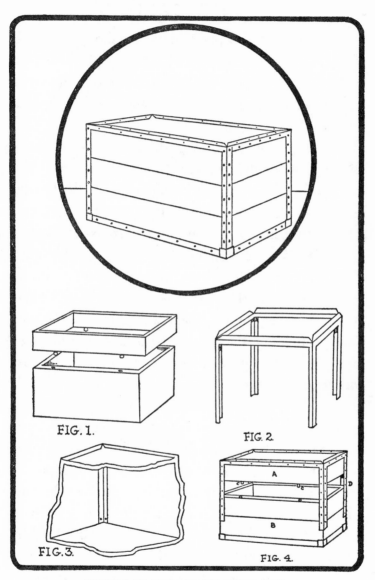

FIG. 1.

FIG. 2.

FIG. 3.

FIG. 4.

DETAILS OF THE METAL-RIMMED BOX

When the escapist pushes upward, the top and half of the box lift, together with all the metal rim except that on the bottom. The rim that runs along the lower edges of the sides and ends is actually attached to the lower section of the box.

The diagrams explaining this trick do not show all the interior details, but it may be assumed that there are pins and sockets in the boards at the broken portion so that the upper half of the box will rest steadily and firmly on the lower part. Nails may be driven freely in the top and part way down the sides, when the box is closed; but they must not continue below the break. The exact position of the break is optional; it may be very near the bottom of the box. Catches holding the two sections are desirable, as they can be sprung by the performer when in the box, and arranged to snap back in place when the box is rejoined.

In a development of this box, Houdini suggests an ingenious type of escape. The idea was to have holes drilled in the sides and ends of the box, at the break, these holes appearing between the boards. His hands, feet, and neck could then be roped and the cords pushed out through the holes and held by the committee outside the cabinet. With his hands and feet against the sides of the box, escape would appear impossible. But by merely lifting up and pushing off the upper section, he would automatically free himself from the ropes.

As a feature to be used with the simple metal-rimmed box in which the break is up high and no telescopic cover is used, the rope trick thus described is an exceptional feature that would make a baffling mystery out of an ordinary box escape. The comparatively light weight of the upper section is to the performer's advantage. Adding to the effectiveness of an escape was Houdini's regular procedure. The breaking sections of the metal-rimmed box gave opportunity for a remarkable rope tie, and he did not overlook its possibilities.

THE LEAD SHEETED AND LINED BOX

HOUDINI'S aptitude for improving good ideas and working them into sensational mysteries is seen in this escape. It is a development of the box trick previously described but is so far superior as to be almost unrecognizable. The performer is placed in a box that is unmistakably solid and lined with sheets of lead or iron, the lining riveted together. The outer portion of the box may be banded or rimmed with metal. Instead of an ordinary cover, a telescopic or deeply rimmed top is placed on the metal-lined box. The cover may also have a metal lining as long as spaces are provided for driving nails through it. The object is to have a cover as formidable as possible. The lining of the box is attached to the box itself with bolts or screws with soldered heads so the two portions are firmly fixed together.

This gives the performer three barriers to meet: the sheet-metal lining, the box itself, and finally the cover that fits over; this comes nearly to the bottom of the box and is nailed in every way imaginable.

Nails and screws may also be placed in the lower edges and the bottom of the box after the cover is on, so that no escape is possible through the bottom. Houdini refers to the escape as the "incredible" box trick, and the adjective is not an exaggeration. If ever a device seemed a positive prison for a human being, this box would appear its equal. Yet fundamentally it is nothing more than the metal-rimmed box previously described, with substantial improvements.

First the box breaks away at a spot very close to the bottom. The metal rim is desirable for the finish; hence it is considered in the explanation. It is secured to the box at the top edge and down the sides to the break; only the lower portion of each corner band is loose. The bottom band is firm, and is apparently part of the entire rim, the cleats hiding the separation between the corners and the bottom. The sheet-metal lining is very cleverly faked. A piece with turned-up edges is set in the bottom of the box. Then a four-sided lining is inserted; this comes *within* the turned-up edges, so the false bottom is effectively trapped and cannot be removed.

False rivets apparently connect the bottom part of the lining; the rivets that join the perpendicular sheets of metal are genuine. All down the sides are bolts or screws with soldered heads that hold the metal lining to the sides of the box. These are gen-

uine, and they serve to hold the lower and upper portions of the box together; hence the box will stand
any test. But as the lower portion of the box is very
small, only four bolts or screws are required to hold
it; these are located in the corners of the box. If
others are desired for effect, they need be nothing
but dummy heads.

When the cover is placed on, it reaches far down
the sides of the box, but does not extend below the
break. This means that nails can be driven anywhere,
in any number. When the performer enters the box
he carries some equipment, including an iron for
melting solder. He uses this on the bolts or screws
that hold the metal lining to the sides of the box.
When the solder is off these, it not only loosens them
but reveals notches for the insertion of a screw-driver.
Thus the performer removes the screws and releases
the upper and lower portions of the box. He pushes
upward, and off comes the entire top, the upper half
of the box, and all the metal lining except the false
bottom! He replaces the screws with dummy heads,
soldering them in place. All of this is put back in
position. As the separate portions are now loose, they
must be fastened; here is where the metal rim comes
in handy. By inserting genuine screws instead of false
ones in the lower part of the corners, the two sections
of the box are made fast.

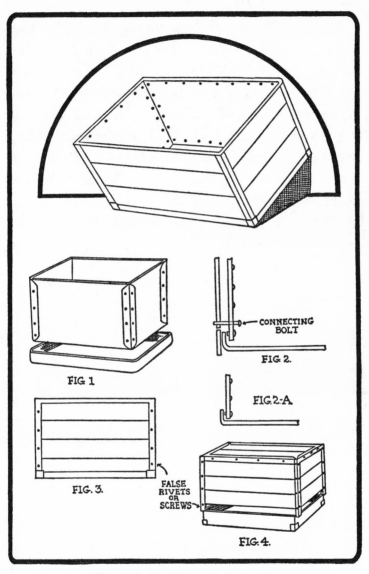

CONNECTING BOLT

FIG. 1

FIG. 2.

FIG. 2-A

FIG. 3.

FALSE RIVETS OR SCREWS

FIG. 4.

THE LEAD SHEETED AND LINED BOX

Houdini also provided for roping the box by passing the rope through the handles of the cover and having it so tied that there would be sufficient slack at the bottom to cut the rope when the upper section of the box was raised. This would be aided by tilting the box, but considerable slack would be necessary because the metal lining extends below the break. Airholes in the cover are necessary in this box; they are usual in all such apparatus.

THE DOUBLE BOX ESCAPE

I N THIS spectacular escape, the performer is placed in a large box, which is locked, strapped, and encased in a canvas cover. This box is placed in a larger box, which is also locked, strapped, and laced in a canvas cover. Nevertheless the performer accomplishes his escape and the boxes may be examined before and after the exhibition.

There are three horizontal boards in the back of each box. The middle board is attached to the lower board only by two long, thin metal rods. But for the presence of the top board, the middle board could be lifted from the rods. There are three catches in the upper edge of the middle board. These engage openings in the highest of the three boards. All are spring catches, and they are actuated or operated by a single rod, which is set horizontally in the middle board. An air-hole is drilled just below this rod, at the center, and the performer is provided with a special U-shaped tool. He inserts this in the air-hole, pushes upward, and thus releases the catches. This enables him to pull the center board inward and raise it upward, allowing space through which he can pass his body.

With the board of the inner box raised, the per-

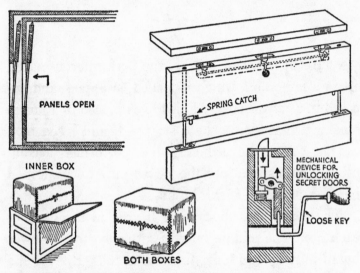

DETAILS OF THE DOUBLE BOX ESCAPE. THE PANELS IN EACH
BOX OPERATE IDENTICALLY

former loosens the lacing on the canvas cover. The lacing runs horizontally and is properly situated for this work. Much of this is done while the outer box is being locked and laced inside its cover. Then the performer finds the air-hole of the outer box, opens it as he did the inner, and attends to the outer canvas cover. Outside of the boxes, he slides the board of the inner one into place, tightens the canvas cover, closes the special board of the outer box, and relaces the outer cover. His work is then completed.

There must be sufficient space between the inner and outer boxes to allow for the raising of the special board in the outer box, for it must be drawn inward a few inches. The boxes used in this escape must be well constructed, with boards that fit closely together, so that they will stand thorough examination before and after the trick.

This apparatus was constructed and used by Houdini. The escape is most spectacular. Yet the mechanical work allows for a rapid release, and the fact that two boxes are employed makes the effect appear miraculous to the audience. As a regular escape in a regular program, the double box trick is far superior to the ordinary box escape.

THE NIAGARA FALLS ESCAPE

THIS was merely an idea that Houdini detailed in his notebook; yet it is quite as interesting as many of his actual escapes, for it shows his aptitude for planning the spectacular. The notes state: "The idea is to be nailed in a packing case, thrown over Niagara Falls, and eventually make an escape!" Houdini's plans for this remarkable escape are merely suggestions that had not reached the point of practical solution; he states that it would have to be a trick test, and not an actual escape in the water.

Here is the description:

"So that the crowd can see that I am being nailed into the packing case, the nailing is done on a platform, into which I can slide after the box is nailed up.

"The best way would be to have the platform on a large wagon, which is drawn down to the landing place, where I get into the water according to opportunity.

"Or else get back into the box when placed on

126

wagon, and be found there, having failed to escape (being 'knocked out' coming over falls).

"This can be worked into an extra good idea and needs doing some time."

THE INDIAN BOX MYSTERY

IN HIS notes on the trick he calls the Indian box
mystery, Houdini does not give the origin of this
unusual title; but he does state the purpose of the
escape, namely that it is "to be used on the stage;
also made portable to use on steamers or in clubs."
The notes were written on August 14, 1910, on board
the *Mauretania*. Houdini's purpose was to have a
wooden box with a hinged cover, well constructed
and strong in appearance, from which he could escape.
The sketches show the top of the box with metal
bands continuing across as part of the hinges, terminating in hasps on the other end. It is not clear
whether the bands were to continue entirely around
the box, or to end at the back.

Bands completely encircling the box would probably be used for stage purposes, as the other end of
the bands would then terminate in staples to receive
the hasps. But Houdini designed this trick with two
ideas: first, to make the box portable, so it could be
easily carried and screwed together; second, so that

it would be necessary to carry only the cover and fit it into any box that might be constructed. In the latter case, especially, the encircling iron bands could not be used, as the size of the box would not be known; in either case, such bands would interfere with the portability of the device.

The box itself was merely part of the proposed mystery. The committee would first strap Houdini in a straitjacket, then chain his legs and place him in the box. Next the men would close the box and put padlocks over the hasps and staples, then rope the box in all directions. The last step would be the addition of a canvas cover, placed over the box and drawn tight, with a rope passing through eyelets in the cover. From the sketches it appears that the end of the rope terminated in a permanent loop, to which a padlock could be attached; hence the rope could not be drawn back through the eyelets. This required a triple escape by Houdini, first from the straitjacket and the leg-irons, second from the locked and roped box, third from the canvas cover.

The escape from the straitjacket was Houdini's first consideration. Inasmuch as space was limited inside the box, he planned a special straitjacket for this escape. The straps coming from the sleeves are used to bind a man's arms to his body; Houdini planned these to release from inside the sleeve, by a firm catch which could be removed by the hand. This made escaping from the jacket very simple, for the arms were freed immediately and allowed an easy method of unbuckling the jacket through the cloth. Out of the jacket, Houdini could easily dispose of the leg-irons; these, he remarks, are to be opened in the regular manner.

The top of the box was to be made in three sections, the center board wider than the others and about ten inches across. These sections were not only fastened together by the outside bands; they were also held together by wooden cleats directly under the bands. The center slat served as a trap. The screws through the iron bands were short, barely entering the wood. The screws through the wooden cleats, however, were long; it was these screws that held the three sections of the box together. The cleats at the sides were provided with long screws, and long screws passed through the bands above the side slats. Removing the long screws from the side slats, when within the box, Houdini would be able to draw in the center slat, or trap. The cleats were not arranged to go clear across the box; their short length made them more easily manageable.

Houdini provided that the rope on the canvas cover should end at the top; hence when the trap was opened, he could spread the canvas sufficiently to push his hand through and pick the lock or undo it. The ropes around the box offered no obstacle, for they were far enough apart for him to pass between them; their purpose was merely to make the box appear more secure. After opening the canvas cover, Houdini's method was to replace the trap. This was to be done without unlocking the box or untying it. Hence short screws were inserted in the ends of the cleats that had formerly been fast, so that the center slat alone held the cleats. These screws were taken from the center of the iron bands. The long screws were then put through the center portions of the iron bands, so that the three slats were held firmly from the outside. This made the trap accessible only from the outside, instead of from the inside, as it had been at the beginning of the escape. Its position was quite as firm as before.

The committee examining the box could not suspect this; for the arrangement made the three slats in the top very tight, and kept the iron bands firm against the box. To all appearances, the top of the box would have to be handled as a single piece, the removal of one slat being the last thing that would occur to any one.

The ropes encircling the box were to be roped

double across the top, so that those running length-wise would pass on either side of the removable slat or trap. This gave the box a very secure appearance, especially to those who naturally examined the entire top of the box as a single piece. A single rope across the top would have been not nearly so convincing; yet it would have interfered with the escape, whereas the double rope did not! For the double rope provided a natural opening that corresponded with the trap itself and could only overlap it to a very slight degree. In making the escape, the double rope proved the least important of the devices used to secure Houdini in the box.

This is an escape that has excellent possibilities, especially for the purpose planned by Houdini. He needed an effective escape that required very little apparatus. A straitjacket, a leg-iron, a canvas cover, and the top of the box (which could be carried in pieces) were the only articles required, with the exception of a few padlocks and tools. It would be a simple matter to have a box made to fit the cover, the staples to be attached by bolts with the nuts on the outside of the box. The cost of the apparatus would be very small. Here again we observe Houdini's ability to build up a highly mystifying act by the combination of several features. The combined effects of the straitjacket, box, and canvas cover make the Indian

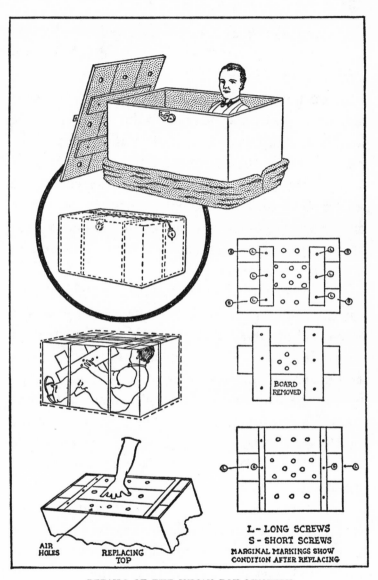

L- LONG SCREWS
S- SHORT SCREWS
MARGINAL MARKINGS SHOW
CONDITION AFTER REPLACING

AIR HOLES   REPLACING TOP

BOARD REMOVED

DETAILS OF THE INDIAN BOX MYSTERY

box a remarkable escape, quite as well suited to the stage as to the special performances for which Houdini actually intended it.

A small diagram in connection with another escape illustrates a box very similar to the one used in the Indian box mystery. Inasmuch as it is through the space between the braces that the performer must escape, the removal of the middle portion of the center slat is all that is actually necessary. In using a box where the cover is nailed on and is not loose as in the Indian box mystery, removal of the entire center slat is impossible.

Hence we find a form of box that is actually a packing case, with three slats in the top and four crosswise wooden cleats, of considerable width, two outside and two inside. The center slat is made in three sections, and the ends of these sections are hidden between the cleats. There are spaces between the ends of the sections. They are held in place by long screws on the inside cleats; the screws on the outside cleats are short. The middle portion of the center slat is provided with air-holes.

The three sections appear as one, but from the inside of the box the performer makes use of the separations. He removes the long screws from the cleats and puts in short ones; then he pushes the middle section of the center slat toward one end of the box, and thus brings a free end into view. Drawing back the free end enables him to pull the faked section into the box. Having made his escape, he replaces this section from the outside of the box and fastens it in place with long screws on the outside cleats. Note that the long and short screw transposition is necessary only with the middle portion of the center slat.

This method of escape from a box is included here because it is primarily intended for the top and is a variation of the Indian box; actually it is more suited to a packing case, where wooden cleats can be used on both sides and the box must be nailed. Houdini mentions it for the box used in the improved milk can escape; also as a form of release from a packing case. Used with a packing case, it can be applied to the side or the end of the box as well as to the top. It can also be placed on the bottom for use in an under-water escape; in such an escape, the performer would not take the time to put long screws in the outside of the box.

THE BURIED BOX ESCAPE

URING the two seasons that Houdini appeared with his full-evening magic show, he demonstrated the test of being buried alive or kept in a box under water during a period of approximately one hour. In doing this, Houdini counteracted the claims of self-styled "miracle workers" who attributed the feat to Oriental parentage plus autohypnosis. Houdini openly declared that the only requisites for this demonstration were self-confidence and endurance, for the air supply in the box used was sufficient to sustain the performer for a period considerably longer than his imprisonment. It is interesting to learn that Houdini considered this trick long before he presented it, and was familiar with the fact that a person could exist for a surprisingly long period of time before his air supply was exhausted. His notes refer to the "buried-alive man secret." The notes read:

"A large box about the size of a large kitchen table. The man enters, his mouth stuffed with cotton, likewise his nostrils.

"He has a hood placed over him, with the eyes cut out; then a longer hood over that which falls over his shoulders.

"He lies down in sand with his arms under his

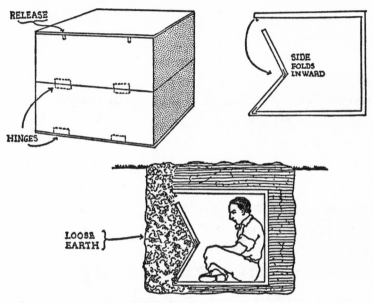

CONSTRUCTION OF THE BOX USED IN THE BURIED BOX ESCAPE, WITH ARRANGEMENT OF LOOSE EARTH

chest; his knees drawn under him. His back is upwards. The secret is that the space made with his knees allows him to have enough air to live fifteen to thirty minutes. Wet damp sand allows longer time. . . .

"When the man takes his place in the bottom of

the box there is some sand already, and he is covered with about 1,500 to 3,000 pounds of sand.

"A challenge test is to build a box with rubber band and a cover put on, which is pressed down so as to make it air-tight.

"I presume that with oxygen one could live much longer.

"In the act of lying down, the cotton is pushed out of the mouth; it then lies against the nose in the second hood, which enables the man to breathe."

Knowing that he could breathe comfortably in an empty box—the way in which he eventually demonstrated the feat—Houdini planned a highly spectacular escape, which he describes and explains thus:

"Get nailed into a packing case; lowered into a six-foot hole; then the earth or sand shoveled on same.

"Box can be made to work on side, so that I could worm my way out towards the air.

"Must have the hole in which box is buried large so that I do not have to strike the solid earth, but can work my way out through the sand or earth that has been dropped on box that contains me. Must be tried out to see how much air I have with me."

Penciled notations follow the typed explanation:

"I tried out 'Buried Alive' in Hollywood, and nearly (?) did it. Very dangerous; the weight of the earth is killing."

Earlier notes on this escape were written by Houdini while on board a North German Lloyd steamer. They are dated "June 14, 1911, near Cherbourg." In these notes he provides for a special type of end trap in the box, which appears to have two loose boards, hinged together and held by a catch at the top of the box. A release of the catch permits the boards to drop inward, one upon the other, thus allowing a large opening for the escape. The notes also provide for bolts to hold the boards in position; when these are released from the inside, the trap is free to work.

Houdini realized that his exit from the box would be but the first part of this difficult escape, and it is obvious that he intended not to be handicapped by any limitations in the trap. Coming out into earth presented a tremendous problem when compared with the familiar escape of emerging into water. In planning his exit from the box and then through loose earth at the sides, Houdini chose the only possible method of escape. Any attempt to raise the cover of the box and the earth above it with a powerful jack would prove hopeless, and there is no indication that Houdini even considered such a method. An escape by raising the cover and thus dislodging the loose earth above would be just about as practical as an exit through the bottom of the box!

THE IRON EXPRESS BOX

THE iron express box is a large, heavy box, made entirely of iron with all parts riveted together. Staples are riveted to the front; the hinges are riveted to the back. When the performer is placed in this device and the lid is held to the box by padlocks, the chances of a successful escape seem very remote. The release is effected by simply cutting the rivets at the hinges or at the staples, according to which is the easier. The staple rivets are preferable, for then the box will open in the usual manner; but if the box can be opened by using the staples as hinges, the real hinges may prove the best place to cut if there are fewer rivets there. The box used in the trick is entirely unprepared; it can be of a standard pattern. The escape artist must conceal a pair of cutters on his person and must be sure of his ability to clip the rivets. The box must be unlocked after the escape so that the staples may be replaced. Houdini planned two escapes which operated on the same principle as the iron express box.

The *metal bathtubs* required two small bathtubs with flat rims that could be set one upon the other. These were to be hinged, the performer placed inside, and the tubs secured by straps passing through staples. He also provided that straps could be used all around to hold two separate bathtubs together, the close-fitting rims preventing the use of a knife to cut the straps. The performer simply cut the rivets at the hinges or the staples. The purpose of the leather straps was to counteract the curve of the tubs. Being flexible, the straps would act as hinges where metal clamps would not! and this would obviate the necessity of cutting and replacing all the fastenings.

The *sprinkling wagon escape* was an idea similar to that of the iron express box. The performer was to be placed inside a regular sprinkling wagon, and the cover would then be clamped down and locked. Here again the method was to cut the rivets in the hinge or staple.

THE IRON BOX CHALLENGE

THIS escape is made from a box of solid iron, the corners and sides being riveted in place. The cover of the box is also made of iron, and fits down over the box itself. Designed as a challenge, this box can be made by any manufacturer or under the auspices of any group of challengers. The box is exactly what it appears to be—a large box of iron that will withstand almost any amount of pressure or hammering. The box itself has no device for locking. It must contain air-holes in the top, as usual in escape devices, and a large hole is drilled in each side near the upper edge, with corresponding holes in the cover.

The sketch provides for four of these holes; one in each side, the box being nearly cubical in shape, and large enough to contain the performer, with allowance for space in which to move. The method of fastening the cover on the box is also convincing. Four solid bolts are used, each with a large head; and these bolts fit into the holes in the sides of the box. The bolts are pushed through from the inside, and

the ends that protrude have holes in them so that padlocks may be attached. The box and the bolts are
placed on exhibition and any one can satisfy himself
that this escape must be impregnable, first because of
the strength of the material used, second because of
the size and solidity of the bolts. The bolts must
necessarily be large so as to allow for holes of sufficient size to receive the padlocks.

When the escape is to be made, the box is brought
on the stage; the performer enters it, and the bolts
are inserted by the committee members. Then the lid
is pressed down on the box; the bolts are pushed
through, and the padlocks are attached. There is no
possible way for the performer to reach the locks;
they are large and of standard pattern, examined or
supplied by the challengers. Apparently the performer is in the box to stay. The box is covered with
the cabinet, and several minutes pass by; then the
curtain opens and the escapist steps out. There is
the box, the padlocks still on the bolts. Everything is
examined inside and outside, and all is found to be
in regular order.

The artifice by which this escape is accomplished
is very simple. It depends upon the method by which
the cover is fastened to the box, a plan which is specially suited to be of aid to the performer. The only
way to hold the cover to the box is by bolts through

the holes. This seems fair enough because the bolts are made of iron, like the box, and are of simple, solid construction. The heads of the bolts must be on the inside, so that the locks can be attached on the out-

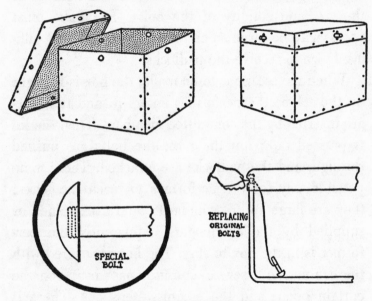

DETAILS OF THE IRON BOX CHALLENGE

side. The heads of the bolts are quite as strong as the box itself. But when the cover is placed on the box, the bolts must be drawn in to allow it to pass. This is done by the performer. When the cover is fitted in place, he pushes the bolts back again.

That is what the committee-men believe he does; actually, when he draws in the bolts, he pulls them all the way in and lays them on the floor of the box. Concealed on his person are four fake bolts, exactly resembling the genuine ones; and these bolts are the ones he pushes out. The difference between the fake bolts and the genuine bolts is this: the fake bolts have heads that unscrew. They are made in two pieces instead of one. As soon as the cabinet is closed over the box, the performer unscrews the heads from the fake bolts, draws them in, and pushes out the free ends. The bolts fall with the padlocks, and the performer is free to lift the cover of the box. The notes on this escape show short chains attached from the box to the padlocks; these serve the ostensible purpose of keeping the padlocks permanently attached to the box; their actual use is to prevent the bolts and padlocks from clattering to the floor when they are pushed out.

The method of replacing the bolts is not given in the notes on this escape, but this detail is not difficult to supply. By using large holes in the box and cover, strings may be attached to the genuine bolts and passed through the holes in the box and the cover. When the cover is replaced on the box, the strings are drawn, pulling the bolts out again. Then the padlocks are picked or unlocked and are transferred from the fake bolts to the real ones.

THE SHELVED BOX ESCAPE

THE shelved box was never built or used by Houdini for escape work, but he invented the trick and gave the idea to another performer, who made a box according to the instructions and used it frequently. The box is an upright cabinet or cupboard made of unpainted wood with a hinged door that opens outward. When the door is closed, a hasp on the door passes over a staple on the side and is held in place by a padlock. The unique feature of the box is a row of shelves that fit in the interior. These shelves go into slides; each shelf consists of two pieces, with semicircular holes in one side.

Three halves of the shelves are pushed into the slides and the performer takes his position in the cabinet. The front halves of the shelves are inserted with the holes inward and the result is that the performer is held in a series of stocks, one at his neck, one at his waist, and one at his ankles. To hold these stocks in position, chains are passed through small holes in the shelves and are locked with padlocks.

Then the performer's hands are crossed, chained, and padlocked. Finally the door of the cabinet is shut and locked. As the shelves come against the door, the performer is doubly secured in the stocks, for he

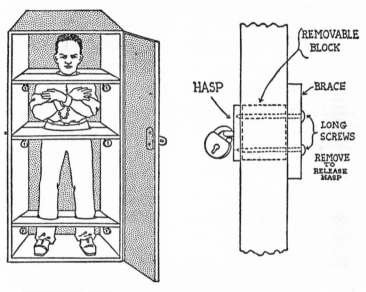

PERFORMER IMPRISONED IN THE SHELVED BOX. DETAILS OF MECHANISM

could not escape from them by pushing them apart even if the chains were open. The diagram accompanying the explanation of this escape shows all the padlocks beneath the shelves; hence the only padlocks that are accessible if the hands should be freed are those on the upper shelf. There is no reason why these should not be under the upper shelf, so that they also would be out of reach of the performer's hands. Every part of the apparatus stands close inspection, and its construction is so plain and simple that the device is very convincing in appearance.

In making the escape, the performer first releases his hands, which is not difficult, as they are chained in one of the several manners that enable him to obtain slack and slip his hands. His next step is to open the door; this is done by operating a faked hasp. The hasp is controlled by long screws or rods which pass through a cross-brace on the inside of the door; when his hands are free, the performer draws a screwdriver from his pocket, turns the special screws, and thus pulls the rods out of the way. Then he pushes the door open. The padlocks are reachable and are opened with duplicate keys, or, if mechanical locks are used, they can be opened with the hands alone.

This enables the performer to release himself from the top shelf and the center shelf; with these out of the way he bends down and attends to the bottom shelf. The rest is obvious: he replaces the shelves, opens the outer lock, replaces the hasp, closes the door, and locks it again. This is a very practical escape and the apparatus is both convincing and inexpensively constructed.

THE PLATE GLASS BOX

THE escape from a box made of sheets of plate glass was performed by Houdini, and also by Mrs. Houdini. It is an interesting and unusual escape, as the performer, when imprisoned, is visible from every angle. The box is of simple construction. The sides are held together by metal angles; these are held in place by heavy bolts which pass through holes drilled in the glass and in the angles. The bolts are very tight; the heads are on the inside; hence the nuts cannot be undone by any one who is imprisoned in the box. There are two angles for each pair of connecting edges. The cover of the box—also a sheet of plate glass—lies flat on the top of the box proper, and is hinged to one of the long sides of the box. Three hinges are used; they are held in place with bolts, just as the angles are kept in position. The use of three hinges makes the cover fit exactly. The front side of the box has two hinged hasps at the upper edge; the top has two metal staples projecting up at the front edge, held by tight bolts and nuts.

When the performer enters the box, the cover is closed; the hasps are folded down on the top, and large, heavy padlocks are slipped through the staples. The glass box may be thoroughly examined. Washers

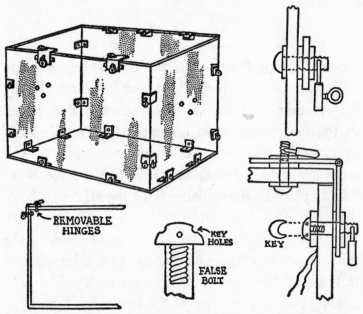

REMOVABLE HINGES

KEY HOLES

FALSE BOLT

KEY

THE PLATE GLASS BOX. NOTE HOW THE BOLTS ARE LOCKED. THE DIAGRAMS SHOW CONSTRUCTION OF THE FALSE BOLTS

are used with the bolts in order to protect the glass, but there is no deception about them. The fact that plate glass is used makes any hidden mechanism an impossibility. Any person can satisfy himself that the box is without preparation, and an inspection can be made in a very few minutes. Yet the performer escapes from the crystal casket a few minutes after the cabinet is placed over it, and the box is found to be as firmly locked as ever.

The secret of the escape lies in the hinges. These are not faked, but the bolts through the back of the box are of special construction. Each bolt is large and consists of two portions, the bolt itself, which is hollow at one end, and the bolt-head, which is provided with a small screw-bolt. When the bolt-head is screwed into the hollow end of the bolt (which is threaded to receive it), the result is apparently a solid bolt that exactly resembles the real bolts used on all the other parts of the glass box. From inside the box, the performer can unscrew the bolt-heads, push the bolts out of the holes, lift up the cover with the hasps acting as hinges, and thus make an escape.

So that the bolts may pass the most rigid inspection, the heads are screwed in so tightly that they cannot be removed except by the use of a special tool. One method of accomplishing this is with bolts that have small holes in the solid heads. The holes are short depressions that do not extend deep into the heads. The performer has a flat key, with extending prongs, which are pushed into the holes of each bolt-head; the key is turned, and the bolt-head is quickly and easily unscrewed. After the escape, the replacement of the special bolts is not a difficult matter. The heads are put back in place, and the nuts are removed. The bolts may be attached to cords which are passed through the holes in the glass so that the bolts may be drawn into position from within the box and the nuts replaced. But if the padlocks are the performer's own or are of a type which may be easily opened, the simplest method is to unlock them, releasing the front of the cover, and thus replace the bolts in the hinges. The cover may then be closed and relocked. Another method is to tilt the box backward, slip the bolts through the holes in the back, and fit the hinges over the ends of the bolts, after which the nuts may be tightened from the outside. It is quite an easy matter to substitute genuine bolts for the special bolts after the escape. The extra bolts may be concealed in the cabinet. This will allow the glass box to be examined with no possibility of any one's discovering the secret.

The only article which the performer must carry into the box is the small flat key, which may be concealed without any difficulty. There are no less than forty-two bolts used in the plate glass box. These are all exactly alike in appearance. All but three of them are genuine. With so many bolts to examine, and without the special tool at their disposal, the committee-men have no opportunity to discover anything amiss. Suspicious committee-men naturally direct their attention to the hasps and staples of the box.

The bolts used there are genuine; that is a subtle feature of the trick. Opening the cover from the hinge side is an excellent procedure. The plate glass box is an ingenious escape, because its secret is so effectively protected. It is effective because it is quickly and easily accomplished and affords no complications. It is convincing to both the audience and the committee because of its simple construction that permits a view of the interior after the box is closed.

PART FIVE.

UNDER-WATER ESCAPES

THE addition of water as an element of danger and difficulty always added to the effectiveness of Houdini's escapes.

The kinds of apparatus described in this section vary both in appearance and in working, but all of them involve water.

RUBBER BAG AND GLASS BOX

O F ALL the escapes explained in Houdini's notes, the rubber bag and glass box most aptly proves that a very simple trick can be made into a spectacular mystery if properly presented. Everything in this trick is designed to mislead the audience. The objects that are used seem free of trickery because of their construction. It appears that the escape must require a long time to accomplish, whereas it is very quick; and finally, the escape seems to be full of complications, while actually it is comparatively easy of execution.

The conditions under which the performer is imprisoned are novel and unusual. He is placed in a bag made entirely of rubber, which will pass close examination. Then the top of the bag is tied with rope and knotted by members of the committee. In the sides of the rubber bag are two small holes; these are fitted with valves, so that two long pieces of rubber hose may be attached. A water-tight box is then required. The committee has been examining this, and the inspection shows that it is a glass aquarium with wooden posts and bottom, sheets of glass set in a wooden frame with a hinged top provided with a hasp and staple at the other side.

The bag containing the performer is placed in the glass box, and water is introduced with a fire-hose. As soon as the water reaches a point above the bag, an assistant begins to let oxygen into one hose from a tank; the other hose passes off to a post, and allows bad air to escape. The cover has two cut-outs, one on each side, so that when the glass box is filled with water and the top is closed, nothing interferes with the rubber hose. Then the box is padlocked, and the cabinet covers the box, leaving the assistant with the oxygen tank outside.

By this time the audience is deeply interested. Here is a double problem. The performer must escape from the rubber bag and then make his exit from the box. Meanwhile he is dependent on the hose for air. To escape from the bag first will leave him without his air supply, and he may not have time to work free from the box; to escape from the box first seems quite impossible, for the rubber bag interferes with the performer's actions.

Yet that is the way he intends to go about it. For when the curtains are thrown aside, the performer is not only free but dry. The glass box is locked and may be examined; the rubber bag is inside, still knotted, and puffed with air!

From the standpoint of presentation, this trick is excellent. It is one that people will talk about; it is therefore a real box office attraction. Furthermore the man who does it has a much easier task than the audience supposes, and to a performer of Houdini's ability, the trick would be nothing more than a simple routine. At the same time, this is an escape designed for a showman, and Houdini's extensive notes on the trick prove that he recognized its great possibilities.

Analyzing this escape, we observe that the performer must release himself from the glass box before attending to the rubber bag. The release from the box must be sure and easy, yet well concealed, for the performer is unquestionably handicapped by being in the bag. Hence Houdini states that the top must come up away from the frame so that by simply standing up, the cover is raised. "This," he wrote, "can be cleverly concealed" in the following manners:

First Method. The glass is attached to the top by a brass binding which is heavy at the corners; that is, the glass simply rests on the wooden frame, and the brass holds it in position. Bolts pass through the brass and enter the wood. These bolts go into holes that have been made in the wood. Hence the glass is held firmly to the top, but the bolts are removable. They appear to serve the purpose of screws, fastened into the wood itself. The top thus stands careful examination, especially as the spectators in the committee are devoting most of their attention to the lower part of the frame, where it fits on the framework of the box.

There is no indication of the bolts inside the box; they cannot be operated from there; hence no one worries about them. The persons examining the box are easily convinced that the glass part is firmly in place. The performer cannot reach the outside of the box. This is where the assistants play an important part. It is necessary for them to move the box slightly so that the cabinet may be set on it. They naturally take hold of the top corners of the box, and their fingers finding the bolts draw the bits of iron back from the wooden holes. The bolts, it may be observed, are not necessarily removable. They cannot come all the way out. Slots from the brass binding down will enable them to slide up with the binding when the ends of the bolts do not engage the holes that are deep in the woodwork.

There may be several bolts at each corner; all may work free (either by slots or by faked bolt heads) except one key bolt at each corner; these hold the glass and the binding firmly enough to pass inspection. Thus when the performer stands up in the rub-

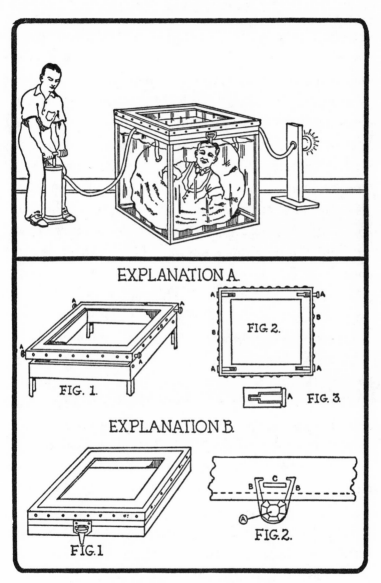

EXPLANATION A.

FIG. 1.

FIG. 2.

FIG. 3.

EXPLANATION B.

FIG.1

FIG.2.

THE RUBBER BAG AND GLASS BOX

ber bag, he can lift off the glass and its broad brass binding and carefully set it alongside of the box, using his hands through the rubber bag.

Second Method. This release is in the hasp on the outside of the box. The staple is on the box; the hasp portion is on the cover. There are no inside connections, but the staple itself is operated in a neat mechanical fashion. Pulling on it will not disengage it from the box; *spreading* it will do the trick. Instead of using a padlock, an examined bolt and nut are used to hold the hasp to the staple. These are placed in position. The bolt is wedge-shaped, and is forced down tight by an assistant. This makes the fastening appear secure; it also spreads the staple automatically, and when the performer presses against the top of the box, the staple comes out, allowing the cover to be raised.

Thus the entire cover of the box is solid and will stand any amount of examination; after the performer is out, a slight loosening of the bolt allows him to put the staple back in its original position. An alternate type of staple is a metal fitting that goes in the woodwork of the box. This is held by strong springs or fastenings, and ordinary pulling will not remove it. When the performer presses firmly against the front of the cover, he pulls the staple clear of the woodwork.

Third Method. This plan, which Houdini considered probably the best, reverts to the extreme top of the cover—where the glass is bound into the box. The binding is held to the woodwork by hidden catches set in the woodwork. Bolts or screws through the binding either are free in the wood (by slots) or do not enter it. Yet the catches hold the binding securely, and there is no way in which they can be discovered or removed by the committee. These catches are actuated by little levers in the woodwork; the levers are horizontal and end in plugs set in vertical holes. On the framework of the box are pins that correspond with these holes. The obvious purpose of the pins and holes is to set the cover squarely on the box and hold it there so that padlocks may be attached to hasps and staples on all sides. Everything undergoes a rigid examination before the trick, for the glass and its framework are actually secure to the top of the cover. But as soon as the cover is fitted into position, the pins automatically operate the hidden catches, and the glass and framework may be pushed upward. The framework should be a tight fit, requiring a certain amount of pressure to free it. After escaping, the performer simply puts the glass and framework on again. As soon as the cabinet is removed, the locks are examined and taken off; then the assistants lift the cover and offer it for another examination. The catches having springs are back in their original position, and the entire top is in perfect condition.

The Bag Escape. Escaping from the bag is an important item; the performer accomplishes this by untying the knots through the bag itself. The bag is made of thin rubber, and the knots can be very effectively handled. Houdini made little mention of this item, for untying knots through cloth or rubber offered him no difficulty. The supplying of a short length of rope makes it impossible to tie intricate knots, and the performer can retie the bag after he is out of it. Yet the use of the bag is extremely effective, especially because of the water. It makes a good box trick into an extraordinary one, and the bag escape and tank escape are an excellent combination when worked together.

Of course the performer does not replace the parts of the glass box until he has released himself from the bag. He puts the bag into the box before making the box as secure as in the beginning, and being free from the bag, he has no difficult operations. It is also essential that the bag should be tied in a regular manner so that no difference will be detected by the committee; furthermore, the knots are wet and are not so easy to handle as dry knots. But well tied with square-knots, the bag will unfailingly satisfy the usual stage committee. As the preparations for the trick are rather elaborate and lengthy, the time allowed for this work is too short to permit delayed tying. In an emergency the performer may simply cut the rope with a sharp-pointed instrument and replace the old one with a new rope, covering the small opening in the rubber; or he can destroy the bag itself by cutting it or ripping it, replacing it with another bag tied exactly like the original. A duplicate bag and rope are therefore items of equipment to be concealed in the performer's cabinet.

THE CRYSTAL WATER CASKET

THIS is one of the most spectacular of all escapes. Consider a man imprisoned in a massive casket entirely filled with water and secured from the outside with genuine locks and massive straps, the walls and top of the casket made of glass! The escape must be effected within a very few minutes, and escape seems impossible, for alert committee-men may examine and seal the contrivance. Yet Houdini not only planned such a formidable device; he devised an ingenious method of getting out of it. The casket as the audience sees it is a strong wooden framework that supports sides of clear glass. A heavy cover fits on the casket; the sides of the cover are of glass, and so is the top. Both parts may be carefully inspected. Brass trimmings are on the edges, and the casket and cover are water-tight. There is a certain peculiarity of the cover that serves a definite purpose. The sheet of glass on the top has a hole in the center. This hole is bound with metal and connected to the brass rim of the cover by flat bars both above and below the glass.

The casket is filled with water, and the performer appears in a bathing suit. Then he enters the casket and stands there with his head and shoulders out of water. The cover is lifted and set on the casket. It has a close-fitting downward flange that goes over the top edges of the casket and makes the whole affair water-tight. Each side of the cover is supplied with a large mechanical lock which operates perfectly. These locks are thoroughly examined by the committee, and they pass inspection. They are inaccessible from within the cabinet. But to render the contrivance doubly secure, there are two staples on each side of the cover and corresponding staples on each side of the casket. As these staples are horizontal, the committee-men can run heavy straps through them. Thus there are four straps, two in each direction, passing over and under the casket, which is mounted slightly to permit the passage of the straps. No effort is spared to make these straps tight, and they are buckled at the bottom of the cabinet. Their purpose is evident. Should the locks fail to hold the cover, the straps would still be an insurmountable barrier. For the lip or flange of the cover is too deep to allow the performer to reach through by pressing the cover upward. The heavy straps are virtually unyielding; pressure can stretch them but the fraction of an inch. The only opening into the casket is the hole in the center of the cover;

it is so small that the performer can merely put his arm through. But a hemispherical cap is designed to fit over it, and this fastens down to solid bolts or clamps that are thoroughly inspected and approved by the committee.

When the escapist is in the casket and the cover is on with the straps and locks firmly secured, a funnel is inserted in the small hole in the center of the top, and water is poured in through a hose. The closed casket is water-tight; hence the water-level rises, and the performer, who has moved to a corner, is entirely immersed, with no possibility of obtaining air, for the water comes to the very top. Then the hemispherical cover is clamped on the hole; the bolts or clamps work quickly, so that the prison is sealed within a few seconds. Curtains are drawn about the apparatus, and the audience realizes that the performer is in a most precarious position. Three or four minutes seem the maximum time permissible for this escape, due to the lack of air within the casket; and the performer has lost a few precious seconds in the closing of the hole in the top. As the minutes go by, the spectators become tense and wonder what is going on inside the curtains. For this escape carries a real element of danger. Suddenly the curtains are thrown aside and there stands the performer, dripping with water. The casket is still locked and strapped; the water-level has dropped because the performer is no longer within. The committee steps forward to inspect the apparatus. Nothing has been changed; everything is secure. The casket may be opened if desired, and an inspection of the interior will show nothing amiss. There is a certain similarity between the crystal water casket and the glass box from which the performer escapes while in a rubber bag. But in the crystal casket, quick escape is much more essential, and the apparatus is much heavier and more formidable. The first thing to consider is the spot where the performer makes his exit. This is at the extreme top of the cover. As in the glass box, the glass lifts off with the brass binding. This part of the apparatus must be secure when the committee examines it; yet it must be capable of quick release. The first method used in the glass box can be applied to the crystal casket also. A loose brass binding, held with bolts that fit in holes and draw back to slots, will serve. These bolts are in the corners and are withdrawn by the assistants while moving the casket. But it is not the ideal arrangement, first because there is no excuse for delay, second because the casket is very heavy and cannot well be moved. The curtains are placed around it or a cabinet lowered over it.

So Houdini planned a special release for the interior, and while his diagrams are lacking in mechanical details, they at least give the fundamental idea of the method he devised. There are hidden catches in the center of each portion of brass framework. The framework is enlarged at these points, because it connects with the hole in the center of the top. The diagrams indicate a single release for each of these catches, operating from the center of the top. This appears to be a twist of the center rim, giving a corresponding turn to the flat rods extending to the brass framework. The rods operating thus are the ones beneath the glass. One arrangement would be for this to turn or operate by moving the cap itself, and it is possible to have the turning take place only when the cap is in position; it is simpler, however, to have everything take place from beneath, in which case the rods can move independently, each being operated individually from a position at the center. Their release may also depend on pressure from pins used to set the cap in place.

These details, while based on a study of Houdini's sketches, are speculative; the important point is that he regarded such a release as being not only practical but also undetectable and preferable to any other. If his plans had proven unsatisfactory, the release used in the glass box could have been applied to the crystal casket also. There are three factors in addition to its mechanical perfection that guard the secret of the release. First, there is much to be done and inspection is sure to be brief: second, every one looks for trickery at the spot where the cover joins the casket, so that attention is centered there; third, the straps seem to preclude all possibility of any mechanical arrangement. It is these straps which are our next consideration. Having released the top of the cover, what can the performer do? The straps are not faked, and he is still in the cabinet.

The brass binding offers the solution. It is not wide except at the corners and at the middle points where it joins with the strips or rods that go to the center of the top. In those spots it is apparently fastened to the woodwork, but the bolts are fakes or short bolts that fit in slots in the wood. Between the middle points and the corners, the binding does not come far below the glass. Now the straps will give, no matter how tightly they are fastened. They will not yield sufficiently to be of any use at the bottom of the cover, where the overhanging edge is thick and deep to make the casket entirely water-tight; but at the binding only a little stretching is necessary to enable the performer to insert a thin-bladed knife between the binding and the woodwork. The straps pass by spots where the binding is not deep, and the knife can be worked through when the performer presses upward on the top of the cover.

Thus he cuts all four straps; then he lifts the top of the cover and leaves the box. There is one important point, however, which must not be overlooked. The performer has released the top; he has cut the straps; but what has he done for air in the meantime? He certainly cannot count on finishing operations on the straps before he is out of breath. The answer to this problem is found in the hemispherical cover that fits over the center of the top. It contains air; and when the performer needs a fresh supply, he goes back to it. The cap is smaller than his head; hence its purpose is not suspected. The performer gets the air by tilting his head backward so that his nose and mouth come out of the water! Houdini evidently estimated that the few breaths the performer would require were contained within the cap, but he also had an emergency measure in case the cap should prove too small for its required purpose. That was to have the bottom of the cap slightly faulty, so that when it was clamped down it could never lie absolutely flat on the rim beneath. As a result the cap would not be air-tight, and the performer's air supply could last almost indefinitely.

Once out of the casket, the performer's task is to remove the cut straps and replace them with duplicates hidden in the cabinet covering the casket. He must also replace the catches so that the top of the

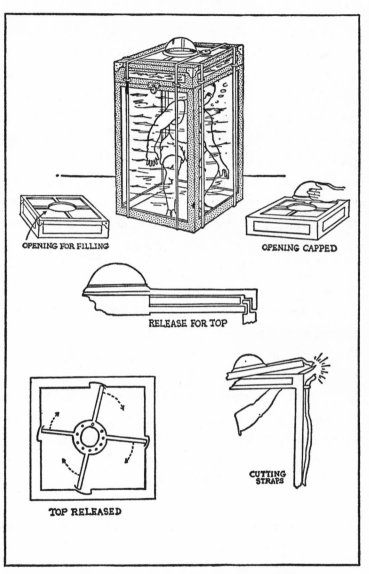

OPENING FOR FILLING

OPENING CAPPED

RELEASE FOR TOP

TOP RELEASED

CUTTING STRAPS

DETAILS OF THE CRYSTAL WATER CASKET

cover will be firmly in position. That is why a turn of the cap is desirable, for the catches can then be thrown back from the outside of the casket. If such a mechanism is too complicated and the catches must be handled from inside the cover, the performer must unlock the locks, remove the cover, and fit the top portion into position. The locks, while genuine, are part of the casket, so that duplicate keys are easily retained by the performer. No water will come from the casket when the top is removed, for the performer's body has displaced a considerable quantity, and the level will normally be below the upper edge of the casket. If the glass box type of release is used (i.e. a release from outside the cabinet) the performer's task is simplified, as he has merely to undo the simple action of his assistants before the escape.

To the audience the crystal water casket is a sensational escape in which the odds are so greatly against the performer that his act of freeing himself seems miraculous. To the performer it is a workable device that requires nerve and ability but is well worth it because of its effectiveness. Houdini, with his fearlessness and strength, his ability and his experience, could attempt escapes of this caliber and present them successfully where others would have hesitated and eventually abandoned the idea.

A GLASS CABINET

THIS method of escaping from a glass cabinet of simple construction is not one of Houdini's originations; it was given to him by the designer, and it is quite obviously inferior to the escapes created by Houdini. It involves, however, a novel use for padlocks of special construction.

The trick requires a glass case or cabinet taller than the performer and made entirely of glass. This would probably need a metal bottom and reënforced sides, as the glass cabinet is to hold water. There are two holes in each side of the cabinet; these are just below the top edge, making eight holes in all. The performer is imprisoned in the cabinet by the simple process of covering it with a sheet of glass which has holes drilled in the edges close to the holes in the cabinet. Eight padlocks are used. These are tested beforehand, and as soon as the performer is under the lid of the cabinet the locks are slipped into place, each lock going through a hole in the cabinet and a hole in the sheet of glass.

As the time element is important, with water in the cabinet, self-locking padlocks are used. They are snapped into place quickly, and curtains are placed over the glass cabinet. The trick lies in the padlocks. These are double-acting. Pressure on a knob or center point on the arm of one of these locks releases it. The performer presses all the locks, slips them from the holes, and lifts the sheet of glass. Coming out of the cabinet, he replaces the sheet of glass and snaps the locks back in place.

With eight locks, the time required to escape would be to the performer's disadvantage unless the cabinet contained some air. Four would be preferable if the cabinet were entirely filled with water. The real merit of the trick lies in the fact that these locks can be neither unlocked nor picked, for the key-holes, hinges, and clasps are impossible to reach. Performed without the use of water, it would make a sure and effective escape.

THE SUBMERGED TRUNK ESCAPE

THE mystery of the submerged trunk was devised by Houdini in 1909, or before; his complete notations and sketches are dated Croydon, England, September 9, 1909. It is one of those rare escapes that carry a double mystery, and it illustrates Houdini's capability for making a seemingly miraculous effect out of a rather hackneyed trick. For with the submerged trunk, the escape seems unbelievable even after it has been accomplished. The trunk used in the escape is large and solidly made. It possesses no air-holes; on the contrary it must be made air-tight, so that it may be submerged in a tank of water. This tank has a glass front; after the performer is locked in the trunk, his air-tight prison is lifted and lowered into the tank, where it is completely under water. Then the curtain is drawn around the tank.

It is obvious that the performer must escape quickly. The trunk has been hurriedly locked and roped, and the expectant audience realizes that no time must be lost, because of the limited supply of air. This adds to the tenseness of the situation. After several minutes have passed, the curtain opens and out steps the performer. He has made the escape, but to the amazement of the audience he is as dry as when he entered the trunk! The cabinet is removed, and everything undergoes the most rigid examination. The trunk is still in the tank, under water. It is lifted from the tank and inspected; the locks are still fastened, and the ropes are intact. The trunk is opened, and the interior is shown to be quite dry.

This bewildering effect is particularly good from the magician's standpoint, for it offers a variety of impractical solutions, all of which, like the trunk, do not hold water. "An optical illusion"—"duplicate trunks"—"the performer is never in the trunk"—"the tank empties and refills itself"—these are the theories that will occur to members of the committee on the stage; yet they will find no evidence to support any of these pet beliefs. This is indeed an escape that can create amazement. Yet the secret is very simple; in fact, it should be, in an escape of this sort, and the practical ingenuity of the trick is something that will not be noticed.

The tank is unprepared; the trick lies in the trunk, which is nothing more nor less than an escape trunk of the well-known style, operating by means of a secret panel in the end, the panel opening inward.

A trunk of this type will stand close examination by any committee, and the trunk used in this particular escape, being water-tight and heavy, is particularly well designed to preserve its secret. In the trunk are two flat metal weights. They may be placed in the trunk beforehand, or they may be inserted just before the performer enters. In either event their purpose is too obvious to excite comment. Without them the trunk would not sink; when they are inside the trunk there is no possibility of their removal while the trunk is under water. The weights are in the bottom of the trunk, rather close to the ends, held in place by hooks or fasteners. On the bottom of the tank are two bars or rollers on which the trunk rests. The apparent purpose of these bars, which are rather close together, is to keep the trunk above the bottom of the tank, so that there is no possibility of exit in that direction, and the audience may see under the trunk when it is submerged.

But the weights and the bars serve a much more important purpose than the spectators suppose. Houdini's method would be to remove the weight, when he was in the trunk, from the end where the secret door was situated, and to transfer it to the other end of the trunk, at the same time moving his body to the end with the weights. The bars in the bottom of the tank, being high, crosswise, and close together, would immediately produce the desired results. The heavy end of the trunk would tip so that the trunk would stand on end, the upper end coming just above the level of the water in the tank! The next step

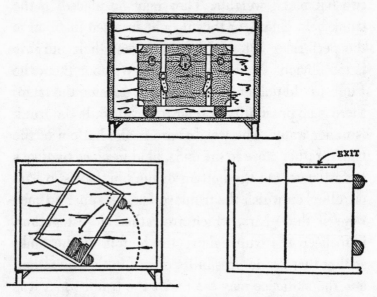

CHANGE OF POSITION IN THE SUBMERGED TRUNK ENABLING
PERFORMER TO ESCAPE CLEAR OF THE WATER

would be for Houdini to open the secret panel and make his escape from the trunk, swinging his body over the edge of the tank and bringing the loose weight along with him. By this system he could re-place the loose weight in its proper position at the upper end of the trunk, close the secret opening, and give the upper end of the trunk a push that would immediately cause it to drop back and resume its original position.

In a sketch accompanying the explanation of this mystery, Houdini indicated that the cross rods should be attached to the bottom of the trunk and not to the tank itself. This was evidently intended to make the return journey of the trunk a positive matter, the bars having a curved bottom to make the tipping easy. This appears to be the final design of the apparatus. The size and depth of the tank are, of course, important. It must be long to allow for the space into which the trunk turns when on end; it must be deep enough to be convincing, yet shallow enough so that the end of the trunk will emerge. Distance from front to back was reduced to a minimum, so that the rear edge of the tank would be within the performer's reach. The use of very heavy weights is justifiable and logical, for the trunk is supposed to be definitely submerged with no chance of floating. Hence the very factors that aid the performer in his escape are accepted by the spectators as obstacles to his success.

Houdini's notes also mention a canvas cover for the trunk, of the type used in the regular trunk escape. This, of course, is arranged so that the two pieces of canvas may be spread apart above the secret panel. This would necessitate a slight delay, particularly because the canvas would be wet, and Houdini was doubtful whether it would add to the effectiveness of the mystery.

Inasmuch as the usual trunk escape has never lost its popularity, the use of the tank and the submerged trunk, with the mystery of the performer's escaping dry, affords great possibilities for sensational showmanship.

HOUDINI'S DOUBLE BOX MYSTERY

THE notes on this escape are dated Berlin, October 29, 1912, 4 A.M. They are written in ink and illustrated with rough diagrams, and it is probable that Houdini had been working since midnight, planning the details of the proposed escape. The notes contain a variety of ideas, and from these a clear impression is gained of the escape as Houdini intended it and of the basic method by which he expected to accomplish it. Some of the mechanical details offer complications, but they do not appear impossible of solution, and the escape is so ingenious and unusual both in effect and method that it offers unusual possibilities. The double box mystery was planned some three years after the submerged trunk escape, and the two escapes are similar in effect, yet entirely different in method of operation. It was Houdini's plan to construct two boxes, one considerably larger than the other, each having a firmly fitting top, particularly the smaller box, which needed to be water-tight. The large box used in the escape is mounted on heavy legs; the smaller box is similarly mounted and is within the large box, its legs being bolted firmly to the bottom of the large box. The large box has a glass front so that the audience can see the smaller box within.

The performer enters the smaller box; it is locked with a hasp over a staple, and the outer box is flooded with water. As Houdini states in his notes: "The small box is filled with me and air; the large box is filled with water, so that I am completely surrounded by water." There is no necessity for weights on the small box; the legs hold it to the bottom of the large box.

After the large box is locked, the cabinet is placed over the affair, and the performer makes his escape, dry. Yet when the curtains are raised the small box is still fast to the bottom of the large one, locked as it was before the escape.

There are two problems here: the performer must open the boxes, and he must not get wet. The only way of doing this, Houdini decided, is to bring up the small box and open both boxes together. Accordingly he planned to have the boxes act with a very simple and sure release, for he knew that the real mystery centered in the dry escape. "The covers of both boxes," the notes state, "work on the hasps. When the hasp of either box is lowered, it releases all catches, and when I lift up the cover of the small box,

I raise it until it lifts up the cover of the large box also."

This was Houdini's original plan; he follows with another arrangement. Figuring that the self-releasing

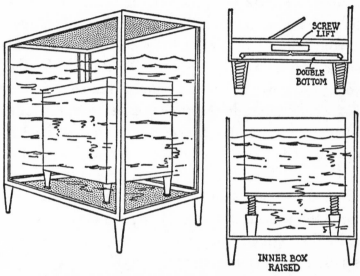

OPERATION OF LIFTING DEVICE IN THE DOUBLE BOX MYSTERY, SHOWING SMALLER BOX ABOVE THE SURFACE OF THE WATER

cover would not prove air-tight, he states: "The small box must be air-tight; so the cover must have a round center, on the style of a ship's porthole, so I can unscrew it from the inside.

"The hinges of the large box can be faked so when closed it may be pulled away from the pin hinge by a strong push from beneath, the lock and hasps acting as a hinge."

To make these methods work, the top of the small box must be up against the top of the large box. Unless that is accomplished, it does not matter how the covers are worked. Therefore the crux of the trick is Houdini's method of bringing up the small box. This he proposed to do by having hollow metal legs supporting the small box, each leg to contain a metal screw device, the four operating together under the control of a wrench in the center of the box. Such a box would naturally require a double bottom, with a small compartment between, and a trap or hidden opening which could be lifted to operate the wrench.

Using such a method, the performer proceeds as follows: first he lifts the bottom of the small box and turns the wrench, thus elongating the legs to nearly twice their original height. This brings the top of the small box against the top of the large box. He clamps the wrench in place and raises the covers of both boxes, or opens the porthole in the small box and lifts the cover of the large box. Now, free, he steps from the inner box over the side of the outer one and uses some simple method (such as a chain or a bar) to hold up the small box, while he releases the wrench and replaces the top securely on the small box. The screws are so devised that when the small box is released it will return to its original position. Then the cover is replaced on the large box and fastened there.

Houdini also suggests a porthole in the top of the

large box. The object of the porthole in either the small box or in both boxes is to enable members of the committee to see the performer when he is under water. Naturally no suspicion is attached to the porthole in the small box, because it is under water and therefore of no value (presumably) to the performer. The fact that the porthole must be unscrewed from within and later secured from without indicates the use of long and short screws. The long screws are on the inside and hold the porthole firmly in place; the short screws are nothing more than heads tightly inserted from above so that when the inner screws are removed the porthole will be free. In closing the box, the short screws are inserted on the inside of the porthole; the long screws are inserted from the outside, and the device is quite as secure as in the beginning.

This is an escape of the most mysterious type. The mechanical arrangement of the legs of the smaller box is something which offers considerable difficulty in construction. The lifting of the inner box may not be practical as described, with the simultaneous operation and automatic lowering of the screw devices. Houdini's notes were not the description of a finished piece of apparatus, but were merely preliminary ideas on a new mystery. There are, however, many possibilities for changes and modifications in design, and it is probable that Houdini had in mind the practical plans of construction that would be required.

MILK CAN ESCAPES

THE escape from a milk can was performed by Houdini on many occasions. It was an escape that held its popularity and was highly effective; for when Houdini did it, the can was filled with water to make the escape more difficult. Houdini's notes do not contain finished diagrams of special milk cans. There are references to "the old style can," the "1908 can," etc., and these prove that Houdini used several types of milk cans.

In his notes Houdini gives rough sketches that show in part the construction of milk cans, but all these notes refer to improvements or new developments of the trick; therefore the working of the milk can is merely mentioned in passing. Before explaining the working of this device, we must consider the trick as it appears to the audience; for then it will be possible to understand the various additions that Houdini introduced or planned.

The performer exhibits a large milk can. It is a cylinder of metal on which a collar is riveted, and a tapering tube goes up from the collar. A smaller cylinder, or neck, is attached to the tapering tube, and this is provided with staples. The can is filled with water, and the performer enters the can. He is attired in a bathing suit, and he displaces a quantity of water which splashes over the sides of the can and pours itself on a canvas carpet. The cover is a flat lid which is fitted with hasps; it is placed on the milk can, and the hasps are locked to the staples with padlocks. The performer must make his escape in very quick time.

It is understood, of course, that the milk can will bear a close examination. Its simple construction and the fact that it is made entirely of metal make it appear very secure and free from trickery. The simple method of escape depends on the fact that the collar of the tapering portion is not riveted to the top of the large cylindrical portion of the can. The rivets are there, but they are shams. Inside the milk can, the performer can separate the two portions at the joint. This is very practical, and despite its simplicity, it cannot be detected. The secret is safe because the collar fits tightly to the cylinder. It cannot be pulled from its position; no one can obtain a good hold on it. The sides of the collar are slippery (they may even be slightly greased), and there is no possibility of any one's budging it.

But from within the can, the performer is in an ideal position to work. With ordinary effort he can break the neck away from the cylinder and thus escape. The stronger the performer, the easier the escape. By removing the loose section and sliding it out of the way, all difficulties are overcome; and after the escape it is necessary merely to replace the loose portion and make sure that it is firmly in position so that it will again stand inspection.

The bottom of the milk can, riveted in place by an iron band, is a solid article. The band there is exactly like the one at the top, where the can separates. It is very important that the bottom should be tightly joined and well constructed so that there will be no leakage. This is not always possible with the joint at the top. The can is actually loose there, and despite the fact that it cannot be removed from the outside because it fits so tightly, leakage may result. But the can is not entirely filled with water—no water fills the neck; for when the performer enters, there will be an overflow even though the can is only partly filled. Hence nothing betrays the secret before the entry; the can appears quite water-tight in every respect. When the performer goes in, water comes up through the neck and down over the sides of the can; its presence accounts for any water trickling down the sides. The cover is quickly locked, and the escape is under way in the cabinet before any alert committee-man can even begin to make a test for leakage. Hence the secret of this milk can is protected from beginning to end, and it forms a most sensational escape. At the same time, a well-made, tightly fitting can will not leak if the parts are closely joined; this is proven by the double milk can escape, which is explained later.

Among Houdini's notes appears a method of using an *unprepared milk can* which could be used as the genuine commercial article. There are three hasps, solidly attached to the lid of the milk can. The staples are held by single rivets; each rivet comes through from the inside, and is square-bolted on the outside. These rivets are made of brass or copper. When they are put through the neck of the can, felt washers are used so that the heads do not press too tightly against the neck of the can. Everything is genuine, but if these rivets are cut from within, they can be pushed through from the inside and the staples will be free.

To make this method practical, Houdini suggested additional features in his notes. The milk can was to be large, so that there would be space to move freely while at work. The staples should be well down on the neck of the can—possibly attached to the collar below the neck, so as to be quickly and easily reached. The lid of the can was to be raised or bulging upward so that air could be obtained if the work took longer than expected, and the cover was to fit high and have the hasps so placed that the removal of a single staple would enable the performer to open the lid, using the other hasps as hinges. Finally the pliers or nippers were to be provided with a bag-like arrangement so that when the rivet was cut it would drop into the little bag and stay there. In this way the clew of a shining rivet head at the bottom of the milk can would be eliminated.

The notes state: "Have the can made in exact imitation of the can now in use, to deceive them," which shows that Houdini intended to use the unprepared milk can on special occasions. A milk can of this type would prove excellent for lobby display, and would also stand inspection from all points. A person placed inside it would be unable to escape; hence the performer could advertise it heavily. It is one of those escapes which Houdini would not have hesitated to attempt, but the average escape artist would not undertake it, even though he knew the secret and had the appliances.

Working under water when a quick escape was necessary was one of Houdini's accomplishments. He was able to cope with unexpected situations and to overcome obstacles that might—and sometimes did —prove disastrous to his imitators. While this escape is referred to as an "unprepared milk can escape," it depends on a special type of milk can designed for the use of the performer, not self-operating, but vulnerable, from the inside. Houdini's notes go still further with this type of escape and deal with a milk can that may be supplied by any one and that may be specially constructed with the definite purpose of keeping the performer in despite all his efforts.

Houdini's method for an escape from an unprepared milk can *on challenge* depends on the concealment of an assistant in the cabinet which hides the escape. The suggested method of concealment is given in the descriptions of Houdini's cabinet plans. Still the escape is not made certain merely by an assistant's being at hand. Houdini refers to important considerations that should not be neglected, and his ideas on the construction of the unprepared can are interesting.

They provide certain factors which **are** desirable, and which could be incorporated in the construction of the can if made by the performer or if built in accordance with his specifications. Houdini's plans were to make the milk can appear absolutely invulnerable, so that every one would be convinced of its genuineness and it could be examined and left on display indefinitely.

One of his ideas was the use of a glass can. He

states: "The top must be made so that it will fit on
the outside of the body of the can so that I can
breathe until the confederate unlocks or releases the
top. Air can enter above the neck, whereas if the lid
fits inside, it will make it air-tight. The top must not
rest tightly; there must be space for air to circulate.

"A good method of locking the can would be to
have heavy steel straps incasing it like a network and
have it made so that only one lock has to be opened;
also have it fixed so that in case all are 'strange' locks,
one rivet can be cut or one nut removed from a bolt,
thus allowing the cover to be lifted or shifted. Or
arrange it so that only one lock with a special hasp
will lock the strap together."

In his notebook Houdini mentions a glass milk
can, but suggests one made of metal, as follows:
"Have the can made of seamless material or of spun
brass. This will show that it is positively impossible
for any preparation; the cover or lid can be arranged
to lock with one to six locks. The best way is to have
the cover fixed permanently with a very heavy hinge
so that only one lock will be required. . . .

"In the first method I write that I could use a seamless or spun brass can; this may lead to the thought
that there is no preparation and might lead to the
fact that I am helped out.

"It would be best to have a suspicious-looking can

SINGLE
MILK CAN

FALSE
RIVET

DOUBLE
MILK CAN

DETAILS OF MILK CAN ESCAPES

made. This will attract attention and make them all look for a fake in the can. It is almost imperative that the bell-shaped top be used, so that in case of danger I could have time to get a change of breath, the hollow just allowing that with ease and comfort."

The following notes on the *regular milk can* were typed on a page of Houdini's stationery; they evidently served as memoranda when making plans for the construction of a new milk can. They are not dated, but they are included here because they are typical of many of the original notations that served as references in the preparation of this book:

"Improvements for can.

"Have one made larger. The circle must be at least 17 inches——

"IMPORTANT. Must have a slot or groove to have 'gag' fit at once and no moving, etc. etc.

"Have the top made so that it has a larger lip, and that when it is filled the water must not run over. This is important. Even if we have to put cork or rubber on top of the ledge.

"Handles must be down lower so no cuffs can be hung on to keep the lid on.

"Have all the rivets run in one straight line, and not three like the one now used.

"Have it made air-tight right from the start!!!!!"

THE DOUBLE MILK CAN

THE greatest improvement that Houdini contemplated for the milk can escape was the use of two milk cans, one inside the other. This is described in his notebook and is also mentioned in separate notes. Under the heading "Two in One Can Trick," dated Chicago, 1908, Houdini planned to set the regular milk can into a larger can that resembled an ash can and fastened with hasps and staples at the bottom instead of at the top. This is nothing more than the regular milk can trick, using an outer can with the top secretly removable; the top is merely a disc riveted to a heavy collar which clamps down on the cylindrical outer can and gives the appearance of solidity. But in a later development of the escape, Houdini planned to turn the milk can in which he was confined so that it would be upside down when inserted in a larger cylindrical can. The outer can would be filled with water like the inner, yet he would effect his escape.

The notes state: "The trick is to have two cans, one

to fit inside of the other. These cans must be large, so that I can stand in them in an upright position and make use of my shoulders in utilizing my strength.

"I am to be placed in one can in a standing position; this is to be turned upside down into the larger can, which is also filled with water. Both cans are locked.

"If the can works on the old style it is best to have the one I get into resting on a bridge or hanging apparatus so the weight of the water will not expose the trick. [This is because the collar that can be pushed upward is fastened to the bottom of the can, the top being genuinely riveted. The bottom will be at the top when the milk can is inverted.]

"The can must be made so that I can turn around and when I am apparently upside down I am turning around and my head and shoulders are up, ready to force the gag so as to get out.

"This wants to be very carefully worked out. The inside can must work at the bottom; the outside can must work at the top, so that both work together and in the same position. If required, the inner can may have a curved top so I can breathe until it is placed into the larger can. This will make the punishment less than if I have to go without breath the entire trick.

"Water can be poured in the outer can so that

when the smaller can is placed in the larger can it will splash all over and will be air-tight.

"The inside can cover must be made so that water will not come out when the can is turned over."

In loose notes on this escape, Houdini specifies certain things that must be guarded against. First the inner can must have handles so that it can be put into the larger can. He arranges for such handles on the collar at the bottom. As a result, carrying the can in an upright position will hold the false bottom in place. The handles are properly situated to appear natural, because the milk can must be tipped over when it is inserted upside down in the large cylindrical can.

"The cover of the outside can," Houdini stated in his notes, "must be high so that water does not really fill it. This is necessary to allow an air space; and the inner fake can be raised a few inches before touching the outside can, so that I do not have to separate both cans at the same time."

The result is obvious. The performer removes the fake bottom from the inner can almost as soon as the cover of the outer can is in position. He gains air immediately. Then he slides the inner can cover aside (allowing time for the cabinet to be placed over the apparatus), and with only the resistance of one cover remaining, the whole affair comes off. A sketch of the outer can shows that the fake lies in the metal collar to which the cover is attached by hasps, the staples being on the collar. Hence it is very similar to the simple method used in the regular milk can escape. From the notes it is evident that Houdini's thought was to create the impression that he could not turn over inside the inner can. With this belief in the minds of the audience, the effectiveness of the escape becomes tremendous.

PART SIX.

TRUNKS—BARRELS—COFFINS

HOUDINI's notes dealt with various methods of escaping from trunks, barrels, and coffins. These may be regarded as outgrowths of box escapes, and the fact that all of them employed standard articles has led to their inclusion in a separate section. Some of the escapes explained here may be performed as challenges with ordinary objects; others require specially designed apparatus.

TRUNK ESCAPES

AN ESCAPE from an unprepared trunk is not difficult, for the lock of such a trunk is usually fastened by a bolt with a nut on the inside. The trunk is made so that people cannot get in it, not so they cannot get out of it. Unless the clasps are fastened also, the performer who attempts this escape has merely to take off the nut and push out the bolt. A few tools and a flash light are all that are required. With the clasps fastened, the usual procedure is to unscrew the hinges, which are naturally on the inside of the trunk; then the lid can be lifted in reverse fashion.

It is interesting to note that the clasps, which are merely used to prevent strain on the lock and to hold down the ends of the cover, become a real barrier when the trunk is used as an object in which to confine a person. Houdini, however, had methods of overcoming them. He mentions these in his description of a rawhide trunk to be used as a challenge. The locks on the rawhide trunk could be made so that no bolt and nut arrangement would be usable. With such a trunk, Houdini planned special locks that could be unlocked from the inside, probably with a small key, or through a tiny hole in the lock which could be managed with a pin.

The first method of pushing back the clasps is to use a thin awl-like instrument; this is particularly adapted to the rawhide trunk, as the trunk itself could be pierced. The other method, which is possible with various types of trunks, is quite simple. The performer puts his head against the top of the trunk and presses upward; then he strikes the front of the trunk with his fist, hitting directly in back of the clasp. A well-directed blow will knock the clasp loose.

Houdini mentions a tin trunk fitted with a lock operating from the inside as well as from the outside, yet able to stand examination. It was used by a performer called Hanco, who escaped from the trunk while under water, by the simple method of opening the cover. While performing in an Australian town, Hanco unlocked the trunk too soon; and as it happened to turn while it was being let down from a bridge, the performer fell out before he reached the water, much to the amusement of the crowd.

An ingenious idea in connection with trunk escapes appears in Houdini's notes. It is specially applicable to an unprepared trunk. Some trunks have linings of cloth, and this must be cut to enable the performer to get at the lock or the hinges. To render the escape effective, the escape artist must repair the damage, unless he does not permit an examination after the trick is over. This work is not difficult; a supply of duplicate cloth and a bottle of glue will suffice. But Houdini developed this idea to the extent of having a solidly lined trunk which appeared to have an interior made of wood that was not removable. Instead of using wood, he planned to use heavy paper which resembled wood; this material would appear formidable; yet it would be no barrier to the performer. By tearing the paper away he could get at the parts of the trunk where operation was necessary, and after the escape he could reline the trunk with whatever amount of paper was needed, utilizing a supply hidden in the cabinet.

There are various forms of trunks designed for escape work. There is a similarity between them and certain types of boxes which have hinged covers. Houdini refers to various types of trunks and boxes in his notes and includes a brief description of a trunk-like box lined with zinc that can be filled with water while the performer is inside. This device was designed to work at the hinges, which had special removable pins. The essential difference between a box escape and a trunk escape is that the former involves a roughly made article which is nailed at the top, while the latter requires a permanently constructed device which is used indefinitely, locks, bolts, or clasps being used to fasten the outside.

The famous box trick performed by Maskelyne in England many years ago was really the original trunk trick. A reward of £500 was offered to any one who could duplicate the mystery, and it was won by Dr. J. W. Lynn in 1898. Dr. Lynn's box had an entire panel that was removable; it slid up and down between the framework at the top and bottom of the box. It was held up by a small marble located in a groove directly under the panel and also by a concealed spring. After the performer was locked in the box and a canvas cover placed on it, assistants moved the box to show all sides, and the tipping process caused the marble to roll to the end of the groove and into a shorter groove that ran along the front of the box at the bottom. By inserting his fingers in airholes, the performer was able to pull the panel downward and inward and then untie or loosen the cord holding the canvas cover. When this box was right side up, with the marble in position, its secret was absolutely undetectable, for the panel could not be opened. When the box was placed on end, the panel worked automatically.

BARREL AND CASK ESCAPES

ONE of the most convincing escapes described by Houdini is that from a large barrel or cask. The simplicity of the article impresses the audience. No locks or attachments are necessary. When the performer is placed inside and the barrel is headed, escape certainly seems to be impossible. Houdini's notes describe several methods of escaping from a barrel. This trick was done as a challenge, and from one set of instructions it is evident that Houdini used it himself. In the construction of an ordinary barrel, the staves are provided with grooves at the inner ends. The bottom is fitted into the grooves and the band is driven on, holding the staves together. The same process is applied to the top. With tight-fitting ends and metal hoops around the sides a strong barrel or cask cannot be broken open from the inside. Yet in this escape, the performer must manage to open the barrel and later show it in its original condition.

For *the barrel challenge* the performer uses a barrel which may be provided by the challengers. It must, of course, be large enough to contain him comfortably. This challenge was usually accepted by a brewery; when delivered, the bottom of the barrel was already in place. All that remained was to insert the top and drive the upper band firmly into place. This system makes the actual imprisonment the work of a very few minutes; the escape from an ordinary barrel requires a much longer time.

Houdini's instructions follow: "My original method was to have the top of the barrel made in several sections, with plenty of air-holes. The middle board should have at least five or six (the more the better) in a cross-row.

"I would take one dozen fine key-hole saws and a strong handle with me in the barrel, having previously obtained duplicate boards from the brewery.

"Inside the barrel, I would fasten two stage screws in the top and then start cutting with the saws, to cut the board in half.

"After cutting the board, I would be able to give a few hard pulls (using the stage screws) and thus draw the sections of the board inside the barrel.

"You can use two rows of holes so that in case the board is in too tight, you can cut both lines of holes, thereby taking out a piece of the board, making the rest short enough to draw out, no matter how tightly it may have been placed in."

The removal of the center board makes it possible to draw the other boards toward the center, where the distance is greater than at the sides; thus these boards are drawn in intact. The performer is provided with duplicates of all the boards, concealed in the cabinet, in case it proves necessary to saw one of the smaller boards.

The instructions continue: "After making your escape, dig up the duplicate middle board, take a muffled hammer (any hammer which you have padded beforehand), and knock up the hoops. This is easy after you have taken the top out. Replace the boards and drive down the hoops.

"Before entering the barrel make a speech stating that you are not certain of escaping and that you will try for at least an hour before giving up. You should be able to do the job in thirty minutes.

"After starting the cutting with the keyhole saw it is a good plan to have a small fine hardwood saw also; this will cut more quickly.

"Be sure and try this escape before you go after it. Also take along a couple of electric pocket lamps; they will come in handy, as this 'gag' will take an awful lot of work."

In another set of instructions on the barrel challenge, Houdini suggests that the bottom be made of several pieces (presumably so that the top may be a solid piece of wood). In this case the performer must saw on the bottom, cutting it and removing; it may be replaced by a board of pliable wood, which can be forced into place, especially if slightly shortened. The smaller boards go back in the same way they came out—by sliding from the center to the sides. This requires air-holes in the bottom; whichever is used, top or bottom, it is important that the air-holes should be placed exactly the same as in the original board. This indicates that they are made when the barrel is constructed. If the committee should make the air-holes just before the performance, the performer would require a brace and bit among the items hidden in the cabinet.

Inasmuch as barrels differ, the performer who accepts this challenge must make arrangements according to the circumstances. If the top is formed of several narrow strips, it will be necessary to cut two of them instead of one. Cleats or wooden cross-braces on the top can be permitted; these are screwed to the boards that form the top, and they add to the length of time required. When outer cleats are used, the performer must cut a hole in the top board, through two lines of air-holes, and thus reach out to unscrew the cleats from the center board. With the center board gone, the other screws are easily reached from within the barrel.

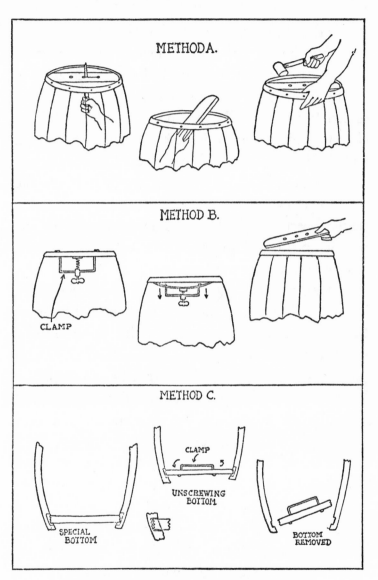

EXPLANATORY DIAGRAMS OF BARREL ESCAPES

Another method given by Houdini requires that the center board in the top be made of pliable wood. The air-holes are in the side sections, of which there are two, and the performer has a strong wrench or screw device specially designed for the trick. Two clamps project from this, and the ends turn at an angle. They are adjustable and are fitted into air-holes in the side boards, hooking on the outside. The performer turns the screw and it presses against the center board, gradually bending it upward in the middle until it is finally forced free. This board must have no air-holes, or it may break.

Having stepped out of the barrel, the performer bends the board and forces it back into the top of the barrel, using the wrench for this purpose. This method is specially suited to large-headed casks, and possesses the advantage of requiring no duplicate boards. It probably requires a great deal of effort, but if conditions are suitable for it, it should save time and reduce the number of operations required.

The *false-bottomed barrel* requires preparation and hence is not suitable for a challenge. It is a very ingenious idea, inasmuch as the bottom may be fitted to a thick barrel of the proper size and everything may be examined before and after the trick. The top of the barrel is put on by the committee. The bottom of this barrel consists of two parts, one a wooden hoop threaded on the inside, the other a wooden disc threaded on the outer edge. The solid portion screws into the hoop, which is fitted in the barrel. Theoretically the hoop should fit in in the barrel so that although the hoop tapers slightly on the outside the interior is straight, and when the false bottom is screwed in the joint will be close enough to the barrel staves to be undetectable.

From the outside of the barrel the join cannot possibly be observed. The inside of the bottom cannot be so closely inspected, because of the depth of the barrel. The sides must be very thick in order to contain the wooden hoop, for the hoop cannot be too flimsy. The false bottom cannot be unscrewed by the hands alone, which makes its secret doubly safe. The performer does the work with the aid of a piece of apparatus shaped somewhat like the handle of a flat-iron. He pushes the projecting arms into convenient air-holes and thus gains sufficient leverage to unscrew the false bottom, which is made from a single piece of wood. He can then turn the bottom edgeways inside the barrel and make his escape. Fitting the false bottom back into position, he can again tighten it with the special apparatus. This escape would require a large cask, allowing plenty of space inside; and it appears that the barrel should be placed on its side in a trestle or turned upside down, as it would otherwise be difficult for the performer to find a suitable place to rest while unscrewing the false bottom.

The *side-trap barrel* is covered in some brief notes. This is another type of specially constructed barrel, having an opening on one side near the bottom. This type of barrel is not intended for very close inspection; it seems to have been designed more for an illusion involving the disappearance of a girl than for escape purposes, although it could be used as an escape. The barrel staves are incomplete on one side; they run two thirds of the distance down and end at a broad hoop. The remaining section is formed by short staves fastened together; these can be removed and replaced; they form a secret trap. Inner hoops should be used on this barrel so that the join of the sections will not be noticed. The lower end of the trap is evidently fitted into the bottom of the barrel; by pushing up the inner hoop, the trap may be removed. When the performer is out, the inner hoop is pulled down and the outer hoop is slightly raised, allowing the proper insertion of the trap, after which the outer hoop is pushed back in place. Well designed, a barrel of this type would appear quite unprepared and would be capable of standing an ordinary examination.

The *double barrel* was not used by Houdini; it was designed by another performer as an under-water escape. Houdini pasted an account of the trick in his notebook and eventually learned the secret, which he added in a brief notation. The barrel was specially designed to come apart. It evidently had hoops inside and out, to cover the break. The two portions were held together by bayonet catches that the performer could release when inside the barrel. By turning the top portion in the proper way, the barrel separated immediately.

This type of barrel was not intended for the stage, but it would evidently have served such a purpose in the average escape act. As a release, it was well suited to a quick escape while under water, for by a simple operation at the desired moment the performer was able to free himself without difficulty and thus be clear before his lungs required air. The top of the barrel was headed in the usual manner. During this delay the man inside had time to free himself from handcuffs and shackles that had been placed on his arms and legs. The bottom of the barrel was loaded with pig iron, and the sides were drilled with holes so that the barrel would sink rapidly. As the performer was unable to put the barrel together while under water, he was forced to leave it at the bottom of the river. A rope was attached so that the barrel could be retrieved some time after the escape.

THE GREAT COFFIN IMPOSTURE

THIS trick was exposed by Houdini in England on September 30, 1904, and an account of the exposé appeared in a London newspaper the following day. The trick had been advertised in England as an escape from a genuine unprepared coffin by one of Houdini's imitators, and Houdini proved that these claims were false. The coffin used in the trick was a wooden one, put on display before performances. It was brought on the stage a short while before the act, and the performer who exhibited it took his position in the coffin and allowed members of the committee to screw the lid down tight. He took longer than half an hour for the escape and reappeared before the audience in a semi-conscious condition, as though completely exhausted by a terrific struggle. Houdini stated that the claims regarding the coffin escape were misrepresentations and that the long time required by the performer was purely humbug. Hence he demonstrated that the trick could be accomplished in less than one minute and that the coffin was prepared before the performance. When Houdini exhibited the trick, he proved these statements. He also offered a large reward to any one who could escape from the coffin without resorting to the preparation. The performer who had advertised the trick did not appear to collect.

The method used in the coffin imposture was quite simple. The coffin could be left in the lobby of the theater up to a short time before it was required, as the preparation was a matter of a very few minutes. The wooden pieces of the coffin were held together by screws on the outside. The lid was actually held down by clamps and could not be opened by the man inside. The head panel, however, was a short piece fitted in between the sides. It was held in place by three-inch screws that extended through the sides, close to the ends. Without these screws, the panel could be removed with ease.

In his exposé of the coffin trick, Houdini simply removed the three-inch screws and replaced them with one-inch screws. The coffin had been open for inspection prior to this; the faking was done when the coffin was off-stage, and the committee was satisfied that the coffin had not been exchanged for another. The cursory examination did not discover the loose head panel. Inside the coffin, Houdini removed the panel, took out the short screws, and put the panel back in place, fastening it there with the three-inch screws that had originally been in the coffin. This was the regular method used by the imitator who introduced the coffin trick; after each escape the coffin was thoroughly examined, then placed in the theater lobby until a short time before the next exhibition.

SHEET IRON COFFIN ESCAPE

H OUDINI describes for this trick a metal coffin which may be made of brass or sheet iron. He wrote the explanation and diagrams on August 10, 1910, while aboard the S.S. *Mauretania*. There have been various escapes from coffin-shaped boxes; this one is based on a novel adaptation of an older principle. The sides, ends, and bottom of the coffin are riveted together, giving a very solid appearance. The top is broken in the center and forms two covers, one opening on hinges toward the head, the other toward the feet.

The performer is placed in the coffin and the lids are lowered. The top and upper edges of the sides have metal flanges, drilled with holes. Bolts and nuts or padlocks are used to fasten these flanges together, so that there is absolutely no possibility of the top's being lifted. As a final assurance, there are bolts on one lid and sockets on the other; these are joined, and the top of the coffin forms as solid a barrier as the bottom. Yet the escape artist can make his exit in less than one minute. This coffin was designed to stand inspection, open and closed, before and after the trick. Furthermore, it is one test in which the performer requires no concealed appliances to aid him in the escape. When the coffin is opened, committee-men may climb in it and test it as much as they please. When it is closed and locked they can try to open it either before or after the performer has made his escape; yet they will have no results, even if they look in the right place for the escape. For there is only one way to operate it; that is from the inside when the coffin is closed, and the performer is the only person who has that opportunity.

The head end of the coffin is loose. The rivets that apparently hold it to the sides are faked and do not enter the end. The end fits very tight, however, so that it is firmly in place and appears to be a solid part of the coffin. When the upper half of the lid is opened, the end acts as a solid piece, the hinges serving the lid. But when the lid is closed and locked down, the conditions are reversed. The hinges now serve for the end, which swings outward when pressed from within.

Houdini's explanatory notes show clearly the principle on which this device operates; they do not, however, include certain details of construction which are necessary. If the end is merely held in by pressure, or by close fitting, close examination such as striking the end is not advisable while the coffin is opened. At that time, the false end must support the weight of the opened lid. A square-posted framework for the interior of the coffin is a natural item of construction, and this will prevent the end from swinging inward when the cover is swung back. When the lid is opened to its full extent, the position of the hinges makes it impossible to swing the end outward. It can only be pushed when the cover is closed. With the cover closed the end cannot be opened from the outside, for it is tightly fitted and there is no projection that will serve as a hold for pulling the end. In brief, the false end operates only from the inside when the lids are shut.

The notes specify that the coffin should be of sufficient size for Houdini to turn over inside it. He planned to lie on his back when entering the coffin, and to turn on to his stomach after the casket was locked. This indicates that the end would be tightly fitted or fastened from the inside; otherwise backward pressure of the hands would be sufficient and there would be no necessity for the performer's changing his position. The fact that the head end and not the foot end was chosen for the fake gives the same indication. Pressure with the feet would be more effective; therefore the use of the hands shows clearly that some mechanical operation was considered.

Special rivets or metal screws attaching the end section to the inside framework of the coffin would hold the end secure, would pass inspection, and would allow any amount of pressure against the trick end while the coffin was open. These would probably require a tool for their removal or loosening. The fake rivets on the outside of the coffin are the important factor so far as the committee is concerned. Their genuine appearance indicates solidity, and the ingenious method of switching the use of the hinges from the cover to the end is the vital principle of the escape. The other details of construction are minor matters that Houdini evidently intended to add in the finished plans.

THE METAL CASKET ESCAPE

THIS is an escape from an oval-shaped casket which is made of solid metal, all parts riveted in place. It is heavily constructed and makes a very good showing, as it will stand close examination. The casket is encircled by a strip of band iron. Instead of a flange, the strip is supplied with metal angles which terminate in flat projections. A similar band is riveted to the bottom of the cover, which fits over the casket, so that when the cover is on, the projections of both bands correspond. The projections are drilled with holes; these admit bolts or padlocks to fasten the cover securely to the casket.

The performer enters the casket and the cover is placed on it. The cover is made in two sections, hinging above the center, so that the top portion may be turned down to show the performer in position. When the cover is entirely closed, the members of the committee fasten the projections alternately with bolts and padlocks; the employment of different types of fastenings is quite effective. After the casket is placed within the cabinet the performer makes his escape in a short space of time, and when the cabinet is removed, the casket is shown still locked.

The casket is quite as solid as it appears. The secret of the escape lies in the metal band that encircles it. This is not part of the casket; the rivets that seem to hold it are false. The casket is slightly larger at the bottom than at the top; hence the metal band slides down to the center and may be pressed firmly into place at the spot where it is supposed to be riveted. In examining the casket, no member of the committee can discover this false condition, for it is impossible to exert enough force on the small projections to move the band. Even with several persons tugging at them at once, the band is too firm to be raised. Committee-men seldom act in unison; even if they should, they would get no results, for the band is very firmly in position.

When the cover is on, the situation remains the same. The small projections are quite as difficult to grasp; the weight of the cover adds to the solidity of the device. But inside the casket, the escape artist possesses a decided advantage. By raising his back against the inside of the cover or by using his feet to exert pressure, he can push the cover upward, and it will take the metal band of the casket along with it. He does not attempt to lift the entire cover; that

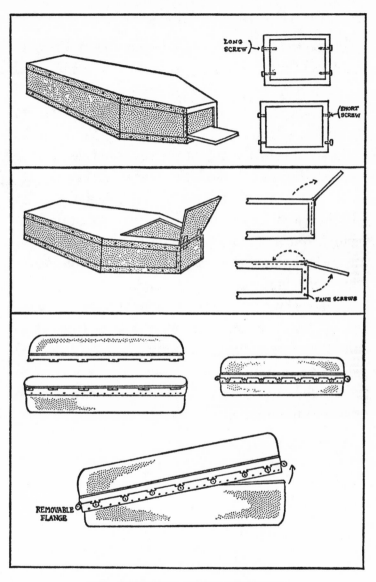

TOP—THE GREAT COFFIN IMPOSTURE
CENTER—THE SHEET IRON COFFIN ESCAPE
BOTTOM—THE METAL CASKET ESCAPE

would be too difficult because of the weight. Pressure at different spots gradually loosens the iron band, and the performer exerts all his strength at one end. This causes the end of the cover to come up, the other end serving as a support.

As soon as he has raised the cover sufficiently, the escapist slips out through the space that he has provided. Then he carefully lets the end of the coffin back into position and pounds it down so that the iron band is once more firmly attached to the casket. Meanwhile the orchestra obliges with loud music, which effectually drowns any noise that may come from the cabinet. After the escape, everything stands the usual inspection. The casket is locked in identically the same manner as before; when the bolts and padlocks are removed, the cover may be lifted and the opened casket submitted to the same examination as before the escape.

THE GALVANIZED IRON COFFIN

THE escape from a coffin made of galvanized iron is explained in unfinished notes which make the idea clear but which end with suggestions of various ways in which the coffin could be constructed. This is because of certain obstacles encountered in the mechanical arrangement; and the interpretation of the notes on this escape was unusually difficult. The coffin is intended to be hexagonal in shape. There are four long, tapering sides and two short ends. At every one of the six corners, there are flat upright posts or braces, both inside and out; also cross-braces at the ends and the center, both inside and outside of the coffin.

The coffin is thus a six-cornered framework into which solid pieces of galvanized iron have been riveted to form the sides and bottom of the coffin. There are eight of these pieces, six for the sides and two for the bottom. The upper edge of the coffin is a wide, flat flange, riveted in place. It extends over the inner portion of the coffin, as well as outward. The cover (which resembles the coffin, but is not so deep) fits on this flange, and it has a similar flange. The outer rims of both flanges are provided with holes for bolts or locks. Altogether it is a most solid-looking device; yet it is designed for a very quick release.

To understand the working of this device we must consider the coffin during its construction. Actually it is nothing but a framework of braces which support the flange. There are no braces at the ends. The cover is not considered, as it is without preparation. Now if this coffin were rectangular instead of hexagonal (a possible construction mentioned in the notes) it would be a simple matter to construct two drawers which would slide in and out between the braces. In position, they would appear solid. Braces or framework at the ends would be permissible then, for they would be attached to the end of each drawer —not to the actual framework supporting the wide flange. To escape from this device, the performer would have very little to do. By pushing in opposite directions, the coffin being short, he could push the two portions apart.

The fault of the rectangular construction is that there is no excuse for the center braces which hide the joint of the two sections. The hexagonal construction interferes with the sliding apart of the drawers, because the sides are tapering. This must be overcome in the construction of the coffin. Each end has four side braces that are upright, two inside the coffin and two outside. The two outside braces are not attached to the flange, but to the sides themselves. Hence when the drawerlike portions are pushed apart, they travel with them. It is not necessary for the bottom to go with the sides and ends. It can be permanently attached to the genuine braces that support the flange.

The coffin should not be too long; by extending his hands and pushing one way while his feet push the other, the performer can separate the parts and make his escape. One end of the coffin—that is, one entire half—may be permanently in position, for the performer can simply push the other end open and make his escape quite as easily. The cover rests on the flange throughout the escape and does not figure in the working. All parts are riveted; many of the rivets are false.

The ultimate construction of this device may be analyzed thus: A framework supporting a flat flange, and permitting the insertion of a drawer from each end. All parts are riveted at the end that does not operate. The end that must be removable is so arranged that no framework is attached both to the flange and to the drawer. All parts are attached to the flange, with the exception of those which would interfere with the operation; those are attached to the drawer. False rivets are used wherever genuine ones would make trouble. The double framework at the center covers up the joint; the wide flange extending inward and outward hides the sliding upper edges of the sides. Properly constructed, this coffin is extremely ingenious, and with tight-fitting parts it cannot be operated except from the inside.

PART SEVEN.

MISCELLANEOUS ESCAPES

ESCAPES of many types—large and small—appear in this section. They represent a wide variety of ideas and methods, and illustrate the scope of Houdini's notes. Miscellaneous related tricks, other than actual escapes, are included in this group.

THE WOODEN LOG ESCAPE

THE escape from a wooden log was an idea planned by Houdini and mentioned in a very short memorandum. The performer was to be bound to a wooden log, with ropes or chains, from which he would escape. In order to accomplish this escape, Houdini planned to have a special log constructed; the log would be cut in two sections and rejoined by a heavy screw. Bound to such a log, the performer, by separating the two portions, could release himself by sliding the ropes or chains to the center. The exact method of binding is not given; it would be planned so that the separation of the log would be possible and would also be of advantage to the performer.

Conceivably the performer might be held by short chains encircling the log, the ends of the log set in solid stands and held there by bolts passing through the outer ends of the logs. In brief, the primary object would be to prove that no chain could be slipped over the end of the log. Houdini suggested that the log be made in Germany and evidently intended to give the device further consideration, for his notes were made while aboard the steamer *Kaiser Wilhelm II*. If the special log could be constructed as Houdini proposed to have it, it would form the important part of a simple but highly effective escape.

PILLORY ESCAPES

THREE methods of escaping from a pillory in which the performer's head and hands are imprisoned are explained in Houdini's notes. The earliest reference to this sort of escape is dated Liverpool, October 22, 1904.

A

Pillory Number One is very ingenious. The lower half is mounted on two posts and is made in two sections. Starting with the inside of one post, a cut runs to a wrist-hole, then curves down below the neck-hole, and comes up to the other wrist-hole and down to the inside of the other post. A secret hinge holds it to the post at one end; a catch holds it to the post at the other.

To hide the cut, the posts and lower part of the pillory are decorated with a brass binding which follows the break, just touching the lower edges of the wrist-holes. Fake rivets in the brass binding reënforce the deception. The performer releases himself by kicking the post that has the catch. This releases the catch and the lower section of the pillory breaks apart, allowing ample space for the performer to remove his head and hands. The apparatus is easily restored to its original condition.

B

Pillory Number Two is a very simple yet effective form of release. The lower half of the pillory is mounted on a frame, while the upper section is either loose or hinged, so that when the performer places his wrists and neck on the semicircles in the lower section, the upper half may be closed to imprison him. Then the pillory is locked and the performer is firmly held in position. Yet his escape is very easy. The holes in the pillory are bound with leather so that they can fit tight against the performer's neck and wrists. The leather binding extends up the sides of the pillory. The pillory is faked beneath the leather. The holes are really much larger than they appear, but are fitted with curved blocks to which the leather is attached. All the performer has to do is to draw his head and hands backward and the curved blocks come out, releasing him completely. The portions removed from the pillory are then replaced.

The notes mention a spring to release these parts of the pillory, but the details are not specified. Some such mechanical device is necessary to make the pillory really effective and to allow it to pass inspec-

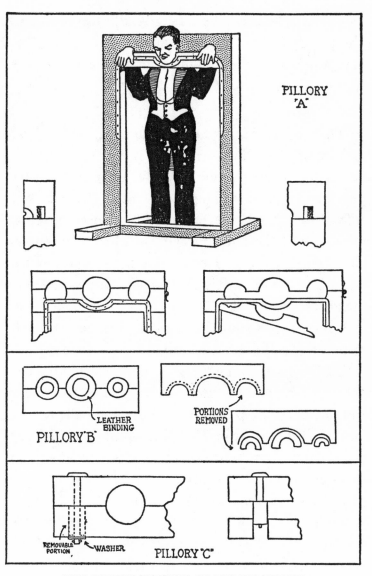

PILLORY
"A"

LEATHER
BINDING

PILLORY "B"

PORTIONS
REMOVED

REMOVABLE
PORTION   WASHER   PILLORY "C"

EXPLANATORY DIAGRAMS OF PILLORY ESCAPES

tion. The release can be arranged with the closing of the pillory or by a spring touched afterward by the performer. The pillory in the form described is simply an idea that requires further development.

C

Pillory Number Three is held together by long bolts which pass through vertical holes in the sections of it. The bolts are genuine and may be sealed after they are in position. The lower half of the pillory is affixed to a stand and the upper portion is set on it. The ends of the holes through which the bolts pass are strengthened by large metal washers which are placed in position. These washers have an outside diameter greater than the heads of the bolts. The lower part of the pillory has large plugs through which the bolt-holes are drilled.

The performer is bent well forward when in the pillory; by a straight upward lift he raises the top portion and the plugs are pulled out of the lower half, so that he is released. The plugs are held by catches which are opened by the performer, who presses nails on the sides or front of the pillory. This mechanical arrangement is not described in detail, but it could easily be worked out. The plugs must be carefully and neatly made, so that they are well concealed in the pillory. They are, of course, much larger than the bolts, and a trifle larger than the washers.

THE GLASS CYLINDER

T HE device used in this escape consists of a cylinder made entirely of heavy glass and a glass cover that fits over the cylinder. There are either four or eight handles or flanges on the cover, which are open in the center. The bottom of the cylinder is solid; everything is made entirely of glass. The sketch shows no air-holes, and it is probable that none were intended, for a reason that will be mentioned later. The performer is placed in the glass cylinder, and the cover is set on it. The edge of the cover extends several inches down on the cylinder, so that the performer is very effectively bottled within. As there are no places for locks, the cylinder is secured with straps. These pass through the openings in the handles on the outside of the cover and are fastened.

The description refers to four straps; this may mean *two* long straps that appear as four when they entirely circle the cylinder, or it may mean four straps that would appear as eight. Two straps seem likeliest. These straps can also be connected by cross-straps, forming a meshwork about the cylinder. The performer makes his escape from the cylinder while it is concealed from view, and after his escape it is still strapped.

The escape depends entirely on the straps; they are ordinary straps that will stand examination, but they are handled to the performer's advantage. When the straps are drawn tight, they bind in passing through the openings on the side of the cover. This makes it impossible to pull them too tight, although they appear tight. The height of the cylinder and the length of the straps aid in this deception. Although the performer is apparently in a tightly sealed device, he can take advantage of the slack in the straps by pushing the cover upward. It takes considerable pushing to draw the straps farther through the openings, but the performer has the advantage of a strong, well-distributed pressure, for he is centralizing his efforts on the cover and is drawing the straps straight up, whereas the committee-men were forced to pull the straps downward from the openings. That is, the straps are a little too large for the holes, but they can be worked through. The performer finally manages to raise the cover sufficiently to slide a knife between the cover and the cylinder and thus cut the straps. A flexible knife with a curved blade is helpful. It is not necessary to cut every strap that appears on the sides

of the cylinder. Two cuts will sever the straps that
appear as four. Then the cover is free and the performer can lift it.

There are several items worth considering: first, a

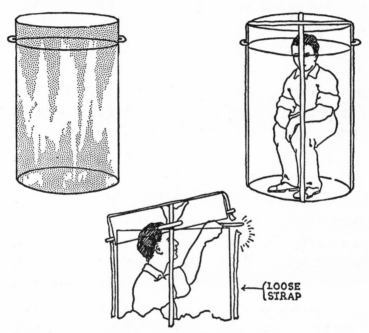

DETAILS OF THE GLASS CYLINDER SHOWING ACTION OF ESCAPE

loose-fitting cover that is helpful when the knife is
used; next, the absence of air-holes. This is an excuse
to hurry the strapping, as it is evident that the performer must hurry and cannot be delayed. Air-holes
would also work against the trick because of the possibility of pushing an implement through them to the

straps. With the straps buckling on top, the tightness is deceptive and seems much greater than it actually is. The object being to hold the cover firmly, the persons buckling the straps believe that the tightness at the top indicates tightness throughout. The meshwork or connecting straps at the sides also give the appearance, when used, of additional security. They are tight and therefore add to the deception.

Out of the cylinder, the performer can replace the cut straps with genuine ones concealed in the cabinet. If the meshwork is used, this, the notes suggest, might not be necessary, owing to the presence of so many straps. The cut straps could be drawn tightly together and fastened underneath one of the cross-straps, and the performer can dismiss the committee before any one has an opportunity to discover this. A few pushes on the top will convince the committee that the cover is still firmly in position. The cylinder can be made of glass and metal instead of glass alone; so constructed it must be designed to prove clearly that it is unprepared. The simplicity of this escape may create the impression that the method would be obvious. This is extremely doubtful. Straps can be straight without being tight, and they will appear tight. The best tricks are often the simplest—when the secret is known—and this escape possesses features that are favorable to successful presentation.

THE GLASS TUBE TEST

HOUDINI was ever active, and it appears that ocean voyages, with their periods of enforced inactivity, either stimulated him to new ideas or gave him the opportunity to set down plans that were formulating in his mind. His notes for an escape from a glass tube, like other excellent ideas, was drawn up on board a transatlantic liner. No date appears on these notes; they were made on the S.S. *Mauretania,* probably during the voyage of August, 1910, when he planned a coffin escape.

In many of his notes Houdini describes a piece of apparatus in considerable detail and adds a very brief and somewhat obscure explanation; in the glass tube escape he followed the opposite procedure. The only part that is doubtful is the appearance of the tube itself; the methods of escape—of which there are several—are quite clear. The tube was intended to be made partly of glass and partly of metal, the purpose of the glass being to increase the effectiveness of the trick; for secret traps and springs cannot be used in glass apparatus. The cover of this device is like the porthole of a ship, a piece of glass set in a metal frame; the tube itself was to be of glass, either a single piece in cylindrical form with a metal bottom, a single piece with metal bands at both top and bottom, or a glass cylinder set in a metal framework with long openings in the sides so that the glass would be visible. This would make the sides of the tube invulnerable, and false rivets at the top or sides would be unusable, since the examiners could see them through the glass.

The tube thus designed holds the performer in an upright position, with just sufficient space in which to move. Turning upside down in the tube is impossible. The top is hinged, the hinges held with rivets to the upper portion of the tube. On the other side a staple is fastened to the upper part of the tube, and the top has a hasp attached. This allows a padlock to hold the cover firmly in place. An optional method is a cover fitting over the top of the glass tube; bolts are pushed out from the inside, and the committeemen fasten padlocks to openings in the bolts. Houdini devised five methods of escaping from this contrivance; some of them were adaptations of methods used in other escapes; others were designed for this trick alone. All of them required working at the top.

In the *first method* genuine rivets are used to hold

the top to the glass tube. The performer has a plier-like cutter that enables him to cut the rivets, either at the hinge or at the staple. The cut rivets are forced through by the performer, and he is able to open the top of the tube so that he can escape. The lock must then be opened with a duplicate key so that he can replace the cut rivets with others that will stand ordinary examination. He then relocks the cover in position.

The *second method* requires the use of bolts. The bolts first shown are genuine; the performer exchanges them for bolts from which the heads may be unscrewed. This would be difficult to do inside the tube, as the performer would be visible to the persons outside. Houdini evidently intended that the exchange should be made before entering the tube, or else that the bolts should be so well constructed that they would pass the examination of the committee. It is probable that he considered the latter method, since he evidently possessed bolts that would stand inspection.

The *third method* is quite ingenious, and well adapted to this particular trick. The tube is not of great diameter; hence the lock is not far distant from the performer. Its inaccessibility is evident, however, and it seems quite apparent that a standard padlock of strong construction is all that is required to keep the performer from escaping. In this method Houdini depended on large air-holes in the glass top. Through one of these, near the side, he intended that the performer should push an extension key—a key that could open the padlock and that could be operated by the rod that holds it. With such a key, the performer reaches the padlock and unlocks it; then he uses the key to shake the padlock from the staple. It is evident that in this method two staples should be used instead of a hasp fitting over a staple, for lifting the hasp with the extension key would require an additional operation; whereas it would be nearly as easy to lift the padlock from two staples as from one. Thus disposing of the padlock, the performer can raise the top of the tube, make his exit, and replace the padlock. In the *fourth method* all parts on the outside of the tube are inaccessible; the air-holes in the glass are small; all rivets or bolts are genuine and are not attacked or manipulated. The top itself cannot be worked from within the tube; in fact the performer is actually bottled up in a most convincing fashion. To make his escape, the performer requires a special device of screw pattern. He conceals this on his person and has it in the tube. The apparatus consists of a disc just the size of the glass in the top of the tube. This has threaded holes which correspond with certain air-holes in the glass.

The performer pushes several iron rods through the air-holes. These rods have projecting angles; the angle of a rod is inserted first; then the rod is turned so that the performer can reach over the edge of the disc and engage the lower end of the iron in the correct hole in the disc. These rods are arranged with threads for the attachment of little levers or winged clamps. By operating these from below, the performer gradually tightens the disc against the glass, and as he continues pressure, the glass breaks or is crushed. He carefully removes enough glass to reach out and operate the lock. Opening the top of the tube, he makes his escape, takes the cover apart from the outside, and inserts a new piece of glass which has been hidden in the cabinet and which is the exact duplicate of the original glass (i.e. containing air-holes of the same size and in the same position). Then he is able to arrange everything from the outside so that the glass tube and its cover are in their original condition.

It would seem as though the performer could make his escape by removing all the broken glass and passing through the space thus provided; then by removing the top rim he could replace the glass without opening the cover. But Houdini does not mention this in his plans; the assumption therefore is that the rim containing the glass is quite large, and the diameter of the hole is insufficient for the performer to emerge without lifting the cover. This, however, has an advantage over the extension key method, as Houdini provided a way of completing the trick in case the hasp was locked to the staple with a lock that

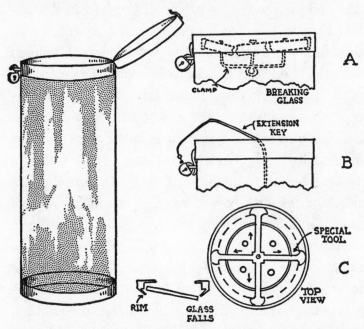

THE GLASS TUBE, WITH EXPLANATORY DIAGRAMS SHOWING THREE
METHODS OF ESCAPE

could not be easily opened—a "strange lock," as he terms it. To do this, the hasp is made in two pieces, the top piece bolted to the lower and also to the cover, but entirely outside the top, so that it cannot be handled from within the tube while the glass is there. If the lock cannot be operated, the performer uses a pair of cutters to clip the upper section of the hasp. This enables him to open the top, and he replaces the cut portion of the hasp with a duplicate section.

The *fifth method* is quite as ingenious as the fourth; the removal of the glass is also essential, but the glass is not broken. The glass does not go deep into the metal rim that supports it; yet it cannot be removed without the aid of a special implement. The performer has an instrument with four flat arms, each terminating in a head with curved edge. These enter a center block which is provided with a screw to force the arms outward. The performer sets this against the glass and turns the screw to force the arms toward the sides. The edges are knife-like, and the glass is forced upward a fraction of an inch so that the heads of the instrument enter between the metal and the glass. The metal rim is not thick, and as the performer works the instrument and slowly revolves it, he forces the metal downward and inward, carefully and evenly.

After the rim has been bent to a certain point, the glass slips down when the instrument is removed, and the performer carefully takes it from the frame. Then he is free to open the top of the tube. Replacing the glass and bending the bottom of the tube back into position is not a difficult process, especially as the performer may have any necessary tools in the cabinet. This brings the whole arrangement back to its original condition, and the escape comes to a successful conclusion. Removing the glass is slower than crushing it, but as the performer has plenty of time in which to accomplish the escape, it is difficult to decide which of the two methods has the greater merit. That is a matter which only experiment could prove; all other factors being equal, removal of the glass would be preferable. The substitution of duplicate parts is something to be avoided whenever possible, and the last method explained eliminates such an action.

ESCAPE FROM A BLOCK OF ICE

I N THIS unusual escape the performer is imprisoned
in a covered iron cylinder which is effectively
closed from the top. A huge block of ice, hollowed in
the center, is placed over the cylinder and comes
down to the platform, which is raised from the stage.
Hence the man inside must not only escape from the
cylinder; he must also overcome the heavy cake of
ice. The cover that fits on the cylinder is not hinged;
it is fitted with hasps that fit over staples on the
cylinder, and it cannot be removed by any usual
method after the cake of ice is in position.

The secret of this escape lies in the construction of
the cylinder, which has very thick walls and will stand
a close inspection. The thick wall is really three layers
of metal. First a thin cylinder with solid bottom is
constructed, and a hole is cut in the side above the
bottom. The hole is large enough for a person to pass
through. Then a double cylinder or shell is made; it
has no bottom, and its walls are several inches apart,
being closed at the top. This fits over the original

cylinder, and when it is in position it hides the secret opening both inside and outside. By lifting this shell, the opening is revealed and the performer can make use of it. If desired, short bolts may pass through the

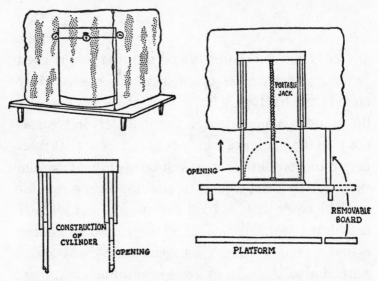

HOW THE CYLINDER IS COVERED WITH THE BLOCK OF ICE; ALSO CONSTRUCTION OF THE CYLINDER AND DETAILS OF THE ESCAPE

inner wall of the shell into the genuine cylinder and thus prevent any one from lifting the shell; if a tight fit of shell and cylinder is obtained, this is hardly necessary. But assuming that the bolts are used, their removal and replacement from the inside will free the shell, and the performer can raise it. The great difficulty then is the cake of ice. It is so heavy that even if the performer can raise it, he cannot hold it up while he makes his escape. That is why the ice is used—to direct suspicion away from the true secret of the iron cylinder.

When the performer enters the cylinder he carries a jack concealed on his person. Inside the cylinder he fits this jack together and uses it to raise the shell and the cake of ice. The sides of the cake of ice make it really an outer shell. Then the performer comes out through the opening. He can lower the jack from below, but this has two disadvantages; it is not only a difficult process, but it leaves the jack inside the cylinder at the finish. To overcome this the ends of the platform are used. They are removable, and the performer places them so that they will block the outer shell and the cake of ice as they are lowered by the jack. Having made his escape, he puts the end boards of the platform in position, drops the jack and removes it, and then knocks the boards out of the way so that the shell and the cake of ice come down to the platform. The ends of the platform are replaced, the jack is concealed, and everything is ready for the committee. When the jack is raised it presses against the inside of the cover, which is attached to the outer part of the shell. The center cylinder does not need to extend clear to the top of the shell; hence the staples for the locks can be bolted or riveted all

the way through. It is advisable to have an air-hole
in the center of the cover, with a corresponding hole
in the center of the cake of ice, as the escape is not
a rapid one and the performer will need air.

THE AUTOMOBILE TIRE ESCAPE

AN ESCAPE from a large automobile tire, mounted on a rim, while the wheel is revolving! This is an idea that has spectacular possibilities. The wheel used is very large; the tire is cut before the escape begins, so that the performer may be imprisoned in it. Then the tire is mounted on the wheel and the ends are vulcanized. The performer obtains air through holes in the tire. The whole wheel is slowly revolved; the curtains of the cabinet are closed, but a space is left open so that the spectators can observe the hub of the wheel as it continues to revolve. The whole tire is set in a special stand that makes this possible, and a belt is connected to a flange on the rim of the wheel so as to keep it in revolution. The wheel, however, does not revolve while the performer is making his escape. The extending hub is large and the end runs independently—the notes suggest the use of clock-work. The belt running to the rim of the wheel is secretly disconnected by an assistant, so the performer can get out of the tire while it is standing still.

Two methods are suggested for this escape. One is to cut the large tire at the point where it has been vulcanized. The performer does this with a sharp knife, and eventually breaks loose. He replaces the tire on the stand, and with a small vulcanizing outfit which has been hidden in the cabinet, he repairs the damage.

The other method depends on a trap in the tire itself. This is a flap, with edges cut at an angle so that it fits very nicely. The trap is four-sided, one side being uncut; this acts as a hinge. The flap is cemented in position before the escape; thus the tire will stand considerable examination. The performer uses a special knife or spatula with which he can do a very neat job of cutting, simply prying loose the flap where it is cemented, without injuring the rubber. Then he can open the long flap and make his escape. The secret trap must then be cemented back into its original position. With a very large tire, this method would not require the vulcanizing of loose ends; the performer would find it possible to enter the tire while it was in its normal shape. Hence it is quicker both as a presentation and as an escape, and is preferable to the vulcanizing method, provided that the cemented flap will pass inspection.

THE MAINE TRAMP CHAIR

H OUDINI'S notebook contains photographs of the
Maine tramp chair, a device that was once employed to confine tramps or suspicious characters
overnight. The escape from this contrivance was introduced by Hardeen, the brother of Houdini, who
performed it in Bangor, Maine, accomplishing it in
eleven minutes. Houdini's notes state that Hardeen
employed the escape and also mention that Houdini
did it in Boston and called it the witch's chair. The
tramp chair forms a miniature portable cell; it consists of two sections, the lower cubical in shape, the
upper square-bottomed but high, so that the prisoner
may be seated in the chair-like interior. When the
door is closed, the open side is fastened by a padlock over a staple. The door is located in the upper
portion of the chair, and a long, heavy pivot hinge
holds it to the framework of the cell. The fact that the
device was used to imprison dangerous characters is
sufficient proof of its formidable construction.

Houdini's notes do not contain an explanation of

the working method of the tramp chair as used either by himself or by Hardeen. There is, however, a method of preparing a chair of this type so that the performer can make an effective escape; yet the device will stand close inspection. The secret lies in the long pivot hinge that holds the door of the chair in position. The hinge cannot be removed because of plugs in the top and bottom sockets. Without these plugs, it would be impossible to push the rod downward because of the bottom portion of the chair. The top plug may be removed, yet still the hinge cannot be pushed upward because the upper portion of the hole in the top socket is too small for it. But when the performer is ready to escape, he reaches out from the chair and removes the plugs from the upper and lower sockets. Then he draws the rod downward, and it goes far enough to free the top end from the upper socket. The top of the rod thus revealed is fitted with a screw-bolt; the performer removes this, and the rod is then free to pass upward through the sockets. The rod is small enough to go through the upper socket; its not moving upward when tested is due to the head of the bolt, which is of greater diameter than the rod.

The ingenuity of this method is obvious. Committee-men who suspect the hinge are easily convinced that the rod will not go downward more than a few inches; hence the only plug that they will insist on removing is the top one. With the plug out of the way, it is still quite impossible to budge the rod. The double action of moving the rod downward and then upward is something that no one will suspect; this

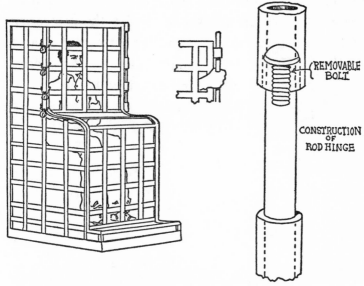

SKETCH OF THE MAINE TRAMP CHAIR WITH DETAILS OF THE ESCAPE

makes the escape from the prepared or faked tramp chair a highly convincing mystery. When the performer makes his exit, the padlocked side of the door serves as a hinge. To show the escape most effectively, he may allow chains to be passed through the network of bars, at the padlocked side of the door. The chains may be equipped with padlocks supplied by members of the committee and may be firmly fastened, for they merely add to the security of the side that is not opened. This method is usable when the escape is made with the performer's own apparatus, as part of a regular performance. Hardeen's escape in Bangor was made from an old tramp chair in the possession of the police of that city, and he performed it as a challenge. Hence the method that he used was necessarily different from the one described here.

THE KNIFE BOX

A͟N ͟ILLUSION, rather than an escape, the knife box
presents an unusual problem for the performer
who is placed within it. The box is an upright cabinet
with a door that opens outward. The interior is filled
with knives projecting from the sides and the back;
when the performer is placed in the box and the door
is closed, there is very little room for him to move
about in without injury. He is placed in the cabinet
upside down, naturally this adds to his difficulties.
Then the box is attached to a chain and is lifted in
the air. It does not leave the view of the audience;
but when the box is lowered and reopened, the performer is standing upright! In some unaccountable
manner he has managed to change his position despite
the knives.

This trick is included among Houdini's escapes because it is a mystery involving the confinement of
the performer in a box; and with certain modifications it could be used as an escape behind curtains.
The box is large enough to permit the performer to

turn over; the problem that must be overcome is that of the knives, which actually prevent motion and are genuine blades. These knives are set on hinges in the sides and back of the box; but this fact is not observed, for the knives are actually attached to plates which appear to be screwed into the wood. Hence, as the notes say, the "knives are shown 'not hinged.'" But the plates or attachments for the knives are fitted to round joint hinges in the walls of the box. The result is that all of the knives can be folded flat against the sides and back of the box, releasing the performer.

To accomplish this, Houdini planned an interior mechanism that is not given in detail. When the box is examined the knives cannot be moved, and the performer, when confined, is unable to turn the knives himself; hence the box will stand the most thorough examination. The release lies in a handle or group of handles on the outside of the box—evidently at the top. These handles pull upward, and when they do, the knives swing flat against the walls of the box. The release is actuated by the simple process of raising the cabinet. Chains are attached to the handles after the door is closed. The chains are drawn tight, and they pull the handles upward for a short distance before the handles actually begin to raise the box. The weight of the box and the performer resist the pull and make this automatic. So as soon as the box is in the air the knives are out of the way and the performer can easily turn over and take his standing position. When the box is lowered, the knives come back into place as soon as it strikes the floor and the chains fall loose or become slack.

The effectiveness of this trick depends largely on its construction. It must be well made mechanically; yet there is no reason why the apparatus should be complicated to any excessive degree. As a self-work-ing device it is ingenious. Some arrangement would probably be necessary to hold the performer in his upside-down position until the box is raised and the knives are out of the way. The release of the knives is clever, as there is nothing suspicious about it. It is quite logical that the box should be opened and closed while on the stage; raising it in the air seems obviously a plan to make the trick more difficult—instead of making it easy. The box can be lifted the instant the door is closed and reopened just as soon as it comes back to the stage. The change can be made in very quick order. All in all, this appears to be a practical and effective illusion that can be pre-sented in a sensational manner.

THE SPIRIT COLLAR

THE collar here described is as much a trick as an escape, and it is a very effective mystery, as the articles used are entirely unprepared. Houdini describes it in a note dated October 26, 1904:

"The collar is made in the shape of an ice-pick, and the rivet can be examined and a new one put in at every show. The lock can be sealed up, but still the collar is removed from the neck, and seals are unbroken.

"The secret: A certain part of the neck is very thin; if you put one point of the collar under your chin near your ear, you can force it way into your neck and you will be able to work the collar from your neck."

A diagram follows the explanation; it shows that the points of the collar have small caps on them, which of course protect the performer. The collar, as described and drawn, is shaped like an ice-pick, with the handles locked; the points of the pick come very close together, and it appears impossible that

the collar could be removed from the neck. By gaining as much distance as possible between the points
and carefully manipulating the collar, the performer
can easily work it free.

THE CHAMPION LOCK CUFF

OUDINI terms this "a splendid freak cuff," and mentions it both in his notebook and in miscellaneous notes. It is a very formidable device, and yet escape from it is simple.

The cuff consists of a long heavy bolt, with a hole in the end. Houdini states that it "is made on the style of the Russian cuffs, like those in Scotland Yard; two bands for hands; the bands are then placed through the rod. Any lock can be hung on, and still escape can be made." The explanation follows:

"Have the holes in the hand loops square, or of some eccentric form. The long bar screws in the center, and is also made square, which allows the hands to unscrew the long bar and take it apart.

"It would be safest to have a round bar with an eccentric bump which would unscrew the bar.

"Another method is to have the bolt-head unscrew; it fits into a key (plate with square hole) that is fixed in the cabinet, to hold it steady while the head is being taken off.

"This can be made into a very sensational-looking cuff, by making use of a very heavy piece of steel for the bar. It should be as weighty as possible; and to show that these cuffs are not slipped it is wise to have

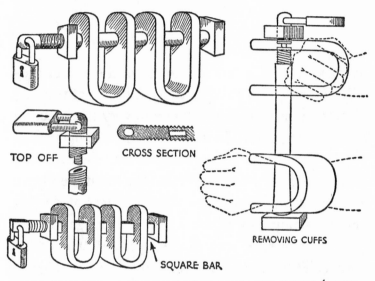

OPERATION OF THE CHAMPION LOCK CUFF. TWO STYLES (ROUND BAR AND SQUARE BAR) ARE SHOWN

a pair of ratchet cuffs on the wrists at the same time."

The ratchet cuffs would, of course, be nearer the hands than the special cuffs; they would be removed with the aid of a key. It is understood that the performer fits the long bolt together after the escape.

TWO TRICKY DOORS

THE "tricky" doors are not used in escapes; they are intended as mysterious devices that will perplex the uninitiated, and they are very ingenious in their construction. These doors cannot be opened by any one who does not know the secret. The first door cannot be shown open at all, for it opens at the hinges and not at the lock. It has dummy hinges at the left and a dummy lock at the right. It is hinged at the right by two rods, one at the top, the other at the bottom. These fit into the woodwork above and below the doorway and act as pivot hinges. At the left of the door a similar rod is concealed in both the door and the woodwork of the doorway, but it is in a horizontal instead of a vertical position.

The man who attempts to open this door will find a real problem confronting him. He cannot pick the lock, for it is useless; pushing the pins from the hinges will be to no avail, for the door will still be solid at that side. The only way to open the door is with the aid of a powerful magnet. This is applied to the woodwork at the left; then it is moved to the right. The rod at the left is not as long as the slots in which it is fitted; so with the magnet working it moves to the right into the door (or it can be drawn into the

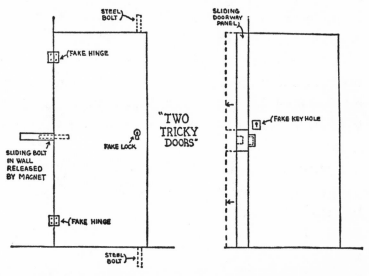

DIAGRAMS EXPLAINING THE OPERATION OF THE TRICKY DOORS

woodwork at the left); and this makes the opening a simple matter because of the pivot hinges at the right!

The second door can be shown either open or closed. It has a lock that is permanently closed and cannot be picked. When the door is open, this lock is still closed; that is, the metal part is extending from the door. The box into which this permanent lock is fitted is attached to the woodwork at the side of the door. If the woodwork is removed, the door will open when pulled, for there will be nothing there to hold the lock. Instead of having to remove the woodwork of the doorway, the performer merely slides it away from the door. The whole vertical piece slides, in grooves at the top of the doorway and in the floor. This is concealed by molding at the top and on the baseboard of the floor. This door is not so ingenious nor so perfect as the one previously described, but it is much more easily constructed, as the door is simply put in position and the woodwork of the door-way fitted afterward. It is easy to operate, requires no tool or magnet, and is so cleverly devised that detection is very unlikely.

THE VALISE CHALLENGE

OUDINI'S method of escaping from a large valise, described in notes dated July 12, 1910, at Chicago, depended on a valise which was not specially prepared, but which required certain specifications in its construction. The valise would have to be made very large, to allow considerable space in which the performer could move; and air-holes were also mentioned in the notes. The method of escape can be understood from a description of the valise. The bag is held by two pairs of straps, the ends of the straps being riveted to the bottom of the valise. The description of one pair of straps shows that one strap is fastened near the front of the bottom, the other strap near the rear of the bottom.

With the performer inside the bag, the front strap is drawn up and its free end pushed through a buckle on the free end of the rear strap. By having a short rear strap, the front strap can be inserted through staples on the top of the bag before it is put through the buckle of the rear strap. A padlock pushed through a metal-rimmed hole in the front strap is the means by which the straps are held together; the padlock obviously cannot be pulled through the buckle. With members of the audience examining and locking the valise, this is a highly convincing escape that seems to border on the impossible.

The method of escape is to work on the rivets of the front strap. By cutting these from the inside of the bag, the strap is released, and by pressing in opposite directions at the top of the bag, an opening is gained through which the performer can pull the strap entirely clear. As two sets of straps are used it is necessary to cut two groups of rivets and to operate both straps simultaneously. The fact that the front straps were marked as the ones to be released indicates that the use of staples on the top of the bag was intended. The release of the rear straps would not be effective, as the buckles could not pass through the staples.

Provision is made for clamps on the metal-work of the rim of the valise; these, however, must be of a standard pattern. Most clamps of this sort, no matter how impressive they may appear, can be easily forced from the inside. The object is to have regulation clamps which seem to add to the security of the valise, yet which offer no great difficulty to the man inside. The clamps are forced open in order to manipulate the top of the valise and release the straps.

The use of a small tool to operate the clamps is not an obstacle, as the performer must carry an instrument to cut the rivets, either hiding it on his person or having it concealed in the valise. When the performer is out of the valise he replaces the cut rivets with new ones. This is accomplished most effectively by opening the locks with a key or a pick, thus releasing the front straps, which are refastened after the rivets have been put in place. In an emergency the rivets can be inserted after the bag is closed, without access to the interior; in this case, only a casual inspection may be made after the escape.

PART EIGHT.

SPECTACULAR MYSTERIES AND ESCAPES

THIS section is a continuation of miscellaneous escapes, but it comprises solely escapes that are capable of highly spectacular presentation.

Some of the most ingenious ideas explained in Houdini's notes will be found in this section, for they represent sensational mysteries that he had planned.

THE CRADLE OF STEEL

AN ESCAPE from a cradle of steel, while suspended from the top, was one of the challenges proposed by Houdini. It possesses the elements of a spectacular escape. The cradle is mounted on a platform. It consists of four upright posts supporting a solid top, all of heavy construction. Metal plates in the top hold rings, one to support the performer's neck, another for his body, the third for his ankles. A metal collar is placed about the performer's neck; it is locked and secured to the ring in the top of the cradle by a chain. A strip of steel belting, attached to the center ring and locked there, holds his body. His feet are secured by a leather strap or by a piece of metal made like a figure 8 which closes over each ankle independently and can be locked to the ring above.

The notes state that the arms are held by steel tubing; no details are given of this apparatus. An additional note describes a pair of cuffs or manacles connected by a chain; these are evidently the device to be used in securing the performer's wrists. The escape depends on releasing the hands. The manacles used are not faked, but the hinge of each one is simply a rivet on which the bars swing. After the performer is in position, and securely attached to the cradle, the curtains are lowered and he starts to work, using a pair of plier-like cutters concealed on his person.

Resting easily in the cradle-like device, he releases his hands. With the manacles in use, the chain between them allows plenty of space for one hand to work on the opposite wrist. With a hand free, the performer reaches to the neck strap and cuts the zinc rivet that supports it. He can support his body by holding the other ring with his free hand. The steel belting offers no resistance. It is tight, but it cannot hold the performer's body, for the belting is pliable. Hence the remainder of the escape depends on the release of the feet. Bound in a broad strap of leather, the feet can be slipped if they have been crossed in fastening. Otherwise the performer must work his way forward, raising his knees and extending his hands until he can reach his feet. If the feet are fastened with a leather strap, the performer cuts the strap. If they are in the figure 8 device, he must use the cutters once more, to remove a rivet at the bottom of the figure 8. In brief, the method is to release the neck and the ankles, then slide free from the body belt.

Free, the performer must replace everything that he has cut—either rivet or strap.

This is an escape that is not so difficult as it appears to the audience, yet not so easy as it may seem from the explanation. Working on rivets that are out of sight and difficult to reach requires both skill and patience. Only an experienced performer could attempt this escape, and in devising it, Houdini relied on his proven ability.

WALKING THROUGH A BRICK WALL

THE mysterious feat of walking through a brick wall was not one of Houdini's originations, but it has become closely identified with his name, for he introduced the illusion to the American stage and presented it with remarkable success. It was an ideal feat for Houdini to perform, for it can be classed both as a magical illusion and as an escape trick; and Houdini's popular reputation was certain to be an attraction for so sensational a mystery.

The wall was built of brick on an iron framework some twelve feet in length. The framework was mounted on rollers so that it could be moved about the stage, and in its final position it stood with one end toward the audience. A committee was invited on to the stage. The inspection proved conclusively that the wall was just what it appeared to be—a solid structure of brick; in fact, the wall could be built in the presence of the audience, if desired. The stage also bore minute inspection. It was covered with a large carpet of plain design and of heavy material, precluding all possibility of any openings. To make everything more convincing, a large cloth, inspected by the committee, was spread over the carpet. Then the brick wall was set in the center of the stage, and

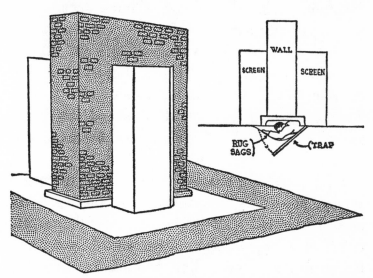

WALKING THROUGH A BRICK WALL—ONE OF HOUDINI'S MOST
FAMOUS MYSTERIES

two threefold screens were placed against it, one on each side of the wall.

Houdini went behind one of the screens, while the committee members stood on all sides, watching the wall from every angle. Houdini raised his hands above the screen for a moment; then drew them within the screen. The seconds clicked by, and suddenly the screen on the other side of the wall was moved away, and there stood the performer! When the first screen was taken down, it proved to be empty. Thus Houdini apparently passed through a solid brick wall, some eight feet in height, under the most exacting conditions. This effect seemed miraculous, as it was apparently impossible for the performer to go through, over, around, or beneath the wall. Under it would have seemed most logical, but with only five or six inches of space and the carpet and cloth preventing use of a trapdoor, that method of passage seemed unusable. Yet Houdini went *underneath* the wall.

A large trapdoor was set in the center of the stage. When the screens were in position, the door was opened from below. Both the cloth and the carpet, which were large in area, sagged with the weight of the performer's body, allowing sufficient space for him to work his way through, the cloth yielding as he progressed. The passage accomplished, the trap was closed, and no clew remained.

Even with people standing on the cloth, the "give" in the center was quite unnoticeable, and the passage from one side of the wall to the other was quickly accomplished by a man of Houdini's agility.

WALLED IN ALIVE!

ONE of the most ambitious escapes planned by Houdini was the "walled-in alive" test. It is very carefully described in his notes, and Houdini gives the effect in his own words:

"The idea is to have on the stage, raised from the floor, extra heavy horses of wood, to support a heavy plate of warship steel. On this is to be plastered a flooring of concrete and huge paving bricks, or rocks, the large square kind.

"The masons start to build up a wall, forming a room, and after it is a certain height, I enter and am walled in.

"It cannot be air-tight, so a cross-shaped opening is left at the top or the side, to admit air. After the whole thing is walled up and I am inside, if I were to attempt to remove a solitary stone, all would tumble down. The curtain is drawn around, and within a certain time limit, I escape, leaving the 'buried alive' chamber intact."

Some details are missing from Houdini's description, but they are easily supplied. The opening in the wall is, of course, too small to be of any use in the escape. The top of the structure would probably require another sheet of steel, covered with stones; but

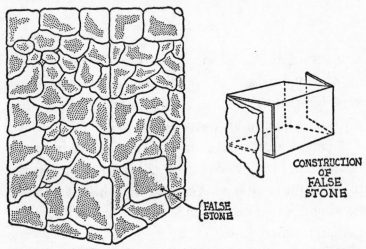

SECTION OF SOLID WALL SHOWING THE LOCATION AND CONSTRUC-
TION OF FALSE STONE THROUGH WHICH THE PERFORMER
PASSES.

with a high wall, this would be unnecessary, as the wall could project above the curtain, so any attempt to climb over the top would be detected. This plan would eliminate the necessity for an air-hole. As Houdini stated, any attempt to remove a stone from any part of the wall would be disastrous. The ingenious method he created made it absolutely unnecessary to remove any stone; in fact the size and weight of the stones is of value in the escape. The secret lies in one stone, which is specially prepared. Houdini's original plan was to have a large hollowed stone, with the ends filled with a plaster to make it look unprepared. The interior of the stone was to hold tools and fresh plaster; so when he broke into the stone and forced his way through it, he would have the materials to repair the damage.

This being rather cumbersome, he improved the method, using a steel box instead of the hollow stone. The box is covered with stone or an artificial stone surface, so that it closely resembles a genuine stone. It has snap doors in each end, with handles on the insides. The only implement needed by the performer is a small key or tool to open the inner door. After making his passage through the fake stone, he closes the doors. In case plaster is needed in the crevices on the outer side of the stone, the necessary material can be kept in the hollow block; and any repair work would be a matter of a very few minutes.

Houdini's diagram calls for the "stone" to be set near the bottom of the wall. Obviously it would have to be large, and the real blocks would be of the same size, with smaller stones for higher portions of the wall. With so many stones required, and the building of the wall being a matter requiring speed, the imitation stone can easily pass the cursory inspection of

the committee. Stones of this size are convincing because of their size and weight, and their use is logical
in a large wall that must be quickly built. The plan of
passing through a solid stone is certainly the last
mode of exit that any one would suspect.

THE CYLINDRICAL CROSS ESCAPE

THERE is a certain parallel between Houdini's theatrical career and the various notes that he made of new ideas. Notes on escapes from ordinary objects such as baskets and barrels bear dates before 1910; the more spectacular tricks are of slightly later date. This conforms with his introduction of the sensational water-torture cell, which was not part of his earlier programs. It seems as though his inventive talents were first applied to devising a variety of smaller or lesser escapes, later to the creation of feature mysteries that could be exhibited almost as an act in themselves. For Houdini was a progressive showman, not content to rest on the laurels of the past, and he had plans for the development of new and spectacular ideas.

The escape from a cylindrical cross stands out as a masterpiece of ingenuity. Its construction would probably have been a matter of great expense; presented as a feature escape, it would have been sensational. The notes on this escape were written while crossing the Atlantic on board the North German Lloyd steamer *Kaiser Wilhelm II*; they are dated August 29 and August 30, 1912. The apparatus planned by Houdini was a cross-shaped device made of metal tubing. This was designed to break apart in the center, along the horizontal tube. Thus the cross consisted of two portions, each shaped like the letter T. The base of each T was a round tube, the top a half tube. One tube was to set right side up, the other to be inverted.

Let us visualize this escape as the audience would see it. A committee is invited on the stage. They examine both sections of the strange cylindrical cross. The two parts are similar, but one stands higher than the other. The ends of the vertical tubes are closed, solidly riveted in place. The performer steps into the taller portion of the cross; it comes up to his arms, and he lays each arm in the trough or half-circle extending from each side of the center section. Attention is called to the fact that there is just about enough space for the lower part of his body. Then the other portion of the cross is turned upside down and set over his head. The horizontal half-tubes correspond exactly to those of the lower section, so the performer is contained in a cross made of cylinders. The arm sections have flanges. These are provided with holes, and bolts or padlocks are fitted so that

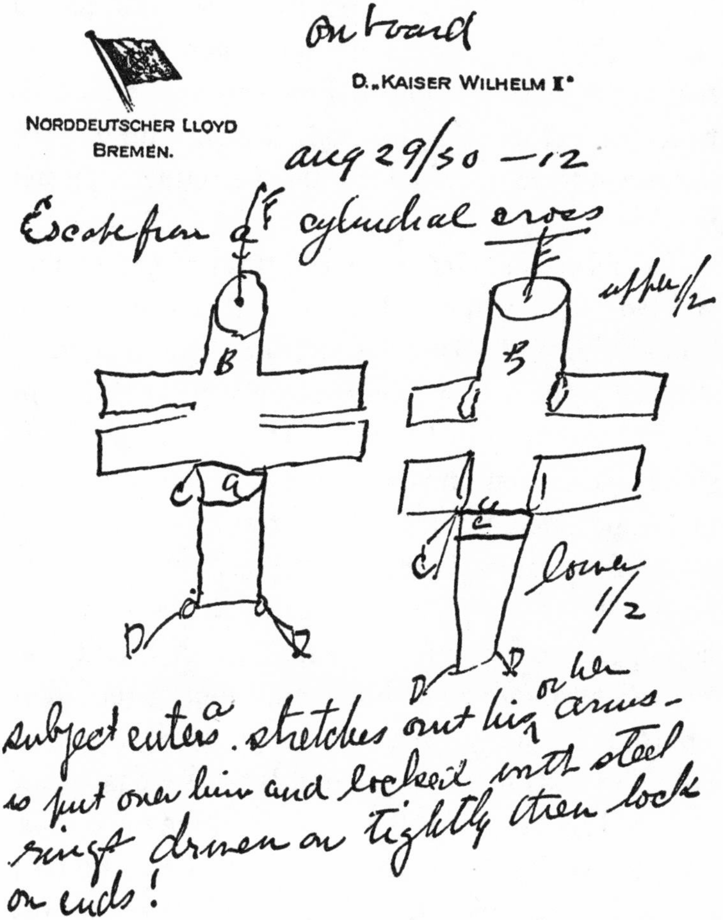

On board

D.ₘKAISER WILHELM Iᵒ

NORDDEUTSCHER LLOYD
BREMEN.

aug 29/50 —12

Escape from of cylindrical cross

upper 1/2

lower 1/2

subject enters a. stretches out his arms.
is put over him and locked with steel
rings driven on tightly then lock
on ends!

REPRODUCTION OF HOUDINI'S FIRST NOTES ON THE CYLINDRICAL
CROSS ESCAPE. THIS IS A TYPICAL SPECIMEN OF THE MATERIAL
FROM WHICH THIS VOLUME WAS PREPARED

the two portions of the cross may be tightly fastened together. When this has been done, the performer is as effectively secured as any one could desire. The horizontal tubes are longer than his arms so that his hands cannot emerge; his body has very little space in which to move. In fact, the performer appears helpless.

To add to the effectiveness of this escape, a chain is fitted into a swivel at the top of the cross and the whole affair is hoisted in the air. The bottom is steadied by chains that serve as guy-ropes; these are hitched to hooks in the floor. The hanging cross is surrounded by curtains, and it is up to the performer to escape from his formidable restraint. The most impressive feature is the fact that he cannot move; no matter how supple his body might be, it would be impossible for him to wiggle clear of the device. To prevent the one possible method—a method possible only in theory—namely, escape through an arm-hole, the ends of the horizontal tube are also closed and held by bolts. All the ends stand the most thorough inspection; all parts of the cross are reënforced by thick metal bands; and the committee and the audience both are positive that only a miracle can help the performer to extricate himself from the device. Yet he gets out, and the cylindrical cross is found in exactly the same position as before, the bolts intact, and the device ready for thorough inspection!

This was indeed an escape worthy of Houdini; had he constructed it and shown it in public it would have created a tremendous sensation. The secret is extremely ingenious; Houdini appears to have hit on the only solution workable with such a device, with the conditions exactly as described—the ends of each section positively solid; the bolts genuine, and no end of the cross reachable with his hands. The vulnerable point of this device lies directly beneath the horizontal cylinder. This point is necessarily reënforced by a metal band or connecting joint which holds the horizontal cylinder to the bottom part. The rivets here are genuine. The same method of connection is used between the horizontal cylinder and the upper section, but that point is not vulnerable.

Note how the cross is suspended. The top is attached to a swivel; the bottom is held firm by two or more guy-lines. It is apparently impossible for the performer to move within the cylindrical cross. Yet he does move; not upward, downward, or sideways, but by a rotary motion, turning around. He manages to do this because at the bottom of the connection between the base of the cross and the horizontal cylinder, the base of the cross is fitted with a threaded screw! This is a tight fit, a close joint that cannot be detected; it withstands all strain and holds the sections of the base firmly together; best of all, it is something that no one would begin to suspect!

As soon as the cross is screened from view, the performer begins to turn. The bottom of the cross is firmly held; the performer's arms, in their metal casings, act as powerful levers. The swivel at the top allows that section of the cross to revolve. Everything is taut. Around goes the performer, and the unseen joint unscrews. Finally he reaches the end; the bottom falls free; and he is hanging by his extended arms. The dimensions of the cylinders are of corresponding size. This factor now comes to the performer's advantage. He is able to do something that would not have been possible with the cross closed; namely, he can draw in his arms, one at a time, by letting his body slip downward. Before, the base of the cross prevented this; now it can be done. Hence by using some agility, the performer extricates himself from the upper portion of the cross. His next task is to replace the bottom. To accomplish this he should have a chair or some object in the cabinet, as he cannot hold the lower section in the air and revolve the upper portion at the same time. Lowering the chain is an alternative; this can be done if the chain runs through a loop inside the cabinet and is attached to the floor. Either is a minor point that is not difficult to manage. The important item is that the performer

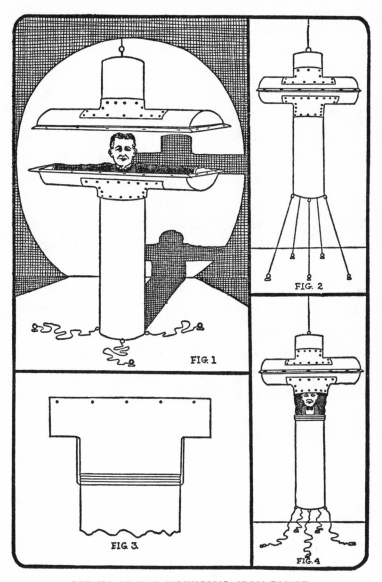

FIG. 1

FIG. 2

FIG. 3

FIG. 4

DETAILS OF THE CYLINDRICAL CROSS ESCAPE

sets the two portions of the cross together and screws them back into position, then leaves everything exactly as it was before the escape.

When the curtains are withdrawn the cross is hanging there as mysterious as ever, and the committee can examine the bolts and every part of the apparatus. The guy-ropes are released and the cross is brought down to the floor. It should be noted that when the cross is loose, unscrewing the two portions is virtually impossible. The bottom portion must be firmly held in order to turn the upper section. The apparatus requires that the top be free to turn while the bottom is held in position. Even inside the cross the secret cannot be discovered, for the necessary leverage to turn the tight-fitting screw cannot be obtained. Any rotary motion inside the free cross would merely upset the device. One or two men would have to hold the base while two others pushed the arms in the required direction. There is no danger of this, for the secret is too ingenious to excite suspicion, and coöperative energy on the part of committee-men is easily overcome.

Considered from every standpoint, this is as nearly perfect as an escape can be. It is a device with remarkable possibilities. Devices built by an escape artist and introduced by him must be formidable and capable of standing the closest examination; the cylindrical cross meets both requirements to perfection. The reader will appreciate that a contrivance of this sort must be well made in every detail. It is difficult to estimate the cost of its construction, but it is safe to say that it could not be manufactured cheaply. Whatever the expense, a trick like this is worth it. There are few escapes convincing enough and spectacular enough to be exhibited as an entire program in themselves; the cylindrical cross is one of these few. It ranks with Houdini's water-torture cell and can certainly be classed as one of his greatest and most ingenious creations.

THE SUSPENDED BRASS TUBE

THE instructions for this escape were written by Houdini on September 1, 1912, two days after he had drawn diagrams and sketches for the cylindrical cross escape. There are certain points of similarity in the two ideas, but the methods of operation are quite different. Both are spectacular escapes. Houdini planned that the brass tube should be built to fit a regulation porthole; this indicates that he evolved the idea aboard the steamship. He also planned that the end of the tube (that is, the top) should contain a sheet of glass.

The effect of the escape is as follows:

The performer exhibits a large brass tube into which his body will fit so tightly that very little motion is possible, even to the extent of raising the arms. The bottom of the tube is a heavy brass cover, riveted to the tube itself. The top is a detachable cover, designed like a porthole, which may be clamped tightly in place. There are hooks or rings in both top and bottom, so that the tube may be suspended between two chains. The committee examines everything. All parts of the tube stand rigid inspection and pressure. The performer enters head first, so that he cannot possibly use his hands to work on the cover; but when the cover is fitted into place, it is so solidly bolted and clamped by a flange provided with holes that every one is positive that inside operation is impossible anyhow. If glass is used in the top, it differentiates the top from the bottom, and also enables the committeemen to see the performer's feet after he has been placed within. Heavy chains are attached to both ends of the tube. The bottom chain is fastened to a metal ring in the stage; the upper end is carried over a pulley on a solid framework and continues off-stage. The result is that the tube is suspended at an angle between the two taut chains and the performer has to make his escape from that difficult position.

The method of release is entirely different from most others, for this is one escape in which the performer is dependent on outside assistance. The bottom of the tube is removable. The rivets on the outside are false; they do not go entirely through the tube. But the bottom fits very tight, so tight in fact that no one can push or pull it loose. The ends of the false rivets hold it firmly in position. Even inside the tube, the performer is helpless; the tube is so long that his feet do not reach the top; his hands are at his sides, and there is no way in which he can exert pressure to push the bottom from the tube. How then, does he escape? The release is effected off stage!

The chain that holds the top of the tube passes off stage and is wound around a winch. The assistant uses this to tighten the chain before the cabinet is placed around the suspended brass tube. As soon as the curtains are closed, the assistant, who has not drawn the chain to its greatest tightness—he may still be winding the winch slowly when the cabinet is put in position—turns the winch farther. The chains, the hooks on the tube, and the ring in the floor are all considerably stronger than the fastenings of the removable bottom. As a result, the tightening of the winch pulls the brass tube apart. The bottom drops off, and the chain remains straight because of the weight of the upper portion, which swings down to the stage. This enables the performer to slide right out of the tube. He puts the apparatus back into its original condition by setting the tube on the bottom and hammering it down into position so that it will again pass examination. The greater part of the work lies in fixing the tube after the escape; the release itself is a matter of a very few seconds.

There are, of course, certain details to be considered. The chain that goes off stage must not betray what is going on within the cabinet. In replacing the tube, the performer can unhook the bottom and move it over to a spot below the tube; he will require some slack in the chain to hook the apparatus back in position, but this can be given gradually. The upper chain can be entirely masked outside of the cabinet, passing behind a scene or a wing; even if visible, slight motion of the chain is not suspicious.

Having decided on this method of escape, Houdini followed with rough plans to work the trick while the tube was filled with water. The required details of this improvement are not complete. The pull-off method was the same, but certain difficulties presented themselves, and these are not entirely solved. The close-fitting bottom of the tube could hold water. The difficulty lay in going into the tube head first, and having the bottom operate as usual; for with this procedure the water would come out before the performer! So Houdini planned an upright stand with swivels fitting into projections on the side of the tube. Here the tube would hang free; apparently to prevent the performer from swinging it, chains would be attached, running off stage—probably to the back, or else to opposite sides.

The arrangement of these chains provided that the upper chain should go down to the floor, while the lower chain would go through a framework above. Tightening the chains would thus have two effects, first to swing the tube on the swivel in the stand so that the bottom would come up to the top and the performer would be head first. The tight-fitting porthole would prevent water from escaping. Further tightening of the chains would then cause the bottom of the tube to pop off in an upward direction. The performer would require sufficient space to move one arm, so that he could either hold to a cross-bar inside the bottom and be drawn with it, or could work his way upward by reaching the edge of the tube. No water would escape; and when the performer had emerged, he could replace the false bottom and jam it into position from the top of the heavy stand. Then by a signal along the chain, the assistants would know when to release the chains letting the tube back to its original position.

It is obvious that this more elaborate escape, while possibly workable, involves many complications in an effect which is ideally simple in its original form. It illustrates very clearly why every feat of magic, escapes included, should avoid difficult systems of operation. It is rather doubtful whether the added effect of having water in the can is worth the extra preparation, especially as the use of the chains becomes suspicious rather than natural. Nevertheless, Houdini possessed the ability to smooth out such difficulties and to make complicated arrangements simple. Having devised a new escape, he invariably found the most satisfactory form in which to present it. With the brass tube escape, he would either have shown it without the water and would have made it a very spectacular effect, or he would eventually have developed the reversing of the tube and the upward pull into a practical method that would have deceived the most critical observers.

THE GREAT CELL MYSTERY

THE description and explanation of this cell mystery are quoted from Houdini's notes on the escape, which are considerably detailed. It is an effective mystery that involves a very unusual principle.

"The cell is large and lined with steel or aluminum. The man is locked in, and from the inside it is absolutely impossible for any one to help himself. The locks are on the outside and there is to be no trap; no faked rivets or faked hinges.

"Then the cell will be either chained or roped as with the trunk escape. After a few minutes the man is free.

"The secret: The locks are to be made of a special pattern. Each lock looks exactly like a very fine Chubb; in fact it is to be a complicated lever lock the same as used on a safe.

"But it is to be made to open from the inside, with a strong electro-magnet!

"The committee has one key, but this locks twice,

and when the lock is locked twice, no man can get out, as the magnet will not work. This is so that a reward can be offered to any one that can get out. I am to do it first and can then change the lock so that a magnet will not work.

"But the safest way is to have a triple lock, and the committee holds the key which locks twice; or if possible have it lock four times: then the committee can lock it twice.

"The door should be held inside by a rather long sheet of steel, which prevents it from coming in; but when this sheet of steel is removed from the inside, it will allow the door to come in just far enough to allow me to squeeze out; or the door may be made so that after the lock is open, you can lift it up from the inside, and thus allow it to be easily pulled inward. Then the closing is easy enough. This must be made to work very quickly.

"The sheet of steel that prevents the door from closing can be made of malleable steel, which only a strong instrument can bend; and this can be bent out of the way of the door. This will not allow the cell to be examined afterward, but it is a good thing to remember.

"This mystery, worked properly, ought to be a great advertising scheme. Advertised as a new system of mystery: no faked hinges, no faked screws. Offer a reward to any one who can find his way out, or can find that the cell is not properly made.

"It would be a good idea to use a good straitjacket and be strapped inside the cell, and then get out of both. This can easily be done by working the strait-jacket like I worked it with Circus Carré. While they are securing the cell outside, this would allow ample time to release myself from the jacket.

"An idea is to have a bolt on the cell, arranged so that by removing a small screw, a stiffened wire may be inserted; pushing the wire will release a powerful spring that will pull back the bolt.

"This can easily be arranged so that it can never come back by accident, but will require pressure. When pressure is released it will relock."

The novel part of this escape is the use of the lock that can be opened with a magnet. Such an ingenious contrivance would never be suspected, but it is interesting to note that Houdini intended to make the lock absolutely certain in case any one else should attempt to escape from the cell. Houdini refers to more than one lock at the beginning of the description and later speaks of a single lock; this means, of course, that any additional locks would operate alike. The door is evidently intended to open outward; secured with chains or ropes, it could not be pushed open; hence the necessity for bringing the door inward far enough to slip through the opening. The replacement of the steel sheet that prevents the door from coming inward is not entirely clear in the explanation, and there are no diagrams accompanying the notes. This, however, is not the important factor of the mystery, and it is evident that Houdini planned some simple and practical method of replacement. Cutting the ropes and replacing them, or undoing the chains temporarily, would make it possible to open the door and put the plate back in position, if no other method could be used. The malleable plate was evidently regarded as inferior, since it might show signs of the work done on it.

THE RACK TEST

⓪LD-TIME torture methods were of great interest to Houdini. They are mentioned in various notes, and it appears to have been his intention to adapt some of these ancient devices to produce sensational escapes. Most of his notes on this subject are incomplete or are given merely as suitable ideas to be studied later on; for escapes of this type were not offered as challenges, since the apparatus was of obsolete design. Houdini studied every object that could possibly be used to hold him, and was constantly creating new ideas for making escapes; where instruments of torture were concerned, research was necessary. The rack escape was worked out in detail. Houdini planned to construct a rack that would closely resemble the torture device of mediaeval times; and he found an ingenious way in which it could be made into a spectacular escape.

Let us consider the rack as it would appear on the stage. The performer is placed on a bench, and his feet are secured at the lower end. There is a roller at the upper end, and his hands are attached there by other ropes. Then the roller is turned with a crank, until the performer is stretched to the limit, as prisoners were once prepared for torture. The handle of the roller is clamped to the floor or is held by members of the committee, through an opening in the curtain. The performer is in a position where he cannot gain slack by any of the methods generally used. The test is therefore an extraordinary rope tie.

Houdini's diagrams show one roller at the head of the rack; from his notes it appears that two rollers would be preferable, one at each end of the rack, so that the ropes could be wound from both ends; hence release of the feet would be more difficult than release of the hands. The indication of only one roller in the diagrams is explained by the fact that the secret lies in the hand roller alone. The use of two rollers has a certain advantage. The rack is of such simple construction that no preparation seems possible, and the device will stand examination by the most careful committee. But it is a fact that slack is required to escape from ropes, and the rack is designed to prevent slack. Therefore to make the escape sure and effective, a hidden mechanism is highly important.

The preparation planned by Houdini concerned the top roller, which passed through two wooden braces or holes in the frame of the rack. These were

necessary to keep the roller in position. The roller
was to be separated at both points where it passed
through the frame; that is, the roller consisted of
three sections, a long one between two short ones.
To keep the roller intact, Houdini designed square-
shaped plugs fitting in holes in the sections of the
rollers. The handles on each side of the roller kept
the end portions from coming out. The divisions between the sections were small, but by pulling the
plugs outward, they would slide back in slots and release the center section, which could not, however,
come free of the braces. The ends of these plugs were
attached to cords running down through the supporting legs of the frame. Both were attached to a single
cord and so arranged that a pull would draw back the
plugs and release the center section of the roller.
The cord ran off-stage or to a place where an assistant could pull it without being observed. As soon as
the curtains were closed, the pull was to be given,
and the center part of the roller would revolve backward when drawn by the performer, giving him plenty
of slack and making it an easy matter for him to
release his hands from the roller. A removable section
would simplify the process, but it would be more difficult to conceal as perfectly; hence it was not so
desirable as the non-removable section. Intricate knots
were not the factor that prevented escape; the ten-

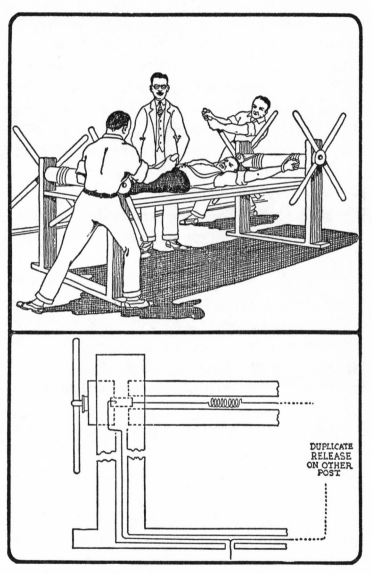

APPEARANCE AND CONSTRUCTION OF THE RACK ESCAPE

sion of the rollers was responsible; hence the reverse rolling of the center section was considered sufficient.

In winding the roller as one piece, a complication would present itself; namely, the turning of the release cord with the roller. This shows the advantage of the roller for the feet, and indicates a method of procedure that was not stated, but that appears quite obvious. First the performer's feet and hands should be bound very tightly, and slack taken up by turning the foot roller. When the hand roller is reached, all slack is gone, and it cannot be turned far without hurting the performer, which is not the purpose for which this rack is intended. The hand roller is not turned far enough to interfere with the pull of the cord releasing the center section of the roller.

Once free from the rack, the performer was able to turn the roller back to its original position, the ropes being slack. To insert the square connecting plugs, a thin pin could be used to push them back into position; but the better plan is to have them return automatically, actuated by springs in the roller either at the ends or by a long thin spring running entirely through the center section and connecting with both plugs. With this mechanical device, the assistant merely draws back the release cord and fastens it so that the plugs are out of the way and the performer can begin his escape immediately. Off the rack, the performer cuts or unhooks the release cord from within the cabinet, and the plugs go back into position.

Houdini typed the description of this trick in Bremen, Germany. The date is not given. A magazine article (date also unknown) which described various forms of torture devices was attached to the material written by Houdini.

THE SPANISH MAIDEN ESCAPE

THE escape from the Spanish Maiden was evidently part of Houdini's scheme to produce some day a scene in which the stage would be filled with strange relics of ancient inquisitions, from any one of which he could effect an escape! The rack and the Spanish Maiden are the only two that are explained in his notes, but there are references to others. The Spanish Maiden is a modification of the famous instrument of torture. It is a box that stands upright, with a hinged section that opens outward. It is shaped roughly like the human body, and the front is painted to resemble a maiden. Both parts of the box are alike —the box proper and the cover—and the interior of each section is lined with spikes. In this detail it differs from the ancient Iron Maiden, for whereas the spikes were arranged so as to pierce the person imprisoned within, those of the modernized device merely surround the prisoner so that it is impossible for him to move freely. When the Maiden is closed, padlocks may be attached to staples in order to make

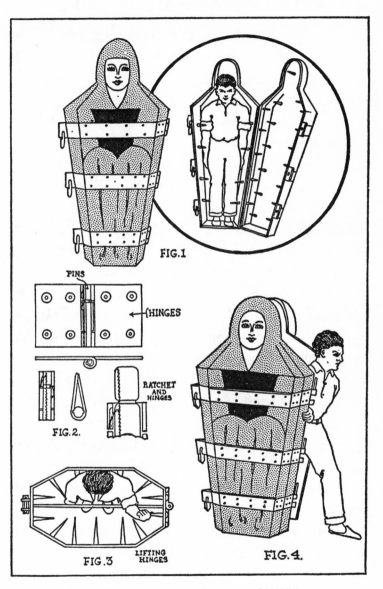

FIG.1

PINS

HINGES

RATCHET
AND
HINGES

FIG.2.

FIG.3   LIFTING
HINGES

FIG.4.

THE ESCAPE FROM THE SPANISH MAIDEN

escape apparently impossible. There are three padlocks; the iron bands to which they are attached pass
around the Spanish Maiden and terminate in the
hinges.

The secret of the escape from the Spanish Maiden
lies in hinges that are specially made. They are pin
hinges, but each pin is cut like a ratchet on one side,
and two springs inside the tube hold the pin in position. When the box is open, the pins cannot be removed from the hinges. This is because the lower
spring swings around with the hinge and engages a
groove in the opposite side of the pin. Any attempt to
pull the pin upward will fail. When the Spanish
Maiden is closed, both springs engage the ratchet; the
upper spring is designed to raise the pin from the
hinge, the lower spring to keep the pin from falling.

By gripping one of the spikes at the hinge side of
the cover (or front section of the box) the performer
can lift the cover upward a fraction of an inch. The
looseness of the padlocks permits this. Each time he
lifts up and releases, the upper spring of each hinge
works on the ratchet in the pin, and thus the pins are
gradually forced out of the springs.

When the operation has been completed, the pins
are clear of the hinges and the performer opens the
box at that side, the padlocks serving as hinges. After
the escape, the performer replaces the pins by push-

ing them up through the hinges from the bottom. Everything is secure once more, and the spiked box may be inspected by the committee. When the box is closed, no one will detect the ingenious method of removing the pins from the hinges; when it is opened, the pins cannot be removed. Hence the mode of escape is indetectable, for it is only workable by the person who is confined inside.

CONCLUSION

IN SUMMARIZING Houdini's escapes, one is impressed by the great number and variety of ideas employed by this famous performer. There seems to have been no limit to the extent of his research and experiment; yet it is safe to say that the material contained in Houdini's notes represents but a fraction of the amazing knowledge that he possessed on this subject. In the literature on magic and conjuring there has been very little reference to escape work, and the known methods have been few and restricted. It is an unquestioned fact that Houdini stands alone as the great creative genius of escapes. There have been other performers who have possessed originality and ingenuity in this field of mystery, but it is probable that the ideas and methods created or planned by Houdini have far exceeded the combined total of all those devised by others. The tendency of escape artists has been to feature one successful escape as long as possible, whereas Houdini was always seeking the new and seemingly impossible; and this collection of Houdini's secrets bears testimony to that fact.

Just as these notes represent a portion of Houdini's total knowledge of the subject, so his escape work represented a portion of his studies and endeavors in the field of mystery. As a magician, Houdini was always seeking the new and the spectacular, always seeking to create some new trick or illusion. As an investigator of fraudulent psychic phenomena he was constantly alert, and he learned many tricks of mediums that other magicians had failed to detect. His unpublished notes on these subjects contain many of the unusual features found in his escape secrets. For in all branches of magic Houdini was a constant seeker of knowledge and a man of originality in ideas and methods.

CONTENTS OF BOOK TWO

CONTENTS

CONTENTS

CONTENTS

PREFACE

by Bernard M. L. Ernst

S OME of the material used by Mr. Gibson in the
following pages was given to me by Houdini for
publication before his untimely death in 1926, and
more was found and sent to me by Mrs. Houdini in
later years. Mr. Gibson had a plethora of material
thrust upon him and the very difficult task of selecting
only enough items to keep this volume within reasonable bounds. The favorable comment on his earlier
work, "Houdini's Escapes," in connection with which
he encountered the same difficulty, furnishes confidence that "Houdini's Magic" will please the reading
public. As in the earlier work, illusions and effects,
now used by professional magicians, are not exposed
because of the Canons of Ethics and Standards of The
Society of American Magicians, of which the author
is a member. With the co-operation of Mrs. Beatrice
Houdini, I turned over to Mr. Gibson note books and
memoranda, largely in Houdini's own handwriting,
which seemed to contain new and original ideas, or
new and original methods of presenting old time dem-

onstrations of magic. Marginal notations by Houdini indicated that unique effects and "moves" were contained in his rough manuscripts. These have been translated, at times rewritten and presented in clear and non-technical form, and in many instances supplemented by carefully prepared drawings. An effort has been made to present the notes of a great artist in the manner in which he would have done had he lived, and according to the wish that he expressed before his death. Amateur magicians will find in the book a fund of information and many examples of technique and misdirection for which Houdini, among other things, was famous. Then too, there is now offered the kind of tricks, experiments, and illusions which appealed to the master. Unfortunately his transcendent showmanship and personality are gone. My collection of magical apparatus includes many of the devices and articles devised and built by Houdini for use in connection with the items which follow. He tested them all and found that they would work. Indeed, he followed his rule of trying them out at least three times before he was satisfied that they were worthwhile. Some of his ideas he gave to his friends while he lived. Others were set aside for his projected books. Some effects were described in meticulous detail. Others were merely sketched in crude form and their possibilities indicated. I have witnessed Houdini's demonstrations of many of the "experiments" at the dinner table, in the open air during summer evenings, and in his private library on 113th Street in the early morning hours. In his hands all were completely deceptive and extraordinarily mysterious. Frequently he would practice several of the effects and present them at private entertainments to test their efficacy. When the reception did not satisfy him he would destroy his notes and abandon the ideas completely. The memoranda which he kept were of things considered by him to be of value for use in magic and are included in this book. Its pages will be of interest and it is hoped that its contents will furnish pleasant days and evenings to young and old alike.

New York, February 15, 1932.

HOUDINI'S MAGIC
PART ONE.

INTRODUCTORY

THIS section is preliminary to the actual explanations of the magical secrets which were found in Houdini's notes. It discusses the scope and purpose of the material which forms this book. It also deals with Houdini and his relationship to magic.

HOUDINI'S NOTES ON MAGIC

HOUDINI'S notes on magic cover nearly every phase of the art. They were assembled over a period of many years and they form an interesting collection of varied and unusual ideas—many of which have never before appeared in a work on conjuring.

The author began his study of Houdini's notes nearly three years ago. A preliminary examination showed that a considerable percentage of the material dealt with methods of escape. That material was selected and revised. It was published in book form under the title of *Houdini's Escapes*. Following the appearance of the first volume, the author turned his attention to the notes that pertained to magic. These compose the present book.

The art of the magician is much broader than the art of the escape king. Technically, the man who performs escapes is simply devoting his efforts to a specialized branch of magic. In the usual collection of notes on magic, one would expect to find a few escape tricks. Houdini's collection was, of course, an exception, as he won fame as the world's greatest escape artist. At the same time, Houdini was primarily a magician and he was constantly searching for new methods that could be applied to magic.

Houdini began his career as a professional magician. He had high ambitions to reach the topmost place in his chosen art. While he was still progressing, he realized the possibilities of the escape act and turned his great efforts to its development. The success that he gained is now a matter of history. The name of Houdini grew to world-wide fame. Yet Houdini never lost the desire to perform magic. He still held the ambition which has gripped nearly every magician: to appear with his own show, presenting a series of magical effects from feats of sleight of hand to the largest of stage illusions.

When Houdini was demonstrating his escape from a water-torture cell, nearly twenty years ago, he prefaced that feature with a presentation of the needle trick. Some years later, he went on tour in vaudeville, featuring both the needle trick and the substitution-trunk mystery. He had performed those same effects many years before. They were a connecting link with his early career as a magician.

It was not until two years before his death that Houdini set out with his road show, a two and one-half hour performance devoted chiefly to magic. Many who knew Houdini were amazed at the enthusiasm he displayed in his work. Houdini, the magician, was a dynamo of human energy, constantly preparing new illusions and seeking new ideas in magic.

Houdini's attitude toward magic must be considered in connection with his notes on the subject. As an escape artist, he stood supreme. He kept his methods to himself and jealously guarded his most important secrets. He raised a barrier of permanent silence where his own escapes were concerned. The notes that he made on escapes were planned for practical purposes in connection with his own work.

When magic became his chief aim, Houdini adopted a different attitude. He recognized the fact that there were many clever and competent magicians. His aim was not to establish a new form of mystery. He wished to take his place in the long line of famous magicians who have mystified the public over a period of many years. He exchanged ideas with those who knew the principles of magical deception. He was receptive to the suggestions of those well versed in magic. In cities where he appeared, he invited local magicians to appear upon his stage and present their best tricks. The author took part in one of these per-

formances during Houdini's engagement in Philadelphia.

Houdini's enthusiasm for magic is reflected in his
notes on the subject. He sought to adapt old ideas to
new uses, to discover methods that would produce
startling and unusual effects. While he had a natural
leaning toward practicability, he would not abandon
an idea simply because its first plans were not entirely
satisfactory. Simplicity is the keynote of many of the
best tricks and illusions; but many performers have
ceased to progress because they have been too content with their old ideas. Houdini was not restrained
in that manner. He frequently took chances with
tricks that involved the danger of failure. He was
determined to get the most out of magic.

Houdini was different from the conventional magician. He lacked the suavity that is frequently culti-
vated by magicians. His escape work had brought him
into contact with difficult situations. He was often at
his best when forced to adopt a challenging attitude.
He frequently depended upon showmanship in preference to smoothness. He liked tricks that were different; and he appreciated and commended good
magic when he saw it performed. He gained many
excellent ideas from his associations with other magicians.

It must be remembered that Houdini was a great

collector of magical literature and data regarding magic. He was not satisfied with gathering a few workable ideas and devoting all his efforts to commercializing them. He wanted to know all that he could learn about magic. Hence his notes were not confined to restricted phases of the art. He set down numerous ideas which occurred to him. He mentioned tricks that he had seen or about which he had heard. He made notes of conversations with other magicians. As a result, the material in his notes varies from obscure references to detailed instructions supplemented by accurate diagrams.

In preparing these notes for publication, the author was often forced to supply certain details that were not mentioned in the actual notes. Many factors were implied or suggested; these required careful study in order to understand the exact idea. Some tricks were explained chiefly by memoranda. It was necessary to visualize the effect from a consideration of the method. In some instances, the condition was reversed. The notes told how an illusion would appear to the audience, but were meager when it came to the actual explanation. By applying known principles of magic to the particular problems involved, the author has managed to reconstruct these ideas and thus to present them in the finished form.

The reader should bear one point in mind. With

his escapes, Houdini was traveling through undis-
covered land. The great percentage of his notes on
escapes gave his original ideas. With his magic, Houdini was utilizing many known methods of a highly
developed art. His notes, like those of any other practical magician, contain effects that were given to him
or which depend to a great extent upon some idea
previously used by magicians.

The author is positive that many of Houdini's
magical ideas were his own originations. Some of
them are entirely unlike anything that has previously
been used in magic. It is impossible, however, to state
exactly what percentage of the tricks was entirely
Houdini's, partly Houdini's, or simply methods that
he obtained from others. Houdini left these notes
with the definite understanding that books should be
prepared from them. Some of the material was unquestionably intended for reference alone—not for
complete publication—for with the notes were various small manuscripts which bore the names of the
authors.

While it is possible that Houdini purchased or obtained the rights to use such manuscript material,
the author has chosen to eliminate it. The notes contained so many interesting and worth-while ideas in
magic that it was quite possible to form a complete
volume without recourse to material that was defi-

nitely proprietary. The purpose has been to make the book chiefly dependent upon Houdini's own ideas. Any other items which have crept in were included for two definite reasons: first, because it was evident that Houdini intended to use them; second, because the tricks possess unusual merit.

The entire preparation of the book has been a matter of selective research. Preference was given to those methods which appeared to be Houdini's own, to those which were explained most clearly, and to those which seemed most practical. Where the notes were unquestionably preliminary drafts, the author has not hesitated to include or suggest modifications and improvements which he considered to be obviously essential. This is a course adopted by every qualified writer on magic when he is preparing a work that is based upon original notations and dependent upon rough diagrams.

The book has been divided into convenient sections, which classify various tricks and stage effects. The preparation of the illustrations has been an important item in the completion of the book. Where an idea is simple, but routine is important, drawings are nonessential; but in cases where unusual or complicated devices are employed, illustrations can tell much more than words. This is particularly true of stage illusions. Hence the sections that explain larger tricks are provided with a greater number of drawings.

This book includes pseudopsychic effects which may be classed as magical methods rather than as the tricks of fraudulent mediums. It also contains a few escapes that were not published in the previous volume. It was evident from the first examination of Houdini's notes that the material which they contained would be of great interest to all persons who enjoy the study of magic. The element of originality is present throughout. The author gained this impression upon first examination of Houdini's notes. Since completing the manuscript, that impression has become a definite opinion. The methods which Houdini considered worthy of publication should prove a welcome addition to the literature of magic.

PART TWO.

IMPROMPTU TRICKS

HERE we have the secrets of tricks intended for close-up presentation. These are not numerous, but they include some very clever items that will interest all who present magic of this type.

COIN TRANSPORTATION

AN EASY trick and an effective one. The magician borrows a coin and two handkerchiefs. He places one handkerchief in an empty glass, crumpling it as he does so. He places the coin in the second handkerchief and inserts it in another glass.

The magician commands the coin to pass from one glass to the other. He lifts the handkerchief that covers the coin. The glass is empty. He lays the handkerchief aside and goes to the other glass. As he draws out the handkerchief, the coin falls into the glass.

The best coin to use is a half-dollar. A duplicate is required. The duplicate coin has a white thread attached to it; on the end of the thread is a small hook. The magician has this coin concealed in his hand. He borrows the handkerchiefs and a half-dollar. Returning to his table, he shows the duplicate half-dollar and lays it with one handkerchief. He crumples the other handkerchief, leaving the borrowed coin in it.

He puts the threaded half-dollar in a glass with the

handkerchief over it, at the same time attaching the hook to the center of the handkerchief. When the handkerchief is lifted by the center, the coin dangles beneath it and is not seen. The handkerchief is placed upon the table, the hook being detached so that the coin drops behind some small article.

It is only necessary to draw out the crumpled handkerchief and the borrowed coin will fall into the glass. It is immediately returned, with the handkerchiefs.

THE MAGNETIC TABLE

THIS is a surprising trick, which may be used as an impromptu stunt or as an effect of pseudo-psychic nature. The magician seats himself beside a card table. He raises the table once or twice; then he moves away and the table begins to follow him.

The secret is a piece of black thread, attached to two black pins. The thread is less than a foot in length; the pins are slightly bent.

Seated at the table, the magician attaches the pins to his trousers, one at each knee, the thread passing between. He moves his knees apart as he raises the table and he sets one leg of the table within the line of the thread. As he makes passes with his hands, he slides backward in his chair. In conclusion, the magician detaches the thread and lets it fall to the floor.

This is the same method as that used in the balanced cane; hence the two tricks may be worked on the same occasion. The cane is set upright in front of the performer so that it leans against the thread and remains balanced. The moving table is a spookier trick, however, and is less likely to be detected.

A SPOOKY BALL

WHILE this trick has been described in print and is known to many persons interested in magic, it is included here because Houdini's notes add an effect that gives the trick a most surprising finish.

The trick is best performed on a dinner table. The magician exhibits a steel ball-bearing that measures about one inch in diameter. He places the ball on the table and makes mysterious passes toward it. Slowly the ball begins to roll away across the table. It stops and advances at the magician's command.

The magician lays a lady's handkerchief in front of the ball. The ball rolls along the tablecloth and on to the handkerchief. The magician seizes the four corners of the handkerchief and raises it while the ball is still rolling. He gives the handkerchief and the ball for immediate examination.

A simple apparatus is utilized—a small thin ring attached to a thread. The ring is under the tablecloth. The thread goes to an assistant at the opposite side of the table. The magician lays the ball on the hidden ring. When the assistant pulls the thread, the ball moves across the table, away from the magician. The assistant is apparently an interested onlooker. Every one is intent upon watching the ball in its course.

The added effect is the rolling of the ball into the handkerchief. This is simplicity itself; the weight of the ball enables it to do the trick automatically. The lifting of the handkerchief is the assistant's clue to pull the ring completely away from beneath the table-cloth.

THE TALKING GLASS

A GLASS, a thread, and a pencil are the required articles. The thread is tied in a loop. The glass is slipped into the loop. The glass should have tapering sides so that it does not slide completely through the loop. The glass is partly filled with water. The

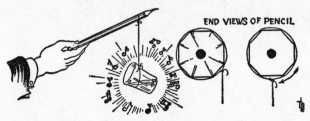

END VIEWS OF PENCIL

TWISTING THE PENCIL MAKES THE STRING CLIMB.

other end of the thread is tied about the pencil. The pencil is raised and the glass hangs suspended by the thread. When persons ask questions, the glass responds. It rings softly and in this manner counts to required numbers or answers questions "yes" and "no," one ring signifying the affirmative, two rings the negative.

The pencil used in the trick is hexagonal. The loop

is tied about it rather firmly. When the pencil is re-volved slowly, the thread begins to climb; then it slips and drops back with a slight jerk, owing to the weight of the glass. This is scarcely observable, espe-cially as the glass is swaying slightly. But each time the string drops, the vibration causes the glass to ring.

If a thin glass is used and the right quantity of water is in the glass, the sound will be quite clear. The proper type of glass can be discovered by experi-ment. The trick is very effective when performed in a dim light, so that the twisting of the pencil cannot be observed. The performer should center his gaze upon the glass. The sound comes from the glass and this heightens the deception.

FOUR-COIN ASSEMBLY

THIS is an excellent impromptu trick. It requires a certain amount of skill, but is less difficult than a pure sleight-of-hand demonstration, as the misdirection is well arranged and every movement is completely covered.

To the audience, the trick appears as follows: The magician borrows four coins, all alike. He lays a handkerchief upon the table. He weights down the corners of the handkerchief by placing a coin upon each corner. He takes two pieces of paper, each about four inches square, and covers two of the coins, one with each sheet.

He picks up a loose coin and places it beneath the handkerchief with his right hand. A snap of the fingers—the coin is gone. The empty right hand lifts the sheet of paper at one corner. Two coins are revealed. The coin has apparently joined its mate. The sheet of paper is replaced above the two coins. Another loose coin is magically passed beneath it. Now there are three coins beneath one sheet of paper; one coin beneath the other. At the magician's command, the single coin passes to join the three. The papers are lifted. The four coins have assembled!

The first deception occurs when the performer is explaining what he intends to do. Having put the four coins at the corners of the handkerchief, he exhibits the two sheets of paper, holding one in each hand, fingers beneath, thumb above.

"When I cover the coins nearest me," says the magician, suiting the words with the action, "you see the coins that are farthest away." He lifts the papers and holds them over the other two coins. "When I cover the coins farthest away from me, you see those that are nearest to me."

It is at this point that the performer makes his first movement. The right hand is holding the paper above the coin at the outer right corner. The second finger presses against the lower part of the coin. The right forefinger raises the edge of the coin. Thus the coin is clipped between the fingers, at the back of the hand. Only the fingers are out of sight beneath the paper. The open palm is clearly seen. There appears to be no chance for deception.

The magician raises the left-hand paper from the coin that it is covering. He brings the left hand over to the right. As the left paper covers the right paper, a few inches above it, the right hand drops its paper and takes the paper that the left hand is holding. During this movement, the right fingers are constantly concealed from view. The right hand places the paper that it has taken upon the coin at the lower left corner. It holds the paper there and still retains the coin. The left hand points at both sheets of paper,

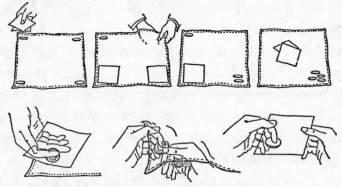

Top, HOW THE TRICK APPEARS. *Bottom*, CLIPPING FIRST COIN— TRANSFER OF EACH "PASSING" COIN—COIN CONCEALED WHEN PAPER IS TRANSFERRED.

while the magician remarks: "When I cover the coins diagonally, the other two coins are visible."

The right hand, still carrying its hidden coin, moves to the upper left corner and covers the coin there. It drops the paper and leaves the coin beneath it. Then both hands point to the coins at the lower corner and the magician says: "I shall use the coins that are nearest to me."

He picks up the coin at the lower left corner, lifting it with the right hand. The left hand raises the corner of the handkerchief. The left fingers are beneath the corner. The right hand slowly slids its coin under the handkerchief. In so doing, it transfers the coin to the left hand, which clips it between the first and second fingers, at the back; just as the right hand previously clipped a coin.

The right hand continues a bit beneath the handkerchief. Then the fingers are snapped. The right hand comes back. It is shown entirely empty. The right hand picks up the paper at the upper left corner of the handkerchief. Two coins are seen there. The left hand is still holding the corner of the handkerchief. The right hand brings the paper over to the left hand. The left moves away from the handkerchief and takes the sheet of paper. This transfer completely covers the coin that is held behind the left hand.

The right hand, being free, moves to the right to take the coin at the lower right corner. The left hand quietly lays the paper upon the two coins at the upper left corner. It leaves its clipped coin beneath the paper and comes back to the lower left corner of the handkerchief. As the left hand lifts the corner of the handkerchief, the magician repeats his previous move. He puts the right hand beneath the cloth. The left fingers clip the coin. The right hand comes out empty. It lifts the sheet of paper at the upper left corner and shows three coins. It transfers the paper to the left hand, which drops the corner of the cloth. The left hand puts the paper upon the three coins, leaving the fourth coin with them. The right hand points to the sheet of paper at the upper right corner of the handkerchief.

The last transfer should be done as mysteriously as possible. The spectators think that there are three coin beneath one sheet of paper and one coin beneath the other. As a matter of fact, all four coins are under one sheet of paper. The magician makes the most of this situation. He commands the last coin to pass and makes a motion with his fingers. He lifts the paper at the upper left corner, with the left hand. This reveals the four coins. The right hand lifts the paper at the upper right corner and shows that the coin has gone. Coins, papers, and handkerchief may be thoroughly examined by the spectators.

If this trick is done properly, the keenest observer will be mystified. The entire routine is natural; the magician is always one step ahead of the onlookers. There should be no great speed. The trick is most effective when done deliberately, as the sleights may be accomplished without fumbling. With a reasonable amount of practice, this becomes a fine mystery, suitable for close-up presentation.

CUT AND RESTORED STRING

NEW versions of the cut and restored string trick are constantly appearing. Like so many others, this one has points of novelty that will be of interest to magicians. It possesses that degree of difference which makes it deceptive.

The string used is about two feet in length. The magician measures off three or four inches and holds the string at that point, between his left thumb and forefinger. The right hand takes the long end of the string and weaves it between the left fingers: over the first, under the second, over the third, under the little finger. He winds the string around the little finger a few times; brings it over the little finger, under the third, then over the second and under the forefinger, letting the long end extend.

He picks the spot where the string passes over the second finger (on its return journey) as the approximate center of the string. He clips the string at that place. Then, drawing the string from his fingers, he shows it to be fully restored!

This trick depends upon a very subtle manipulation. It should be noted that the string, on its return journey, apparently crosses the knuckles of the little finger and the center finger, the back of the hand being upward. But the string does not go over the second finger. When his right hand draws the string

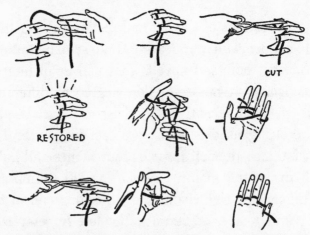

THE ILLUSTRATIONS SHOW THE THREADING AND CUTTING OF THE STRING—ALSO HOW THE SHORT END IS DOUBLED BACK.

under the third finger of the left hand, it is hidden from view. It picks up the short end of the string (which is still downward between the left thumb and forefinger) and brings the short end over the second finger of the left hand. The long string passes clear under the second finger of the left hand and also under the first finger. It extends between the left thumb and forefinger. Thus there is just a tiny end over the second finger and that end is clipped between the second finger and the forefinger. Yet it appears to be the center of the entire string.

The magician uses a pair of scissors to clip the string at the point designated. When he draws the string from the left hand, the short end is retained between the fingers and is later dropped on the floor.

This is a good version of the cut and restored string, as it is almost impossible for any one to note the switch. It should be practiced carefully until the performer can weave the string is a natural, easy fashion. Once the idea is fully understood, the trick presents very little difficulty. It is advisable to start slowly with the weaving, to show that everything is fair. The left fingers should be spread after the cutting, to let the string pull free; at the same time, care should be taken to retain the bit of string that was cut from the short end.

BALANCED DRINKING STRAW

THE feat of balancing a drinking straw depends upon a neat bit of deception. Any straw may be used. The straw is set upon the tips of the first two fingers, which are held together. The palm of the hand is upward. There the straw remains, balanced.

The secret is an ordinary pin, which the performer has in readiness. It may be kept in the lapel of the coat until needed. The pin is clipped between the first two fingers of the hand. The hand is turned downward, the pin projecting inward. The other hand receives the straw. As the hands approach, the pin is pointed upward as the hand is turned over. The straw is placed over the pin. A careful balance is made and the pin easily keeps the straw in position. It appears to be a bit of skillful jugglery.

In conclusion, the hand is turned slightly and the straw is taken by the free hand. The fingers are opened to allow the pin to fall to the floor; where it will not be noticed.

TWO FROM ONE

THIS is a neat knot trick with a large handkerchief —preferably a silk handkerchief. The secret is little known. Houdini used the trick in his show, in

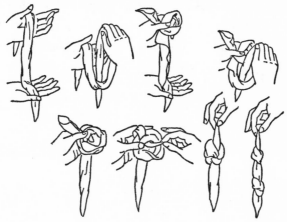

SLOW MOTION ILLUSTRATION OF THE DOUBLING KNOT. NOTE THE FORMATION OF EACH LOOP AND HOW THE TWO ARE ARRANGED TO APPEAR AS A SINGLE KNOT.

connection with a series of handkerchief tricks. The handkerchief is tied in a single knot; the magician shakes the handkerchief and two knots appear at different parts of the handkerchief.

It is simply a case of tying two knots in one. The drawings illustrate the method. While one hand holds the end of the handkerchief, the other hand loops the center once and then again. The knot is tied by thrusting the end of the handkerchief through the double loop. It looks like a single knot when drawn fairly tight.

To make the two knots separate, the handkerchief is held by the upper end and given a quick snap. One knot jumps down the handkerchief. Both knots tighten, and to the observer, the magician has made one knot break apart and form two. The movements of tying should be practiced until they can be performed quickly and naturally.

THE DISSOLVING KNOT

THE old dissolving-knot trick is simple but difficult to follow. The magician twists a handkerchief and apparently ties a fair knot in its center. But the

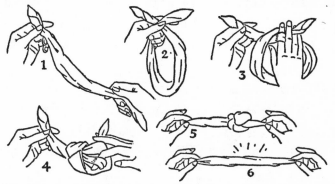

1-2-3, FORMATION OF THE DISSOLVING KNOT. 4, DRAWING A LOOP IN THE CENTER. 5-6, PULL ENDS TO MAKE KNOT VANISH.

knot is not, as the saying goes. The handkerchief comes out knotless.

The move is as follows: Hold the ends of the handkerchief, one in each hand. Bring the right end over the left hand and under the knuckles so that it points upward, in front of the loop. Push it through the

31

loop from above. Pull the end with the right hand and away goes the knot. It is never formed at all.

The improvement includes the following movement. Cross the ends of the handkerchief so that the end on top projects to the right. The left hand takes the left end. The second and third fingers of the right take the right end. The right forefinger reaches through the loop.

The finger can then grip a point near the center of the handkerchief and draw it upward through the loop. This is facilitated if the left fingers assist. The right thumb and forefinger pull the center of the handkerchief so that a false knot is formed when the ends are tightened.

The handkerchief is exhibited in this condition and the false knot adds to the illusion that the magician has tied a genuine single knot. When the ends are drawn, the false knot comes out and the handkerchief is seen to be untied after all.

VANISHING POCKETKNIFE

THE magician can use a borrowed pocketknife in this trick. He opens the blade of the knife and places the instrument in his left hand, from which it immediately vanishes.

A dull knife-blade is used to aid in this vanish. A

SHOWING KNIFE AND DUPLICATE BLADE WITH LOOP. ALSO HOW KNIFE IS CARRIED AWAY WHILE BLADE IS EXHIBITED INSTEAD.

piece of catgut or thin white thread is fitted to the extra knife-blade, at the lower end. The loop is put over the left thumb. The blade hangs out of sight behind the left hand. The magician keeps the palm of the hand toward the spectators.

He asks for an opened knife. He takes it in his right hand and closes the blade while he steps away from the spectators. He lets the onlookers get a glimpse of the handle as he brings the right hand over to the left. Under pretence of squeezing the knife between his hands, he brings the false blade into his left hand. The right hand moves away, carrying the real knife. The left hand lets the false blade come into view, thus giving the impression that it holds the knife. The magician pockets the knife. He brings his hands together and with a rubbing motion forces the hanging blade in back of the left hand. Both hands are opened and the palms are held toward the spectators. The knife has vanished. The false blade is later removed from the left hand.

PART THREE.

CARD TRICKS

THE card tricks found in Houdini's notes are of various types. There was very little reference to sleight of hand. Most of the tricks required only simple manipulation or depended upon special forms of apparatus. The reader will find some novel effects with cards in this section.

A GOOD KEY CARD

MAGICIANS who perform card tricks know the value of a "key" card in a pack which is otherwise unprepared. Many clever tricks can be performed with such a card. When a chosen card is taken from the pack, the magician can find his key and cut the pack at that spot for the return of the selected card. The chosen card can be obtained later by finding the key.

This key card is prepared by taking any card from an ordinary pack, dampening it, and peeling it in half. (Playing-cards are in two layers, glued together.) A thin piece of silk is inserted between the portions of the card, and the front and back are glued together. The prepared card is kept under a heavy weight for two or three days. It then bears no signs of preparation that can be ordinarily noticed. But the performer can detect the card at any time and can use it as a key card. It is stiffer and heavier than the other cards in the pack and can be located by riffling the end of the pack.

HALF AND HALF

THIS is an interesting variation of an older trick, in which a chosen card appears in the magician's pocket. The mystery in this instance is quite different, inasmuch as the magician apparently causes a card to pass from one half of a pack to the other.

A spectator shuffles a pack of cards and divides it in half. He gives one half to the magician. The spectator notes a card in his own half, remembering its distance from the top—for instance, the jack of clubs, eight cards from the top of his half.

The magician then asks the number from the top, referring to the card in the spectator's half. The answer it, "eight." The magician counts off seven cards from his own heap and calmly places the eighth card in his pocket. He palms it, however, and secretly adds it to his half of the pack upon removing his hand from his pocket. The observers believe that the magician has left the eighth card of his own heap in his pocket.

The magician now asks for the spectator's half. In taking it, he places his thumb below the pack and draws off the bottom card. He slaps his hand upon the pack, telling the spectator to hold the pack tightly between his hands. The magician has secretly added a card to the top of the spectator's half.

The spectator now counts down to the eighth card and is told to remove it, the magician taking the remaining cards from him. When the spectator looks at the face of the eighth card, he is surprised to see that it is not the card he selected!

At this point, the magician palms the top card from those that are in his hand. It is the card which the spectator selected. Reaching in his pocket, the magician produces the card and shows his pocket otherwise empty.

The effect is that the *eighth* card of the magician's half changed places with the *selected* (eighth) card of the spectator's half of the pack. While this is a trick requiring sleight of hand, the movements are not difficult. The principal requirement is good patter, convincing showmanship.

THE TRAVELING CARD

A CARD is selected by the audience. It is placed in a clip on the front of a small stand. The magician shows an envelope. He lets the audience examine it and mark it. The envelope is sealed. The card is taken from the clip and the envelope is placed there instead.

The card is now inserted in another envelope. The magician strikes the envelope and immediately shows it empty. He tears the envelope into tiny pieces, leaving no doubt regarding the disappearance of the card. He shows his hands empty and picks up the sealed envelope from the clip. He tears open the envelope and brings out the card.

A mechanical stand answers this problem. The original card is forced. There is a duplicate card flat on the stand behind the clip. It is attached to a short lever, which has a spring and is actuated by pressure upon the clip.

The sealed envelope is not faked. It is actually marked and put in the clip after the forced card has been taken by the magician. The envelope in which he places the card has a slit near the flap. The magician is holding the pack. He rests the envelope on the pack as he inserts the chosen card. He pushes it right through the horizontal slit, so that it joins the pack. The envelope may then be shown empty and destroyed.

To produce the duplicate card in the sealed en-

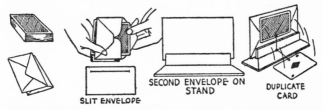

SECOND ENVELOPE ON STAND

DUPLICATE CARD

SLIT ENVELOPE

DRAWING SHOWS SLIT ENVELOPE, THROUGH WHICH CARD IS PUSHED. ALSO SPECIAL STAND WITH DUPLICATE CARD SNAPPING UP BE-HIND ENVELOPE.

velope, the magician simply presses the clip. This causes the lever to rise, so that the duplicate card is in back of the sealed envelope. In taking the sealed envelope from the stand, the magician grips the card also. He cuts the end of the envelope and pretends to draw the card from it. In reality, he draws the card from in back of the envelope.

This mechanical stand is an ingenious idea and is indetectible. Houdini's notes indicate that the trick is intended for several cards—all forced. Each card can be placed in a separate envelope. At the finish, all are found in the marked envelope. They all come up together in the clip end of the lever. The base of the clip hides the duplicate cards prior to the operation of the lever. The sealed envelope is considerably larger than a playing-card.

CARD-READING TRICK

A PACK of cards is given to the audience. The cards are thoroughly shuffled. Various spectators take cards and place them in envelopes—a card to each envelope. The envelopes are sealed. They are placed in a hat.

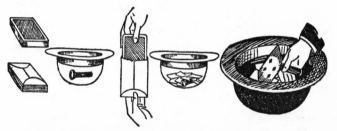

HOW CARDS CAN BE READ THROUGH SEALED ENVELOPES PLACED IN A HAT.

Upon the platform the magician removes an envelope from the hat. He holds the envelope to his forehead. He names the card within it. He tosses out the envelope. It is opened and the card is identified. This is repeated with the remaining envelopes.

The envelopes are thin. The playing cards are of a special type, also very thin. Neither the envelopes nor the cards are ordinarily transparent, but they are thin enough to become so under the glare of a light.

The magician works with considerable light about him. He secretly places a small pocket flashlight in the hat after he receives it, and turns on the light. As he removes each envelope he holds it directly above the glare of the electric torch. The card can then be distinguished through the texture of the envelope.

The reason that the magician chooses a well-lighted position is to overcome the glare of the flashlight. He keeps the mouth of the hat turned toward himself as he removes the envelopes. The holding of each envelope so that it rests against the forehead is merely a bit of byplay intended to mislead the audience.

This principle may be applied to the reading of sealed questions. Where questions are used, the magician supplies very thin cards and can use envelopes that are fairly thick. No spectator can read his own card through the envelope; hence there is no reason to suppose that the magician can read the question.

An effective part of this trick is the immediate returning of each envelope to its owner. Every envelope is given back sealed and the spectators wonder how the trick is possible. The placing of the light in the hat is by no means a difficult matter. A small flashlight is easily palmed and the magician has plenty of opportunity to insert it while he pretends to arrange the envelopes in a pile inside the hat.

A NEW CARD BOX

THE familiar card box is simply a mechanical box in which a card appears through the aid of a falling flap. This trick is a variation of the card box, with a different ending. The magician states that he will make a chosen card appear in an empty box. He invites some one to stand beside him and hold the box, which is shown to contain nothing.

The card is vanished by the magician, but when the box is opened it is still empty. The magician begins a conference with the person who held the box. In talking, they turn their backs to the audience and the chosen card is seen attached to the back of the volunteer assistant.

This trick is done with the aid of the card box. The box is actually empty, but it has a double bottom on the outside. There is a thin space between the bottoms. This holds an inserted card. The card has a projecting hook.

When the magician gets the box, he holds it in his right hand, and in pointing with his left, he holds attention while he presses the box against his assistant's back. By simply drawing away the box, the magician leaves the card on the person's back. The box is then shown empty and the trick is ready for its conclusion. The card that is vanished is a duplicate of the one on the assistant's back.

THE IMPRISONED CARD

A CARD is chosen from a pack. It is placed in a prison, namely, a thin oblong box, fitted with crossbars, just large enough to receive the card. The magician also exhibits an envelope. He shows that the envelope is large enough to hold the entire box. He seals the envelope and throws a handkerchief over the box. When he removes the cloth, the card is gone from its prison. Every one can see through the spaces between the slats. The card is found in the envelope.

The box that is used has special slides behind the slats. These fall into place when the box is inverted, so that they fill the spaces between the slats. The slides are portions of a playing-card; they duplicate the card that is used in the trick.

The box is first held upright; the opening into which the card is inserted points upward. The real card is put in. It goes behind the slides. The back of the box is shown and the back of the real card is seen there. At this moment, the box is inverted; the slides come down, but their movement is not seen because of the card.

Turning the box to show the front, the magician picks up the envelope and shows it empty. He starts to put the box in the envelope but does not do so. At this point, he releases the genuine card. It falls into the envelope. Its progress is invisible because of

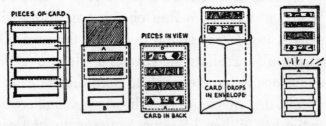

CONSTRUCTION OF SPECIAL BOX FOR VANISHING THE CARD. NOTE HOW SECTIONS OF CARD SLIDE FROM SLATS; ALSO HOW GENUINE CARD IS SECRETLY DROPPED IN ENVELOPE.

the presence of the front slides, which cover it. The envelope is sealed. The box is covered with a handkerchief. It is inverted beneath the cloth. The slides go back out of view. The box will now appear empty.

The magician removes the handkerchief in a suspicious manner. He shows the box empty from both sides and lays it on the table. Every one suspects that the card is in the handkerchief. The magician appears annoyed for a time; finally he shows that the handkerchief is empty. In fact, he passes it out for examination.

This puzzles the spectators, as they no longer have any suspicion of the box. A member of the audience is allowed to open the sealed envelope, and when the chosen card is found therein, the trick arrives at its surprising conclusion.

A SPELLING TRICK

A SPECTATOR removes a card from a pack. He looks at the card and places it in his pocket. The pack is handed to the man and he is told to spell the suit of his card, dealing a card from the top of the pack as he names each letter. For instance: S-P-A-D-E-S—six cards. He must turn up the final letter of his spelling. The card proves to be of the suit he spelt. Continuing from that point, he spells the value of the card, as Q-U-E-E-N; when he turns up the last card, it proves to be a queen—or whatever value he named.

This trick depends upon an arrangement of the cards. There are eighteen cards on top of the pack, in the following order:

three of hearts
queen of spades
seven of hearts
deuce of spades
eight of hearts
knave of spades
knave of hearts
ten of spades
four of hearts

eight of spades
king of hearts
three of spades
queen of hearts
seven of spades
deuce of hearts
eight of clubs
knave of clubs
knave of diamonds

Note that the two-spot is called the "deuce," while a jack is referred to as a "knave." This is in accordance with the system found in Houdini's notes.

The routine is as follows. Cut the pack, bringing the pre-arranged group to the center. Spread these cards so that the spectator will take one of the top seven of the special group. When he takes the card, immediately cut the pack at that point so that the card below the card removed becomes the top card of the pack. This is done by separating the halves of the pack and it is so natural that no one will ever notice it. The pack is scarcely considered at all, as the spectator still has his card, which he notes and places in his pocket.

The pack is given to the spectator and he is instructed how to spell—first the suit, then the value. The arrangement of the cards makes the last card of the first spelling show the suit, while the last card of the second spelling reveals the value.

This is an unusual idea and it has possibilities of greater development. The individual performer can work out his own system if he chooses to do so. With the cards properly arranged, the trick is automatic.

CARD-COUNTING TRICK

THE magician borrows a pack of cards. A spectator shuffles the pack. The magician demonstrates
how he wants the spectator to count down to a certain
number, look at the last card dealt, and place the
pack upon the little pile of cards. Having explained
this, the magician writes the name of a card upon a
piece of paper and folds the paper. He goes away
while the spectator counts to any number he wishes,
looks at the last card dealt, and drops the pack on top.
The pack is then cut several times. The magician
does not know the number to which the person
counted.

Now the pack is given to a second party. The first
person whispers to that person the number that he
dealt. Meanwhile the magician writes something on
a second slip of paper. The second person takes the
pack and counts down to the same number as the first
person. He looks at the card last dealt. When the slips
of paper are opened, they are found to bear the names
of the cards that were chosen by the spectators!

This is a very neat trick, yet it depends upon a comparatively simple routine. Before the counting, the magician receives the shuffled pack. He secretly bends up the inner left corner of the top card, which serves as a "key" from then on. In spreading the cards from hand to hand, the magician carelessly demonstrates that the suits are well mixed. This gives him a chance to turn up the lower corner of the seventh card from the top and to note its index. This corner is allowed to fall back after it has been turned far enough to note the value of the card. We will suppose that the card is the ace of hearts.

Turning the pack face down, the magician says: "I want you to count off any number—say five—dealing the cards one by one." He suits these words with the action. Holding the fifth card, he adds: "Look at the last card you deal, drop it on those already dealt and put the pack on the heap." He also demonstrates this. The counting has reversed the order of the five top cards. The key card is now on the bottom of the pack. The known card (ace of hearts) is second from the top.

The magician writes "ace of hearts" on a slip of paper. He marks the paper with the figure 2. He folds the paper so that no one can see what he has written. A spectator now deals to any number—let us suppose ten—looks at the tenth card dealt, and drops the pack on top of the heap. Suppose the tenth card is the four of clubs. After the deal and the placement of the pack, the key card is upon the four of clubs.

The pack is now cut several times. The magician makes the final cuts. This enables him to cut the pack at his key card and to bring the key to the top of the pack. He carelessly lifts the two top cards of the pack. He glimpses the four of clubs, which is directly below the key card, namely, the second card from the top. He hands the pack to the second spectator. On a piece of paper he writes "four of clubs" and marks the paper with the figure 1. He folds the paper. Now the first man whispers the number he counted—ten —to the second man, who deals ten cards. The last one dealt is the one he looks at. It will be the ace of hearts.

The magician hands the slips to the spectators. They open the papers and find that the predictions are correct, that the performer has written down "four of clubs" and "ace of hearts" and has numbered the slips 1 and 2, respectively. This is a most bewildering result.

Note that the slips are numbered in reversed order. They should be handled rather carelessly when they are picked up so that no one remembers which was the slip first written. The spectators naturally suppose that the slip marked 1 was the first slip and the slip marked 2 was the second.

This trick should be rehearsed with the actual cards, and with a little practice its details can be learned thoroughly. Note that each deal reverses the order of the cards dealt; that the last card dealt is the one looked at; that it is laid on the heap dealt and the pack is put over all. Cutting the pack does not disturb the rotation of the cards.

If the magician is using his own pack of cards, he can have a key card—either the familiar "short card" or a key of the type described elsewhere in this section on card tricks. With a key card, the magician simply cuts the pack after it has been shuffled, thus bringing the key to the top. He uses the key in place of the bent corner that is necessary with the unprepared pack. When the bent corner is used, the bend should be sharp enough to enable the performer to locate the card by simply looking at the corner of the pack.

PART FOUR.

SLATE TRICKS

HOUDINI made a specialty of all tricks of a pseudopsychic nature. The slate tricks which he mentioned in his notes are both practical and novel. Most of them are specially suited to magical presentation.

SLATE IN BAG

THIS is a unique slate-writing effect that may be presented as a duplication of mediumistic methods. A slate is placed in a large cloth bag. The bag

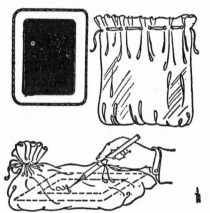

THE SHARP SLATE PENCIL IS PUSHED THROUGH THE CLOTH OF THE BAG.

is tied or sewed so firmly that there is no opportunity to open it. The bag and its seals are marked—the slate may also be marked.

The performer then retires to a cabinet or leaves the room. Upon his return, he delivers the bag in-

tact to the spectators. When the bag is opened, writing is discovered on the slate. Everything stands
complete examination.

The only special feature of the bag is the type of
material used. A dark-colored baize is suitable, although some other coarse cloth will do. The performer has a slate pencil that is sharpened to a point.
The bag is much larger than the slate. The performer
squeezes the cloth and takes up a fold. He pushes the
point of the pencil through the material and writes
the message with the point. He then replaces the slate
pencil in his pocket.

Carefully done, this leaves no telltale mark on the
cloth of the bag. Both the bag and the slate can be
thoroughly examined before and after the trick, for
there is no substitution of either slate or bag; nor
are the knots or seals touched in any way.

IMPROVED SLATE-WRITING

THE trick of producing a written message upon a slate is one which magicians have often used. The standard method involves two slates, which are cleaned, placed together, and held for a few moments. When the slates are separated, a message has appeared upon one or both of the slates.

The usual apparatus is a "flap" or thin piece of material. This may be made of a silicate or of black fiber. It fits within the rim of one slate and appears to be the surface of the slate itself. The message is written on that surface of the slate which is covered by the flap. When the slates are placed together and turned over, the flap falls. Thus the message is revealed when the slates are separated.

With an ordinary flap of this type, the slates cannot be examined unless some method is used to dispose of the flap. If this is done, the slates can be inspected after the trick is over. It was Houdini's idea to present a slate trick in which the slates would be examined *before* the message appeared; then to repeat the trick by obtaining a second message.

To accomplish this, he devised a special box into which the slates could slide, the box being open at

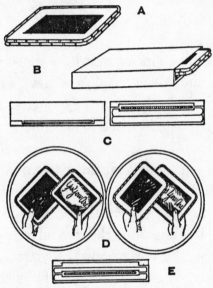

A, TWO EXAMINED SLATES. B, SLATES SLID IN BOX. C, NOTE HOW FLAP DROPS FROM BOX TO SLATE, WHEN BOX IS INVERTED. D, SLATES SHIFTED WITHOUT SHOWING MESSAGE. E, FLAP FALLS BETWEEN SLATES WHEN THEY ARE REPLACED IN BOX.

one end. The box is of flat construction, just large enough to receive the slates. It appears to be simply a carrying case for the slates.

The slates are slid from the box and are given for examination. They are pushed back into the box. In the lower surface of the box is a depression that holds a flap. There is writing on both sides of the flap. After the slates are pushed in, the box is turned over. The flap drops upon the slate that is then uppermost. The performer tilts the box toward himself and removes the slates. He separates them and pretends that he sees no writing. He puts the slates together again; in so doing, he alters their position so that the writing (on the flap) is between the slates. He replaces them in the box. Upon removal, the writing is discovered on the inner surface of the lower slate.

Before the audience has an opportunity to pick up the slates, the performer takes a damp cloth and wipes out the message which he has revealed. He puts the slates together and replaces them in the box. He turns over the box in raising it. The flap drops from one slate to the other. Now, when the slates are separated a second message has appeared on the inner surface of the lower slate. It is the reverse side of the flap which bears the message.

This is shown; the message is erased and the slates are again replaced in the box, which is turned so that the flap falls into its original depression. The performer then proceeds with another trick. Should any one demand to see the slates, they can be taken from the box and given for inspection. The inside of the box is painted black, so that the flap—without its writing—is invisible at the conclusion.

This is a highly effective routine that possesses puzzling features. Needless to say, a great deal of its effectiveness depends upon well-planned presentation.

NOVEL SLATE-WRITING

THIS is an improvment on a slate-writing trick. To understand its usefulness, we must first consider a very clever method of spirit slate-writing which was first explained more than thirty years ago.

The magician has a large thimble which fits upon his thumb. One end of the thimble is fitted to hold either a thin piece of chalk or a slate pencil. The old stand-by of magicians—the flesh-colored thumb-tip —is a useful device for this purpose. The apparatus should be well made, not merely a crudely fashioned article.

In the original version, the magician produced the message on the slate by holding the slate in his hand with one side toward the spectators. His thumb, in back of the slate, secretly inscribed the message. This trick required adept work and it had certain limitations that rendered it inferior to other accepted methods.

Now, however, it appears in a new guise. The magician uses two slates, which are examined. They are placed on a table and each side is numbered with a piece of chalk—1, 2, 3, and 4. The slates are immediately placed together; a message appears between them. Each side, it must be noted, is turned toward the spectators during the numbering process.

Even magicians may wonder how the thumb-tip and its chalk enter into this slate-writing trick, for the method has been improved by the addition of a very clever form of manipulation.

HOW MESSAGE IS WRITTEN AND COVERED.

The performer writes the message on one slate as he carries the slates to the table. To do this effectively, he has the table set a considerable distance away. He holds the slates together with one surface toward the audience and writes with his thumb on the rearmost side. When he lays the slates on the table, he puts down the front slate first; then the back slate, with its writing side down. The writing should be near one end of the slate; and this end is toward the back of the table.

Reaching in his pocket for a piece of chalk, the wizard disposes of the thumb-tip. He picks up the

uppermost slate, with his thumb on top and his fingers beneath. He writes the figure 1 on the upper
surface. In turning up the other side of the slate he
sees to it that his hand covers the message, the extended fingers doing this to perfection. He writes the
figure 2 on that side and puts the slate on the table,
turning it writing side down. There is no trickery in
marking the other slate with numbers 3 and 4, but
to be consistent, the magician holds the slate just as
he held the first one. He puts the slates together, side
2 going on side 3. The slates are then ready for the
appearance of the message.

This trick requires rather small slates. The message
must be very short—say a number of four figures, or
some initials. For the writing cannot cover much
space, otherwise the fingers would not be able to conceal it.

SPIRIT SLATE EFFECT

THIS version of the spirit slate-writing trick is both simple and convincing. It requires very little skill, yet is well designed. The articles used are two slates and a pocket handkerchief. Both sides of both slates are shown clean; each is marked with an identifying letter or numeral. Yet when the slates are tied together and placed in the hands of the audience, a message appears on the inner surface of one slate.

Preparation is made beforehand. A short message —preferably a single word—is written across one slate, between the sides. A handkerchief is folded into a long strip. It is placed upon a table and the slate with the message is placed upon it. The message side of the slate is down and runs directly along the line of the kerchief.

The second slate is placed upon the first and the ends of the handkerchief are knotted above the upper slate. In this condition the broad center of the handkerchief conceals the message in the middle of the lower slate.

The magician brings on the slates. He carries a piece of chalk with one hand, holding the tied slates carelessly with the other. He speaks of psychic manifestations and his ability to reproduce them. Advancing, he brings the slates upward and reveals the side that bears the message. The word, of course, is hidden by the broad center of the handkerchief.

The magician taps the surface of the slate with the chalk and asks for a figure or a letter. This being

HOW HANDKERCHIEF COVERS MESSAGE ON SLATE.

given, he marks the corner of the slate accordingly, say with the letter A. He turns the slates over and taps the opposite side. This he marks with a letter— B, for instance—and sets the slates on the table, with the handkerchief knot upward. He does this to untie the knot. He picks up the upper slate in a careless manner, letting the spectators observe the side marked B. Then he picks up the lower slate, showing its clean, unmarked side. He turns the upper slate so that the unmarked side is toward the audience. He lays down the lower slate so that he can mark the clean side of the upper slate with the letter C. Laying down the upper slate, he lifts the lower slate and marks its clean side D. At no phase of this routine is the side that bears the letter A revealed.

He puts the A and D slate upon the other one, keeping the D side up. The message (on side A) is now between the two slates. The slates are set upon the center of the handkerchief, which is twisted slightly. The ends of the handkerchief are knotted on top of the slates. The slates are given to a spectator to hold. When the handkerchief is untied, the message is found on the side marked A.

While this routine requires no manipulation and involves no special apparatus, it must be performed in a decisive manner, with every possible effort to sell the idea to the audience. It is an excellent deception from a psychological standpoint. The very boldness with which side A is shown with the handkerchief in place serves to divert suspicion. Side B, it will be noted, is marked while the handkerchief is upon it; but the fact that the knot is untied and the surface of the slate is casually exhibited leads the spectators to forget that side A was not also shown in that manner.

The showing of the blank sides of both slates and the marking of each in turn are also effective. The placing of the upper slate upon the table before the lower brings the message within the slates in a subtle manner. The final touch is the narrowing of the handkerchief, before tying up the slates. When the hand-kerchief is taken off at the conclusion, its width is less than the height of the letters in the message. This completely eliminates any suspicion that might lurk in the minds of the observers.

This is a slate test of the highest efficiency and it will deceive all who look for complicated methods or who suspect some mechanical secret. The message used should be forced upon the audience in some manner. The name of a playing-card . . . a word from a book . . . or the total of added numbers—these are all usable. The forcing is done while the slates are tied and in the possession of the expectant audience.

SINGLE-SLATE TRICK

THIS is a very useful spirit slate for close work. It is simply a single slate, which is shown blank on both sides. It is wrapped in newspaper or placed in a paper bag. When it is removed, it bears a message. The slate is given for inspection. The paper is crumpled and thrown away.

The slate has an improvised flap, which is merely a piece of black tissue paper or carbon paper. This covers a message that has been written on the slate. The paper flap is held in place by dabs of wax on the corners.

When the slate is wrapped in paper or put into a bag, the magician pushes the tissue paper so that it comes loose. Then the slate is withdrawn alone. The paper is crumpled and thrown away with the black paper inside it, taking away suspicion from the paper. The slate itself furnishes no clue to the mystery.

The very simplicity of this method makes it useful and eliminates many complications that are apt to arise when the flap slate is used at a small gathering.

NEWSPAPER TEST

THIS is a special test which may be shown on certain occasions. It is particularly good with a fair-sized group of people present. The magician sends some one to obtain the day's newspapers. He wants a copy of every local paper and may also call for a few out-of-town papers, as he can use any number up to ten.

The papers, when procured, are laid in a row on the table. They are numbered from left to right. The magician shows two slates and puts them together. He takes a pack of cards, shuffles it, and places it in a hinged wooden box. He states that the numbers on the top three cards will indicate: first, the newspaper; second, the page; third, the column. Face cards stand for eleven, twelve, and thirteen (jack, queen, and king).

The box is opened. The first card (say a three) enables the magician to select a newspaper. The next two cards (say eight and five) tell the page and column. The magician reads the headline of the chosen column. The slates are opened. On one slate appears the headline, written in chalk.

Old methods are used in this trick. The message is written on a "spirit slate." It is covered with a flap. The wooden box is a "card box." It has a flap in the top portion. The flap hides three cards, which are arranged to indicate the desired numbers, say three, eight, and five. The magician picks the fifth column of the eighth page in one of the daily newspapers. He simply places this newspaper number three in the line.

From that point, the trick virtually works itself. The card box forces the three cards, the proper headline is discovered, and the message is revealed on the slate after the slates are separated.

The magician should explain that face cards mean to continue counting: for instance, eleven would be three columns over on the next page, as most newspapers have only eight columns. A face card indicating a newspaper in the row would mean counting to the end of the row and then continuing from the beginning. It is best to have a small card indicate the newspaper; then the magician is not dependent upon any particular number of newspapers. He is sure to have at least three or four. Others may be added to the row, according to the quantity that is procured.

Another plan is to have a pack with all cards above

the eights removed. It is also wise to have more than three cards above the flap in the card box; otherwise the flap will show when the top three cards are removed. A few more cards in place will keep the flap concealed.

PART FIVE.

MESSAGE-READING

HOUDINI made a careful study of various methods employed in the reading of sealed messages. From those, the author has selected the ones that are evidently designed for performing magicians. These are more effective than the usual billet readings used by fraudulent mediums, as they can be shown before larger audiences.

CRYSTAL-GAZING MYSTERIES

HOUDINI's notes contain various references to methods used by crystal-gazers who answer questions written by the audience. This act is done by trickery. It gradually reached a point of widespread presentation, and in order that the reader may fully understand the act, it is necessary to give a brief résumé of the usual methods before discussing improvements noted by Houdini.

The performer allows spectators to write questions and to seal them in envelopes. These questions are brought on the stage and are burned. Then the performer gazes into a crystal ball and begins to give "impressions" of questions that have been written. His statements are accurate and he follows by giving answers to the questions.

There are gullible persons who believe that this exhibition shows genuine telepathic power on the part of the crystal-gazer, and it is a regrettable fact that some charlatans have taken advantage of that situation to prey upon the susceptibilities of their audiences. But from the magician's view, the crystal-gazing act is merely a form of trickery. To be presented legitimately, it should be simply a form of entertainment, in which the spectators are mystified by the performer's ability to state what they have written—not by his ability to give answers to the questions.

There are two essential elements in this act. First, the performer must secretly preserve some of the questions written by the audience. Second, the wording of those questions must come into the performer's possession.

The conventional crystal-gazer adopted two methods. His assistants collected the written questions in long-handled velvet bags. These were known as "changing bags," because they had a double lining which could be changed by a simple turn of the handle. With the aid of this device, questions were gathered; the interior of the bag was changed to open the other compartment; and when the bag was apparently emptied, a mass of duplicate envelopes fell into the burner. These dummy envelopes had been previously placed in the hidden section of the bag.

The assistants carried the apparently empty bags from the stage. Off stage, they opened the original envelopes while the performer was burning the duplicates. They learned the questions in the envelopes;

MESSAGES DROPPED IN BURNER. SOME GO THROUGH PEDESTAL TO
ASSISTANT BENEATH STAGE.

their next step was to transmit that information to the performer.

The usual crysal-gazer wore a Hindu costume, with a large turban. There was a purpose in the costume. His turban concealed earphones; wires passed down to his shoes, which had metal plates on the bottom. The stage was fitted with plates, connected by wires to a transmitter. By stepping on the plates, contact was formed, and the crystal-gazer could hear the voice of his off-stage assistant, telling him the contents of the envelopes.

This system was used by many performers. Despite its effectiveness, there was a constant effort to supply some improved method. The electrical system was expensive and needed considerable attention. It sometimes became dead during a performance. There was always the difficulty of misunderstanding information given by the man off stage. The last-named objection was counteracted by a double system; the performer carried a microphone beneath his costume and the concealed assistant could hear what was said on the stage. This enabled the performer and the assistant to carry on a veiled conversation between themselves. It did not, however, solve the problem of trouble with the electrical apparatus.

The various methods of doing away with the wires and the Oriental costume are too numerous to give in

PERFORMER READING MESSAGE. NOTE ASSISTANT'S WORK BENEATH
STAGE.

detail, especially as some of them are far inferior to the electrical system. The methods explained among Houdini's notes are given here as representative of improved methods. They do away with both the changing bag and the wires.

There is no actual exchange of questions. The performer simply preserves some of the questions. That is suffiicient, as no performer attempts to answer all of the questions submitted. Time would be too short.

The questions are gathered by assistants, who use network bags with which an exchange would be impossible. The envelopes are delivered to the performer, who drops them into a burner that is mounted on a pedestal. In back of the burner is an opening in the pedestal. This passes to the stage and there is an open trap beneath the pedestal.

In dropping the envelopes, the performer takes only a portion in his right hand. He drops this cluster into the burner, then another cluster of envelopes. He continues thus until all the envelopes have been dropped. With each action of the right hand, the performer inserts his second finger between the envelopes, dividing them into two groups—one in front of the second finger, the other in back. He spreads the front group so that the envelopes there obscure those in back. As his hand approaches the burner, the rear group is behind the burner. When the envelopes are dropped, those in back drop behind the burner and go through the pedestal. This movement is perfectly natural and cannot be detected. Thus, from each cluster of envelopes the performer saves some, which are invisibly passed to the assistant under the

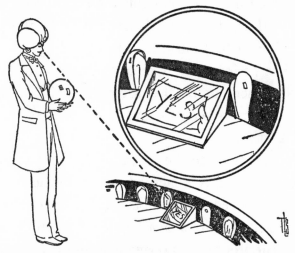

MAGNIFYING GLASS METHOD OF SHOWING MESSAGES BETWEEN FOOTLIGHTS.

stage. The questions in these envelopes are transmitted to the performer on the stage.

The first method of transmission is accomplished by means of another pedestal, upon which the crystal ball is set. Behind the pedestal is a slit in the stage. The assistants below stage write the questions in large letters on pieces of cardboard. One by one, these statements are pushed up behind the pedestal. Standing behind the pedestal, with the crystal in his hand, the performer sees each message as it comes into view.

The second method of transmission is even more ingenious. At the front of the stage, between the footlights, is an opening, covered with a lens of magnifying glass. Two of the footlights are turned to illuminate the glass, which can be seen only by the performer. The actual questions are placed against the glass. The performer sees them and has no difficulty in reading them, unless they are virtually illegible, in which case they are either rewritten by the assistants or are ignored.

Referring again to the obtaining of the questions, Houdini's notes give a method of actual exchange by the aid of the pedestal and burner. This is obviously intended for use with a small audience when the performer is desirous of answering most of the questions.

The pedestal has the opening which leads through the stage, but in this case there is a slide that covers the opening. At the back of the burner is a clip which contains a stack of dummy envelopes. The performer holds the envelopes in his right hand and approaches the pedestal, with his left side toward the audience. He reaches to pick up the burner. His right hand goes in back of the burner and drops the envelopes into the opening in the pedestal. The hand moves forward, drawing the slide shut, and with the same movement gathers up the dummy envelopes from the clip.

The left hand picks up the burner, the right hand assisting momentarily. Then the right drops the dummy envelopes into the burner. The supposed questions are ignited; the burner is set back on the pedestal.

These methods of performing the crystal act do away with the Hindu costume.

SEALED-MESSAGE READING

THIS routine involves old principles in the reading of sealed messages. It possesses certain points of effectiveness that make it a decided improvement over the well-known ideas.

The performer approaches a person with a stack of small envelopes. He passes one envelope to the person. There is a card inside the envelope. The performer holds the envelope while the person writes something on the card. The writer turns the card downward and slides it into the envelope which the performer is holding. The envelope and card are burned; the performer then states what was written.

A special envelope is used. The face of the envelope is cut away. This envelope is the bottom one of the stack. The flap side of each envelope is downward. The top envelope of the stack is ordinary. It contains a card. It is given to the person. The card is removed. The performer takes back the envelope and puts it on the stack. While the person is writing the performer casually turns his hand over. He holds out the stack and turns back the flap of the envelope that is now on top. The person inserts the card. It is the prepared envelope which receives the card; but the entire procedure is so natural that every one assumes that the envelope is the same as the one originally given to the person.

In going toward an ash tray or burner, the performer holds the special envelope with its flap toward the writer. This enables the performer to read the message through the open face of the envelope. The burning of the envelope and the card destroys all evidence of trickery.

For reading a series of questions, the performer can apply this principle to the old "one ahead" system, which is described herewith. All the envelopes are flaps upward. The prepared envelope is on top of the stack. The cards are separate from the envelopes. They are given out to the persons present.

After questions have been written, the performer goes to one person and says: "Put your card in the envelope like this and seal the envelope." He demonstrates by placing the card; writing downward, in the prepared envelope. He retains that envelope, after sealing it. He gives out the other envelopes and lets the spectators insert their cards. No one suspects that the first envelope is tricked.

Having gathered all the envelopes, the performer

notes the message on the first card. He puts that envelope at the bottom of the stack. Holding the top envelope to his forehead, he calls out the question that is in the prepared envelope. The writer verifies

INSERTION OF CARD IN OPEN-FACED ENVELOPE.

the fact that the question was written. Every one supposes that it is in the envelope now held by the performer. He opens the envelope, looks at the card and states that he was correct.

In so doing, the performer notes the words on the card from the ordinary envelope. He lays that card aside, takes another envelope from the stack and names the question which he has just read. It is verified, and the envelope is opened for the performer to check. He continues thus, always reading the question one envelope ahead of the answer. The last envelope is the prepared one. The performer states the question that he read in the previous envelope. He gives back the cards and throws away the envelopes, the prepared one among them.

SEALED-ENVELOPE TEST

THIS is a method of discovering questions that have been written by individuals who seal their papers in envelopes and retain the envelopes. It is particularly good because nothing is used except paper, pencils, and envelopes.

The performer has a stack of envelopes. On top of the stack are several prepared envelopes. These envelopes are double. The face is cut from an envelope. It is inserted in an ordinary envelope. A sheet of carbon paper is placed between the two faces. The flaps are sealed together. This has the appearance of an ordinary envelope.

In each of the prepared envelopes the performer has a slip of paper. One envelope, however, has an extra slip of paper, for a purpose that will become evident. The prepared envelopes are faces up. The ordinary envelopes—which are greater in number than the prepared ones—are faces down. They contain no slips of paper. Armed with his stack of envelopes, the performer is ready.

He approaches his audience. He gives out the prepared envelopes, drawing the slip of paper from each one. He lets the inside of each envelope be observed by the person who receives it. He puts the slip of paper on the envelope in each case and instructs the person to write and to hold the paper writing side down.

When this has been done, the performer remarks that he had an extra piece of paper in one envelope. He picks up the envelopes one by one, placing them upon the stack in his left hand until he obtains the one that has the extra slip of paper. He puts this envelope on the stack and places the stack under his left elbow. This enables him to use his hands in folding the blank piece of paper. He tells the spectators to fold their papers in that manner.

Bringing the stack of envelopes from his elbow, he naturally turns it over, and gives out the uppermost envelopes to the persons from whom he took envelopes. They naturally suppose that they are receiving the original envelopes. Instead, they are getting ordinary envelopes, while the performer is retaining the ones that have the carbon impressions.

Each person seals his paper in his envelope and retains the envelope. In case there are any additional persons from whom the performer did not take envelopes, a special procedure is adopted. The performer stops those persons while they are about to insert their papers. Dealing with each in turn, he takes the person's envelope and lays it on the stack in his left hand while he uses his right hand to show the blank piece of paper which he has folded. The person is careful to fold his paper properly enough to suit the performer. Then the performer gives him the envelope, but in so doing he turns the stack of envelopes so that an unprepared envelope is on top.

In brief, the performer, by subtle, natural procedure, exchanges for other envelopes the envelopes given out originally. There is nothing suspicious about this, as the writers do not know that the envelopes were prepared. They believe that they have written questions and have sealed them in ordinary envelopes, which are kept in their own possession.

Actually, the performer has the carbon impressions of the writing and can use them to reveal what the spectators have written. He can do this in several ways. He can open the envelopes secretly and learn the questions. He can pass the envelopes to an assistant who carries them off stage or from the room and later passes the information to the performer.

There are several simple and effective methods of doing this. The author is suggesting them here in order that the reader may utilize the principle of the prepared envelopes.

One method is for the assistant to write the questions in large letters on blank cards and to hold them so that the performer can see them, while they are invisible to the spectators. In this way, the first question is quickly sent to the performer, and while he is concentrating and answering it, the assistant prepares more large cards.

Another method is for the assistant to write the questions on a strip of paper and to bring the performer a crystal ball that rests upon a velvet-covered board. There is a shelf behind the board and the strip of paper rests upon it. The performer, in gazing at the crystal, learns the questions.

A new method, never before described, may be employed. In this system, the performer calls for some slates. The assistant does not appear immediately. He is transcribing the questions on the slates. The performer meanwhile tells the writers to concentrate. The slates are brought on with their blank sides toward the spectators. It is well to have one slate entirely blank. Holding the slates, the performer notes the writing on the rear slate. He lays down the slates and wipes both sides of the slate that is entirely blank. Then he writes an answer to one question on one side of the slate; and an answer to another question on the other side of the slate.

He picks up a second slate, but this time does not

show both sides before he wipes the slate. He is noting the questions on the back of the slate as he cleans it. He cleans the front also, and writes the answer to a question on one side, the answer to a second question on the other side.

He continues thus with the remaining slates. Only three or four slates are necessary. This method leads

DOUBLE ENVELOPE WITH HIDDEN CARBON PAPER.

up to a very effective conclusion. The performer fails to answer one question. Perhaps he writes a wrong answer on a slate. He is determined to answer the question; and he does not care to rub out anything that he has written on the slates, because these writings are evidence of his answers to the questions.

So he calls for two more slates and the assistant appears with them. Both slates are shown blank; between them, the performer causes the correct answer to the last question to appear, apparently of its own accord. This is simply a spirit slate-writing trick, the methods of which are described in this book. The assistant has placed the correct answer on the spirit slates and the performer uses them.

A BILLET READING

Two persons work in this performance—the magician and another who is seated in a chair on the platform and who intends to reveal words that are secretly written by members of the audience.

The performer gives out small slips of paper, measuring about one by two inches. Words, numbers, or other notations are written on the slips. The performer then gathers them in a basket. The slips are numbered on the reversed sides or are of differently colored paper, so that each person can recognize his slip when it is to be returned to him.

Each slip is folded before it is placed in the basket. Nevertheless, the performer's assistant answers the question. The usual procedure is for the magician to have a lady assistant, who is blindfolded and seated with her back to the audience.

This ingenious performance depends upon the manner in which the magician secretly passes some of the slips to his female assistant. The transfer is accomplished despite the fact that the magician does

TAKING TIP
FROM BASKET

REMOVING
TIP

THE THUMB TIP CONTAINING MESSAGE IS HELD BEHIND THE SLATE.
THE MEDIUM REMOVES IT WHEN SHE TAKES THE SLATE. HER
BACK IS TOWARD THE AUDIENCE.

everything to prove that such action is impossible.
The basket that he uses to collect the messages is
small but deep. Its interior is covered with a dark,

pleated cloth. There is a small secret pocket in the cloth at the side of the basket. This pocket contains a false thumb-tip made of metal. The tip will fit loosely on the magician's thumb and it is painted flesh-color.

When the magician hands out the slips, the basket is on the table with the thumb-tip in the secret pocket. The thumb-tip is mouth up. In collecting the slips, the magician allows them to be dropped into the basket; but with one person, he takes the slip himself and drops it. The magician lets it fall into the thumb-tip and with the same action he inserts his thumb into the metal device and brings it out of the pocket. He keeps his hand in motion as he carelessly shows it empty; hence the thumb-tip is not observed.

When all the slips are in the basket, it is replaced on the table at the front of the platform. The lady appears and seats herself in the chair with her back toward the audience. In arranging this position, the magician has ample opportunity to drop the thumb-tip into his assistant's lap. While he is preparing to blindfold the lady, she removes the slip from the thumb-tip, reads it and replaces it. The performer puts the bandage around her eyes and then picks up the thumb-tip from her lap.

The performer goes to the basket. He reaches in and inserts his thumb into the pocket, leaving the thumb-tip there; but he draws out the message which was in the thumb-tip. He also picks up another slip and drops it into the thumb-tip, which he brings out on his thumb. These actions take place while he is apparently choosing one folded slip which he wishes the lady to reveal. He gives the original slip to the person who wrote it—the slip being identified by its number or its color. It is obvious that the performer has had no opportunity to open the slip.

The performer now picks up a slate and carries it to the lady. She reaches above her head to receive it. The magician holds the slate vertically, with his thumb and its false tip out of view behind the slate. In taking the slate, the lady also carries away the thumb-tip.

She now lays the slate in her lap and writes the words that were on the original slip of paper, which is at present *held by the spectator*. She also has opportunity to read the second slip. The blindfold does not prevent her from seeing downward into her lap. She replaces the second slip in the thumb-tip. She holds up the slate with the writing away from the audience. Behind the slate she holds the thumb-tip in readiness for the performer. He takes the slate and inserts his thumb into the thumb-tip. He carries the slate to the spectators, who read the writing aloud and check it with the slip that the individual holds.

This is a very mystifying effect. The performer is ready to repeat it, for everything is set for a continuance of his procedure. He goes to the basket and obtains a third slip in his thumb-tip. He gives the second slip to the person who wrote it. He erases the writing on the slate and carries the slate to his female assistant.

The second slip is duplicated on the slate; the routine continues and a third message is written by the lady, then a fourth, and so on until the entire supply is exhausted. In giving the last slip to its owner, the performer merely removes it from the thumb-tip as he leaves the device in the secret pocket of the basket. He announces that he has reached the last slip and that the lady will answer it in conclusion. No more deception is necessary at that point.

This is a highly effective exhibition that will puzzle the shrewdest observers. There is very little chance of the thumb-tip's being detected. It is practically invisible when on the magician's thumb, especially as he can keep his thumb partially obscured from view except when his hands are in motion. The most important part of the demonstration is its smoothness. The entire routine requires careful rehearsal, and all hesitation or clumsiness should be avoided. It may be performed deliberately but pains should be taken to make it convincing throughout.

PART SIX.

PLATFORM TRICKS

THIS section will appeal to all who are interested in magic, as it contains tricks designed for presentation at close range or before a large audience. It is a section of small magic that includes new ideas and improvements over well-known tricks.

RED AND GREEN SILKS

THIS is an entertaining routine with a silk hand-kerchief, which disappears and returns after the magician has completely misled his audience. It requires the following preparations:

(1) A red silk handkerchief under shirt collar at the right side of the neck.

(2) A green silk handkerchief under the left side of the shirt collar.

(3) A piece of red silk ribbon tucked under the right side of the vest.

(4) A metal finger-tip [1] which contains a corner of red silk.

(5) Two silk handkerchiefs on the table. One red, the other green.

The performer begins by showing the two handker-chiefs that are on the table. He asks the spectators to choose either color—red or green. It makes no difference which they choose; he uses the red. If they

---

[1] The finger-tip is similar to the thumb-tip, mentioned in this book. It is painted flesh-color and is hardly visible when on the tip of the finger, especially when the hand is kept in motion.

select red, he uses the red silk. If they call for green, he remarks that they have chosen green, which leaves him red. In either event, he calmly tucks the green silk into his coat pocket.

He rolls the red silk into a ball and places it in his left hand. He moves the right hand to the vest and pretends to push an imaginary silk out of sight. He draws out the end of the ribbon. The spectators see it and think it is a corner of the silk handkerchief. The magician observes their glances. He pulls the red ribbon from beneath his vest and looks at it in surprise. Then he opens his left hand to show that the red handkerchief is really there. This turns the laugh on the audience.

Again the magician rolls the red silk into a ball; this time he pretends to hold it in his left hand but actually palms it in the right. His hand goes to his vest as before and he boldly pushes the silk unseen beneath the vest, remarking: "It would be too apparent to try to place a handkerchief under my vest." He draws the hand away, leaving the silk, and continues to the trousers pocket, saying: "I would not attempt to hide it in the pocket, either."

This movement enables him to insert his forefinger in the finger-tip. He brings out the right hand and pokes the forefinger into the left fist, leaving the finger-tip. Then he draws the red silk corner into view, remarking: "With such keen observers watching me, it would be impossible to take the handkerchief unseen from the left hand."

He pokes the silk corner back into the finger-tip. He removes the right hand, with the tip on the finger, keeping the hand in motion. He points to the left again and opens the left hand. The red silk has vanished. The right hand goes to the collar. The finger-tip is left beneath the collar while the duplicate red silk is drawn into view.

While the audience is still wondering at the deception, the magician adds: "If you had selected green, the result would have been the same. Here is the green handkerchief, waiting under my collar." The left hand draws the duplicate green silk from its hiding-place and the performer makes his bow holding the red handkerchief in one hand and the green handkerchief in the other, just as when he began the trick.

THE VANISHING GLASS

HOUDINI'S notes attribute this trick to De Kolta. A small glass is partly filled with water. It is placed in a cylinder of paper. The sheet of paper is crushed. The glass is gone.

The paper cylinder contains a metal ring which has two projecting clips, painted flesh-color. The ring is in place at the beginning of the trick. Its projecting clips extend through a slit in the side of the cylinder. This is kept to the rear.

The glass tapers slightly. It is set in the paper cylinder. Its bottom fits in the metal ring. The magician turns the cylinder (in his left hand) so that the slit is toward the audience. At the same time his right hand starts to smooth the paper; the projecting clips are gripped between the fingers. When the back of the right hand is toward the audience, the hand moves straight upward. The ring carries the glass, safely hidden in the palm of the right hand.

Meanwhile the left hand twists the cylinder so that the slit is not viewed by the audience. The left arm is raised as the right hand goes to the breast pocket of the coat. The pocket is held open by a strip of bent whalebone. A handkerchief projects from in front. The right hand drops the glass into the pocket. It fits rather tightly and the water does not spill. The pocket

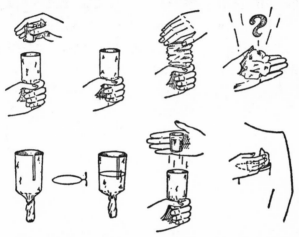

ROUTINE OF VANISHING GLASS. NOTE SLIT IN PAPER—ALSO WIRE RING WHICH IS CLIPPED BY FINGERS. THE GLASS IS DROPPED IN THE POCKET.

should be lined with rubber in case of emergency.

The right hand then comes forward and the empty paper cylinder is crushed between the hands. The glass has unmistakeably vanished and the paper may be torn to bits to conclude the trick.

This is an effect with good possibilities if performed smoothly and naturally. The removal of the glass is an excellent idea. The passage of the right hand to the pocket is covered by the left arm and the magician can create the impression that he is reaching for his handkerchief, which he finally decides not to use. If the glass is "stolen" neatly from the cylinder, there will be no suspicion on the part of the audience.

The illustrations show the effect and also give the details of the apparatus and the method by which the glass is secretly removed from the cylinder with the aid of the unseen wire ring.

A CLINGING WAND
(WITH THE WAND VANISH)

THIS is intended as an additional effect in conjunc-
tion with the "vanishing wand" used by many
magicians. The wand in question is made of rolled
paper, which is painted black on the outside. The
nickeled metal tips of the wand are genuine; they are
made of wood covered with metal tubing and they
have short projections which fit tightly into the rolled
black paper. Thus the wand is simply a hollow paper
tube with solid ends.

The magician displays the wand as a solid one.
He can drop the wand upon the floor or rap the ends
against the table in the course of his performance. It
passes as a wooden wand. When he is ready for the
vanish, he wraps the wand in a sheet of paper; then
proceeds to tear the paper to fragments. It is torn in
half a dozen pieces, which are tossed carelessly upon
the floor to prove that the wand has vanished. Only
the end pieces must be handled carefully, for these
contain the metal tips. They are reclaimed afterward

and the tips are fitted into another black paper tube to form another wand suitable for disappearance.

There is another effect in which a wand clings to the magician's fingers. These notes of Houdini's show how the clinging effect may be adapted to the vanishing wand. The wand is prepared beforehand by pushing two black pins through it about three inches apart. The points of the pins are dulled. The pins lie parallel through the wand. They are invisible when the wand is held, as it is kept so that the pin points are out of view. Before wrapping the wand in paper, the magician places his fingers upon the center of the wand and turns the wand so that the pins are perpendicular to the fingers. One pin is at one side of the hand; the other pin is at the opposite side.

By simply spreading his fingers, the performer exerts pressure against the extended pins. The wand then clings to his hand in a most mysterious fashion. This can be performed at fairly close range. While one hand supports the wand in air, the other picks up the paper; the wand is wrapped and immediately disappears.

The paper wand is admirably adapted to this trick, as it is formed of tightly rolled layers of paper and the pins are held firmly in place. The lightness of the wand also makes it possible for the performer to turn the hand about and move it in all directions without danger of the wand's slipping.

The usual aftereffect of the wand trick is the reproduction of a solid wand which is made of wood with nickeled tips. This is taken from the pocket, as though it had passed there in some mysterious manner.

When performed as an opening trick, the solid wand may be carried in the left sleeve. To produce it after the vanish, the magician places a small pocketbook in his left hand, opens the purse, and extracts the wand with his right hand. The pocketbook is bottomless. Reaching through the opening with his fingers, the magician grips the end of the wand and pulls it through the pocketbook into the view of the audience. The back of the left hand and the left arm are turned toward the spectators during this production.

A VANISHING WAND

A WAND is tapped against a table or another wand to prove that it is made of wood. It is dropped into an envelope. The envelope is crushed and torn to tiny pieces. Nothing remains of the wand.

The old familiar paper wand is used in this trick but with a new arrangement. The wand is made of black paper with silver paper tips; inside it there is a round piece of wood considerably shorter than the wand. This wood makes a noise when the wand is struck against the table.

The rounded wood is attached to a piece of cord elastic which runs up the magician's sleeve or beneath his coat; the elastic is stretched, but the wood is held within the wand by pressure of the hand.

When the magician picks up the long envelope, he releases the piece of wood and it leaves the wand. Only the paper wand goes in the envelope, and this can be completely destroyed. The notes suggest two wands for this trick, one in each hand. The magician first strikes the wands together, then vanishes them. This would be an excellent effect, but one somewhat more difficult than the trick with the single wand.

THE TRAVELING DIE

THIS trick requires a plate, a hat, a red silk handkerchief, and a large die. These are the principal properties seen by the audience. The die is shown to be solid. Attention is called to its large size—it almost fills the interior of the borrowed hat. The die is placed upon the plate. It is covered with a sheet of paper, which is pressed around it and twisted at the top.

The magician exhibits the silk handkerchief and rolls it between his hands. The handkerchief disappears. The paper is lifted from the plate. The handkerchief is found there; it has replaced the die. The hat is turned over and the solid cube of wood falls to the floor.

A reference to the accompanying illustrations will show the effect of this trick and also the principal points that form the explanation. The construction of the die has a great deal to do with the trick. The die is covered with a thin shell, which is open at the bottom. The shell is white on the inside, to resemble the paper that will later cover it. A duplicate silk handkerchief is pressed between the top of the real die and the inside of the shell. It is held in place by a rubber band, which can be instantly released by removing a blackened bit of match stick that holds one end of the loop.

It is a simple matter to demonstrate that the die is solid, by tapping the bottom of the genuine die. In showing that the die almost fills the interior of the hat, the magician dips his hand and releases pressure on the thin shell. The genuine die drops into the hat. Only the shell is retained by the performer.

The shell is placed upon the plate and the paper is molded about it. This action gives the magician the opportunity to release the rubber band so that the silk handkerchief fills the interior of the shell die. Now the magician vanishes the handkerchief. This may be done in various ways. The most suitable is with the aid of a "pull"—a cup-shaped metal container which is beneath the coat, fastened to the end of a length of cord elastic. The magician obtains the pull, works the handkerchief into it, and releases the cup. The silk and its container fly beneath his coat. The hands are shown empty.

When the paper cover is lifted, there is no trace of the die. The shell is picked up with the paper and the space formerly occupied by the die is now taken by the silk handkerchief. The solid die is in the hat and the magician concludes the trick by tilting the hat and letting the cube drop to the floor.

If desired, the shell die may be made of light cardboard; this will permit the magician to crumple the

THE SILK REPLACES THE DIE BENEATH THE PAPER. THE SOLID BLOCK IS DISCOVERED IN THE HAT. EXPLANATORY DIAGRAMS SHOW HOW DUPLICATE SILK IS KEPT BETWEEN DIE AND SHELL; ALSO HOW DIE IS LEFT IN HAT AND SHELL REMOVED.

paper after lifting it from the plate. This adds to the effectiveness of the trick; it also means the destruction of the shell each time the trick is performed. The cost of the shell die is a trifling matter, however, if the magician finds that the apparent destruction of the paper makes the deception more convincing.

WITH THE LINKING RINGS

[I]N PERFORMING the well-known Chinese ring trick, magicians have long desired a method whereby two rings could be unlinked and given for immediate examination. Here is a way of accomplishing it. Two ordinary rings are used. Before the performance, they

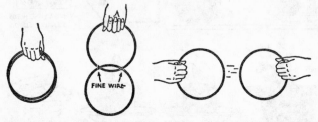

SILVER THREADS OR FINE WIRES MAKE THE RINGS SEEM LINKED.

are tied together by two thin, silver-colored strings, so that they appear to be attached.

The magician can pick these up as if they were separate rings; then turn one ring downward so that the rings appear to join. The upper ring is held with the lower dangling beneath it. Apparently one ring is linked to the other, as the silver threads are virtually invisible while the rings sway back and forth.

By taking one ring in each hand and moving them back and forth, the magician easily breaks the strings, which drop unnoticed to the floor. The result is two single solid rings, which can be immediately given for thorough inspection.

The threads should be tied tightly, a few inches apart, the space being arranged in accordance with the diameter of the rings. The purpose is to create an illusion of two rings actually joined and this is by no means difficult to do, especially as the magician is performing the usual ring routine.

A NEAT PRODUCTION TUBE

THIS tube is designed for the production of silk handkerchiefs, flags, ribbons, and other articles. The tube is shown empty and is set on a tray. Then the articles are produced.

It is simply an adaptation of an old principle. There are two tubes; the inner one is smaller than the outer. The inner tube is loaded with the various articles that are to be produced. It stands upon a chair, against the back. The tray is on the chair, leaning against the back, its upper edge above the tube.

After showing the outer tube empty—to the audience, this is the only tube—the magician reaches for the tray with his left hand. He swings the upper edge of the tray forward before he lifts it and his right hand simply sets the large tube over the smaller one. The magician holds the tray with both hands, striking it to prove it is solid. Then he places it upon a table and sets the tube upon it, lifting both tubes as one. He is ready to produce the various articles from the tube. The outer tube should be made of cardboard or very thin metal, so that the inner tube can be gripped by squeezing the outer.

The author has added a great improvement to this trick, without altering the routine. The addition also simplifies the working, as will be seen from the following description:

Instead of using a simple inner tube, the performer has a metal bottle of a type used in several magical

NOTE HOW BOTTLE IS "LOADED" IN TUBE WHEN LIFTING TRAY. SILKS ARE PRODUCED; THEN GLASS AND BOTTLE.

effects. This bottle is hollow and bottomless. Just below the neck is a horizontal partition that forms the bottom of a compartment which contains liquid. The bottle is about the size of a quart bottle; it is painted black and bears a label. The compartment is filled with liquid, and the bottle is corked.

A glass is placed in the bottom of the trick bottle. The glass is bottom upward and the rest of the space is packed so tightly with silk handkerchiefs and flags that the whole load is kept in place. This bottle simply takes the place of the customary inner tube. It is covered by the outer tube, which has been shown empty. The bottle is much easier to cover than the ordinary inner tube because of its neck and tapering shoulders. The cardboard tube can be virtually dropped upon it.

When the magician places the tube upon the tray, he inverts the tube and thus gets at the handkerchiefs and flags. Having produced them, he lifts the tube and tilts it toward himself. He shows surprise, and reaching in, brings out the glass. This gives him the opportunity to invert the tube again, in a very natural manner.

He still holds the glass in his hand. He peers into the tube, then lifts it with his free hand and reveals the bottle. He sets down the glass, draws the cork from the bottle, and pours out a glassful of liquid.

This makes an excellent conclusion to the trick, as the bottle appears to be quite ordinary and the production of so solid an object makes the previous production of silks even more mysterious. Inasmuch as the inner tube is a necessary evil, its production in the form of a bottle is in this case turned to the magician's advantage.

PERFECTION PAPER-TEARING

THIS is a variation of the paper-tearing trick in which a strip of tissue paper is destroyed and is later reproduced whole. In the usual method, the trick is performed with the aid of a false thumb-tip made of metal. The magician shows his hands empty and proceeds to tear the strip of tissue paper. As he gathers the torn pieces, he draws the thumb-tip from his right thumb and retains it in the left hand. At this point he brings his right thumb noticeably into view. While the thumb actually wears the false tip, it is not made conspicuous.

In wadding the torn strips, a duplicate, folded strip is brought from the thumb-tip and the torn pieces are put there instead. Then the right thumb regains the thumb-tip. When the tissue paper is unfolded, it is apparently restored and the hands are shown empty.

The trick in this form has been long used by magicians ever since the time when the celebrated Chinese wizard, Ching Ling Foo, brought it into popularity. Much depends upon the presentation, as a capable performer can make the trick appear almost miraculous.

The improvement in the present method lies in the use of three strips of paper instead of one. These strips are of different colors: black, orange, and green. In the thumb-tip is a strip formed into a circle; black, orange, and green pasted together. There are also three cards: black, orange, and green, respectively. The thumb-tip is concealed beneath the three strips of loose paper, which lie on the tray. Each strip is approximately two feet long. The individual portions of the circle in the thumb-tip are of corresponding length.

The magician advances with the tray and asks some person to take the cards. The magician picks up the three strips of paper; in doing so, he obtains the thumb-tip with his right thumb. He lays the tray aside and proceeds to tear the three strips. He asks the spectator to decide in what order he desires the restored strips to appear: black, green, orange; orange, black, green; or any possible combination. The spectator names his choice, showing the three cards in order. The performer restores the torn papers so that they form a long single strip corresponding to the spectator's choice.

The secret is very simple. It has been mentioned

that the duplicate strip is a circle formed by three strips. It is possible to form any combination of the three colors by simply tearing the circle at the proper join. For instance; if orange, green, and black is required, the circle is broken between orange and black; if green, orange, and black is desired, the circle is broken between green and black. The combination runs from left to right or from right to left according to the manner in which the performer exhibits the restored strip.

The simplest rule is to remember the color first named and the color last named and to break the paper where those two colors join, then retain the end of the color first named, letting the strip hang downward. The free hand may point out the three colors from top to bottom, showing that they have met the requirements imposed by the selector.

CONE AND EGG

HOUDINI enjoyed performing old tricks that were classics in magic and which had been almost forgotten in the modern era of conjuring. His notes contain many references to tricks of this sort. In the material was the following routine with the old cone and orange. It is probably intended for a small-sized cone, as an egg is used instead of an orange.

The cone is a wooden article. It is actually a truncated cone with a special rounded top. The magician borrows a hat and places it on a side table. He exhibits the wooden cone and wraps a piece of paper about it, fastening the paper with pins. He sets a large plate on the hat and puts an egg on the plate. He lifts the paper cover from the cone and sets the paper cover on the egg.

He raps the solid cone with his wand and covers it with a handkerchief. He walks forward and tosses the cloth in the air. The cone has vanished. The magician lifts the paper cover and reveals the cone upon the plate. A moment later he produces the egg from his elbow.

He replaces the cover over the cone. He makes several passes with the egg and finally squeezes it between his hands. The egg disappears completely. The cover is lifted to reveal the egg upon the plate. The magician sets the plate aside and places the cover

THE DRAWINGS SHOW VARIOUS PHASES OF THE TRICK AND GIVE A "BACK STAGE" VIEW OF THE IMPORTANT MANOEUVRES.

with it. He tilts the hat and shows the cone inside it. He concludes by breaking the egg, crumpling the paper, and returning the hat to its owner, at the same time bringing the wooden cone for examination.

There are actually two solid cones used in this trick; also a thin metal shell that fits over a cone and is painted to resemble it. At the outset, one cone is on a servante (hidden shelf) behind the side table. The magician borrows the hat and uses it for some by-play, finally taking it to the table, where he secretly "loads" the cone into the hat. It remains there awaiting the finish of the trick.

Next the magician exhibits the second cone—the first seen by the audience—which is already covered with the thin metal shell. He forms a paper cover, using the cone as a mold and when he raises the cover, he carries the metal shell along inside it. He sets a plate upon the hat and puts an egg on the plate. He covers the egg with a supposedly empty paper cover.

He vanishes the solid cone by covering it with a handkerchief of double thickness. Between its layers, the cloth has a pasteboard disk. The magician inverts the cone as he places the cloth over it. He is standing behind his center table at the time and he lets the cone drop to a servante at the rear of that table. The cardboard disk retains the shape of the bottom of the cone. The spectators believe that the cone is still in the large handkerchief. The cone seems to vanish when the magician tosses the handkerchief in the air.

While the cloth is still falling, the magician turns toward the side table. As he steps in that direction, he obtains a duplicate egg from beneath his vest. He lifts the paper cover, leaving the metal shell cone.

The vanished cone has apparently replaced the egg. The magician produces the duplicate egg at his elbow. He puts the paper cover back over the shell cone.

Now comes the byplay—false passes with the egg. In one maneuver, the magician pretends to carry the egg beneath his coat with his left hand. He suddenly shows the egg in the right hand and smiles at the suspicious glances of the spectators. This false movement to the coat enables the magician to obtain a special "pull"—a spring-wire holder attached to a length of cord elastic that passes beneath the coat. The egg is wedged into the pull. It flies beneath the coat under the cover of the arm. The hands are shown empty.

The magician approaches the side table and lifts the paper cover. He carries the shell cone with it. The egg has returned. Lowering the cover behind the hat, the magician releases the metal shell. It falls into the servante behind the table. The cover is laid on the center table with the egg and the plate. The solid cone is produced from the hat.

Having disposed of the shell, the magician can now crush or otherwise destroy the paper cover. He breaks the egg to show that it is genuine and when he returns the hat to the audience, he carries with him the only remaining article—one solid wooden cone.

HOUDINI'S AFGHAN BANDS

AMONG Houdini's notes on magic is a finale for the Afghan band trick. It appears without diagrams; hence the details of working it must be left in some degree to the individual performer. The instructions given here are more specific than Houdini's actual notes; but the author has adhered quite closely to the original rather than depart from the idea itself. The trick has all the elements of practicability but requires actual experiment in order to determine the best method of presentation. It should prove of unusual interest to readers of magic, as there have been more experiments with the Afghan bands than with almost any other trick in small magic.

The original Afghan band trick was performed with three circular strips of paper. The ends of the strips were glued to form the circle. One band was cut in half and it quite naturally formed two separate circles. The second band was cut. Like the first, it formed two loops, but they were linked together—a most surprising result. The third band was cut. The result was even more remarkable. The band came out in one large, narrow circle, double the size of the original.

The Afghan bands were highly recommended, but seldom used, chiefly because the cutting of the paper was a tedious process. Some years ago, magicians began to perform the trick with circles of muslin instead of paper. By having a slit in the center of each muslin loop, it became a question of ripping instead of cutting and the trick was worth while. Credit for first using bands of muslin has been given to Carl Brema, the well-known magical dealer.

The strange behavior of the bands is due to their formation. To make a band form two separate loops, simply place the ends together and glue them. To make a band form two linked loops, give one end a double twist before gluing. To make a band form a large circle twice the size of the first, give one end a single twist before gluing. It may be noted that with paper, it is difficult to conceal the twists. This is not so with muslin, which can be pressed flat.

The modernized version of the Afghan bands came about through experiments made by James C. Wobensmith, past president of the Society of American Magicians. He applied the principle to one wide band. The band is first split a few inches at the center of one end, before gluing. One half of the split end is given a single twist; the other half is given a double twist. Then the ends are glued. The result: the band, when torn in half, forms two separate bands. When one of these narrow bands is torn, it forms two bands linked together. When the other narrow band is torn, it forms a band of twice the size. Muslin is used as the material. The trick is highly effective.

Houdini used this trick in his matinée performances, and he refers to it in connection with the finale that he devised. The finale is performed with three bands of muslin: red, white, and blue, each separate.

These three bands may first be used to produce the old effects; if this proves too complicated, the performer can have a number of bands available and pick up three fresh bands for the finale. The author recommends this latter course. The three single bands are looped one within the other, the blue band being on the outside. The magician tears the bands in half. He drops one portion and reveals the other. The result is a triple link, formed by red, white, and blue bands.

The secret lies in the use of two extra bands—one red, the other white—and a double blue band. In preparing, the red is linked into the white; and the white is linked into the blue, which is double width. The blue band is folded in half and the red and white bands are pressed inside the fold, which is stitched along the open edge. This bears the appearance of a single blue band and it is laid folded on a table, care being taken to cover the spot where the link of the white band shows through.

In presenting, the performer picks up an ordinary red band and an ordinary white band and places them with the prepared blue band. The magician pretends to tear the three bands. In reality, he merely rips open the double blue band, the sound of the tearing creating the required illusion. At the finish, the single bands are tossed aside and three linked bands are exhibited. Apparently three of the bands have not joined, while the other three have formed a chain.

Houdini suggests a further finale to the trick—a very large band concealed beneath the top of the vest. This band could be a single color, or it could be composed of three colors—red, white, and blue. The lower part of the band is weighted. Attached to the upper part of the band is a fine loop of thread or catgut, which extends from the vest. The band is rolled or pleated within the vest.

Finishing his triple link effect, the magician gathers in the colored bands so that they form a bundle. His hands come close to his body and his right thumb engages the loop that extends from the vest. The hands move quickly upward and outward. The large band follows and appears instantly as it begins to unroll. The magician drops the smaller bands and whirls the huge band around his forefinger, the weight at the bottom of the loop aiding him in this maneuver. The effect is that the large band has been conjured from nowhere and its appearance, as it whirls above the magician's head, marks an effective conclusion to the routine with the Afghan bands.

THE VANISHING TABLE LEG

THIS is an elaboration of the "Vanishing Wand" trick. It concerns the vanish and reappearance of the nickel-plated rod which forms the center leg of a typical table used by a magician.

The table consists of three parts; a tripod base, the center rod and the top. It is taken to pieces. The top and the base are laid aside. The center rod is rapped to prove its solidity—the fact that it supported the top being silent proof of the same fact—and it is wrapped in a sheet of paper. The paper is crumpled. The rod has vanished. Taking a silk hat, the magician draws forth the missing table leg.

The center rod used on the table has an outer shell of glazed silver paper. This does not detract from its appearance of solidity. It is necessary to dispose of the solid leg within the paper shell. This is accomplished with the aid of another table at the side of the stage. The side table has a long drape and a well in the table-top. A long bag extends downward from the well.

On the side table is a sheet of newspaper; upon this a hat. The magician carries the rod in his right hand. In order to lift the hat and remove the sheet of paper, he finds it necessary to use both hands. Holding the end of the rod behind the hat, he lets the solid rod drop into the well, his hand retaining the paper shell. This shell is wrapped in the newspaper. Inasmuch as the rod never leaves the sight of the spectators, the ruse is not suspected.

The newspaper is crumpled, destroying the paper shell. The metal rod has apparently vanished. Beneath his vest and in the right side of his trousers leg, the magician has a duplicate table leg. There is a hole in the bottom of the hat. By holding the hat against his vest, the magician brings out the solid table leg that matches the original.

SOLID
LEG
DROPPED

DUPLICATE
PRODUCED

TABLE TRICK. SOLID TABLE LEG VANISHES WHEN WRAPPED IN
PAPER. THE LOWER DRAWINGS SHOW HOW SOLID LEG LEAVES
PAPER SHELL; ALSO THE PRODUCTION OF THE DUPLICATE
TABLE LEG.

PART SEVEN.

STAGE TRICKS

THESE are large tricks, suited to the professional magician. Some of them were planned or obtained by Houdini for use in his own stage performances. They comprise a varied array of large and effective magic.

THE TRAVELING BALL

THIS is a stage trick that requires two cubical boxes, each set upon a metal rod. Each box has a solid bottom and a solid top. The four sides drop downward.

The magician takes a large, heavy ball and places it in the box at the right. He closes the doors of the box. He also closes the box at the left. He then commands the ball to pass from the box at the right to the box at the left. When the boxes are opened, the ball has obeyed the order. It is in the box at the left. The box at the right is empty.

The trick depends upon the use of two rubber balls —thick toy balloons. The balloon used in the box at the right has a special valve which allows an even discharge of air when released. This ball is placed in its box. The rear door is the last one closed. The valve is at the rear. The performer opens the valve just before he closes the door. To aid the disappearance of the ball, the box has a double top. A flat board descends upon the sinking ball and presses the deflated balloon flat, so that it is finally lost between a double bottom. This special top is released by a catch at the back of the box and it is arranged to move downward evenly.

The box at the left also contains a balloon, which is deflated at the outset. The sliding board is not es-

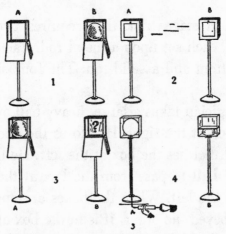

1, BALL SHOWN IN STAND B. 2, STANDS CLOSED. 3, BALL ARRIVES IN A. 4, WORKING DETAILS OF APPARATUS.

sential to this box, as the balloon can be carefully pressed in the bottom of the box. It can be covered by a thin false bottom if desired, for the false bottom will rise to the top of the cabinet when the balloon expands. The valve is beneath the balloon and a hose is attached. The hose runs through the rod that supports the box. As soon as the box is closed, air is forced through the hose and the balloon is inflated.

The main details of the trick are shown in the explanatory diagram. The hose can come up through the stage, or it can run behind the scenes under a carpet. A hand pump may be used for the inflation, or a small container of compressed air may be utilized. The assistant who handles this should know the approximate amount of air required.

The bottoms of the boxes are slightly lower inside than outside, as this aids in the concealment of the balls. Each ball should be colored to represent a granite ball or a cannon ball, whichever the performer chooses to use.

Just before the trick, the performer introduces a ball that is actually solid. He exchanges this for the rubber ball that goes into the first box. There are several methods of effecting an exchange. Perhaps the best is to drop the solid ball near the side of the stage. It rolls off and is overtaken by an assistant who brings back the rubber ball, carrying it as though it were very heavy.

Houdini suggests an exchange by means of a trap in the stage, first covering the ball with a cloth and then disclosing it after placing it in the box. This method is hardly suitable, as the special preparation of a trap would be a great deal of unnecessary trouble for anything less than an illusion.

KELLAR'S WINE AND RIBBON

O N A table in the center of the stage stands a large bottle. The magician picks up the bottle and pours out glasses full of wine. These are served to the audience. The magician points to the bottle. A piece of ribbon emerges from the neck. The magician draws the end of the ribbon. He continues to pull, bringing many yards of white ribbon from the bottle. While he is drawing the ribbon, he calls for a color. Suppose that green is named. When the white ribbon is exhausted, the magician walks away. The end of a green ribbon suddenly appears from the neck of the bottle. The green ribbon is drawn forth. The same effect is repeated with other colors.

The magician asks for the names of various countries. One by one the flags of those countries bob up and each flag is taken from the bottle and displayed. At the conclusion, another flag appears without being called for. The magician shows it and places it upon the bottle. At his command, the flag suddenly disappears back into the bottle.

Finally, the magician asks a volunteer to aid him. Many more yards of ribbon are extracted from the bottle and at the conclusion of the trick the bottle is broken with a hammer to prove that it is quite ordinary.

Two bottles are used. The first is made of metal. It has a cavity running right through the center. The diagrams show its construction. Wine is contained around the sides of the bottle. The bottle rests upon a table which has a hollow top and a hollow leg. The white ribbon runs up through the leg and in the top of the table. A thread passes from the ribbon, through the bottle and out to the stage. The thread is loose. Hence the magician can use the bottle to pour out wine.

When the serving is finished, the bottle is stood upon the table. The thread is drawn tight, either by the magician or by a concealed assistant. The final tightening of the thread causes the end of the white ribbon to put in its appearance. While the white ribbon is coming out, another color is demanded. An assistant below stage fastens the required ribbon on the end of a thread which is attached to the lower end of the white ribbon. After all the white ribbon has been produced, the magician gathers it up. As he steps away from the table, the thread draws the next ribbon into view.

This continues with all the ribbons. During the production of the last ribbon, the magician stops and calls for the names of countries. The assistant below hears his replies and arranges the various flags in their proper order, each connected to the one above by a length of thread. Stepping away with the last ribbon,

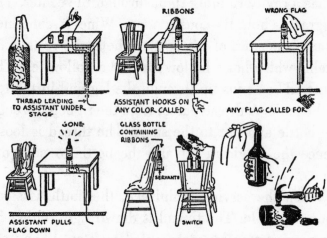

DETAILS OF WINE AND RIBBON TRICK.

the magician causes the first flag to appear. Each flag is produced in succession by the same method. The final flag is one that is not wanted. The magician removes it almost entirely from the bottle; in so doing he breaks the thread that connects it with the flag previously produced. Deciding that he does not want the flag, he drapes it over the top of the bottle and commands it to disappear.

A strong cord is attached to the lower corner of the flag—the corner which is never removed from the bottle. The assistant pulls the cord when he hears the magician's command. The flag is drawn down through the bottle and into the table. The magician corks the bottle. He carries it to a chair upon which he has placed the ribbons. On the back of the chair is a servante—a bag large enough to hold the bottle. A duplicate glass bottle is also resting behind the chair. Under cover of the flags and ribbons, the magician has ample opportunity to drop the metal bottle secretly and bring out the glass bottle in its stead.

The glass bottle is packed with ribbons of various colors. They are fastened together, having been previously pushed into place with the aid of a wand. The ribbons are hidden by the cork in the neck of the bottle. The magician simply removes the cork and, with the aid of a volunteer assistant, produces quantities of silk ribbon. As a quart bottle will hold yards and yards of ribbon, this is very effective, as it appears to be a continuation of the productions that took place while the bottle was on the table.

When all the ribbons have been produced, the trick is brought to an effective conclusion by the breaking of the bottle. This convinces the audience that a real mystery has been performed. An ordinary glass bottle that has held a large supply of wine and innumerable yards of ribbon is indeed a marvelous article.

The illustrations show various details of the apparatus.

HAT SUSPENSION

THE magician appears wearing evening clothes. He stands at the back of the stage, between two draped curtains. He removes his hat and bows to the audience. He places his hat upon his head and then slowly stoops forward. The hat remains suspended in the air. The magician looks up at the hat. He steps behind it and makes passes with his hands. The hat slowly descends. It rises at command. It reaches the level of the magician's hand. He plucks it from the air, twirls it between his fingers and walks forward to make another bow to the audience.

This is a good opening trick. It depends upon two assistants who are standing well behind the curtains. Each assistant is mounted on a footstool. Threads pass from one asistant to the other. There are two threads, the ends being hooked to the shoulders of the assistants.

When the magician appears, he bows while he is behind the threads. He removes his hat as he does so. In concluding his bow, he stands up beneath the threads and his head presses against the threads. He places his hat upon his head. The hat actually rests upon the threads, due to its broad brim. The threads are taut and when the magician stoops, the hat re-

THE FLOATING HAT—WITH SPECIAL VIEW OF ASSISTANTS CONCEALED AT SIDES OF ARCHWAY.

mains upon the threads above him. He looks upward in surprise and moves backward. From that position he commands the hat to descend and to rise. The assistants step down slowly from the stools, taking care to control the hat by correct handling of the threads. By lowering and raising their bodies, they can cause the hat to go up or down, but it never reaches its original height. It is finally taken by the magician. While he twirls it, the assistants detach the threads from their shoulders. The threads fall upon the stage. The magician is free to walk forward without disturbing the threads.

This is a good opening trick. It requires coöperation on the part of the assistants to make it successful. Properly done, it should prove a real mystery. According to Houdini's notes, this trick was shown by Ching Ling Foo, at a special performance in a club in New York.

A NEW DYEING TUBE

THIS device will be of special interest to magicians, as it is an improvement over the old tubes used for changing the colors of silk handkerchiefs. In order to make the idea plain to the reader, we must first briefly consider the effect of the usual "dye tube." The magician rolls a sheet of paper and pushes white silk handkerchiefs through it. One silk comes out red, another white, the third blue. These three are then pushed through the tube. They are transformed into a large American flag.

The tube seen by the audience is simply made of paper or cardboard, but there is also an inner tube, which may be termed the "fake tube." The fake holds the other handkerchiefs and the flag. When the different silks are pushed into the bottom, the others emerge from the top.

The whole problem of the dye tube—from the magician's view—is the secret insertion of the fake and its subsequent removal. These are necessary to make the trick convincing, since the paper tube must be shown empty before and after the deception. In the dye tube about to be described, two devices play an important part: one is a nickeled tube with small holes in it. The other is a special fake to which a hook

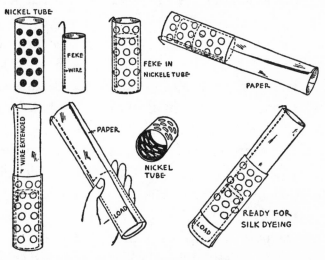

DETAILS OF THE NICKEL TUBE, SHOWING PHASES OF THE TRICK.

is attached. This hook is in a groove, so that while it cannot come free of the fake, it can be drawn upward or dropped downward.

At the beginning of the trick, the fake rests in the nickeled tube. The metal tube is standing on an undraped table. The hook of the fake projects over the upper edge of the nickeled tube, which is slightly longer than the fake. The fake is painted black. The interior of the nickeled tube is black. Hence the nickeled tube appears to be empty.

The magician exhibits an empty tube of cardboard. It is slightly less in diameter than the nickeled tube, but its diameter is greater than that of the fake tube. It is twice as long as the nickeled tube. The magician picks up the nickeled tube. His finger and thumb enter holes in the side of the tube and thus keep the fake from dropping. The left hand holds the nickeled tube. The right hand pushes the cardboard tube up into the nickeled tube. At this point, the left finger and thumb release their hold. The fake drops to the full length of its loose wire. It hangs in the cardboard tube. The magician may pause to turn the nickeled tube in front of a light. The spectators glimpse the light through the holes and know that the nickeled tube is empty. The cardboard tube is now pushed up through the nickeled tube. The white cardboard shows plainly through the holes. The cardboard tube disengages the hook, so that it alone holds the fake. The cardboard tube is very long, so the hanging fake does not emerge at the bottom.

Now comes the dyeing. Handkerchiefs are pushed into the bottom of the cardboard tube. The nickeled tube is centered on the surface of the cardboard tube. As the fake is pushed upward, the left thumb and finger press through the holes of the nickeled tube and hold the fake firmly in the center of the cardboard tube.

When the flag is produced, an assistant aids the magician. The flag is quite large. The assistant drapes it over his outstretched arm. As soon as the flag is completely produced, the magician, standing at the assistant's side, removes the nickeled tube with one hand, drawing it downward from the cardboard tube. The hand that holds the cardboard tube goes up behind the flag. The projecting hook of the fake is deftly attached to the back of the assistant's arm. This is done under cover of the flag. The cardboard tube is drawn straight downward, leaving the fake hidden behind the flag. The magician walks forward and exhibits both tubes, pushing the cardboard tube back and forth through the nickeled tube, demonstrating quite plainly that both are empty.

During this procedure, the assistant folds the flag over his arm and gathers it up with his free hand, lifting the fake tube with it. He walks from the stage with the flag and carries with him the only clue to the mystery—the fake tube with its load of silk handkerchiefs which were supposed to have been blended together in the formation of the flag.

CHING LING FOO'S PAPER TRICK

MAGICIANS have long connected Ching Ling Foo, the genuine Chinese magician, with the torn and restored paper trick. The trick now under discussion is a different paper trick entirely. It was performed by Harry Kellar and attributed by him to Ching Ling Foo. Kellar passed the secret along to Houdini.

The magician has a glass bowl which contains water. It is resting on a stand. Beside the bowl are sheets of tissue paper of different colors. The magician sets the stand to one side. He picks up the sheets of paper and tears them into strips, constantly showing his hands empty. He lets some of the paper strips fall to the floor. Finally, he gathers them all together and drops them into the bowl of water. He shows his hands empty, takes out the wet strips of paper and squeezes them. He holds the strips in his left hand. He starts to draw them forth. They come out in the form of a long strip of paper, composed of various colors. There are many yards of the dry paper.

Now for the subtle secret. The restored paper is in the form of a tight roll. The outside is pasted to-

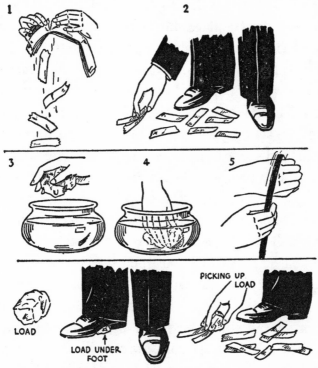

1, STRIPS OF PAPER TORN. 2, PAPERS DROPPED UPON FLOOR. 3-4, SOAKING PAPERS IN BOWL. 5, PRODUCTION OF DRY COIL. *Bottom drawing*, HOW "LOAD" IS OBTAINED.

gether. In the center is a whisk of straw, which is attached to the end of the paper at the center of the coil. This roll is previously dipped in melted parafine. The roll must be very tight, so that the parafine will not penetrate but will merely form a protective film.

The prepared roll of paper is placed on the floor behind the stand which supports the glass bowl.

The magician walks to the stand and shows his hands empty. He places his foot over the coil of paper so that it rests beneath his instep. He sets the stand to the side and shows his hands empty. He tears up strips of tissue paper. He lets some of the strips fall to the floor. When he leans forward to pick up the strips, he sweeps them toward his foot. He steps back a trifle and scoops up the coil with the loose strips of paper. He wads the coil with the strips of paper when he places them in the glass bowl.

The paper coil remains dry. It is taken from the bowl with the wet strips. They are squeezed and are retained in the right hand when they are apparently transferred to the left. Only the coil of paper goes into the left hand. The magician pulls the straw in the center of the coil. The paper begins to unwind. It comes out in a long strip. Meanwhile the magician disposes of the torn pieces. He can do this as his hand sweeps downward, by dropping the wet papers on a small shelf behind the stand. He can wait until the coil is unwound, then drop the wet papers behind the stand. Or he can give the massed coil of dry paper to an assistant, handing him the wet papers under cover of the dry.

The really subtle part of this trick is the obtaining

of the coil of paper. It is done in a natural manner and in a most unexpected way. Both the stand and the magician's body are free from suspicion. The paper strips must be taken from the floor and the magician uses that movement as a perfect excuse for getting his coil. Houdini's notes state that Kellar kept the coil under his right foot.

A DUCK PRODUCTION

THIS is the production of ducks from a tub of water. A tub is brought on the stage. It is rolled about and shown to be entirely empty. It is set in a heavy frame of wood that is raised from the stage. The frame is nothing but a skeleton stand.

Several buckets of water are poured into the tub. Then a lid is placed on the tub and a mat is spread in front of the improvised platform. The magician fires a pistol shot. The lid is lifted. Half a dozen ducks emerge, dripping with water, and drop from the tub to the mat.

A very novel method is employed to produce the ducks. The actual number of ducks is limited only by the size of the tub and the time that the performer desires to spend with the trick. The tub is actually empty at the outset. Its only peculiarity lies in two traps near the top; these may be pushed inward, and they move back to their original position when released, by the operation of springs.

The stand is merely a skeleton arrangement; but

it is heavily constructed, and therein lies the secret.
The back legs are actually hollow metal tubes, painted

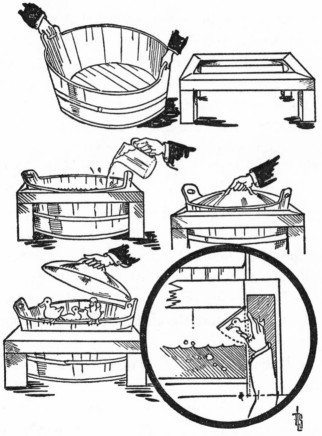

HOW DUCKS ARE PRODUCED FROM AN EMPTY TUB AFTER FILLING
WITH WATER AND COVERING. INSET SHOWS DUCKS PUSHED
UP THROUGH LEG OF STAND.

to resemble wood, and are set over holes in the stage.
As soon as the cover is in place on the tub, the magi-

cian gives a cue. Two assistants set to work and push
the ducks up through the back legs of the stand, one
at a time.

The ducks pass through openings at the top of the
legs. These correspond to the traps in the back of the
tub. The ducks are pushed into the tub and when
the last have made their entrance, the traps close,
leaving no clue. The magician fires the pistol after
sufficient time has been allowed. When the cover is
taken from the tub, the ducks appear.

The laying of the mat, the obtaining of the pistol,
and other bits of byplay give the men below stage
time to work. If the stand is painted jet-black, there
is no need to conceal the openings in the back legs.
These can be obscured, however, by the previous insertion of an inner leg or lining, which is removed
before the ducks are pushed up. The tub is not taken
from the stand, hence the closed traps hide the openings at the end of the trick.

It is better to use very small ducks and to produce a
large quantity of them than to use a few large ducks.
With small ducks, the loading takes place more
rapidly and the back legs of the stand do not have
to be too large in size. The stand presents an innocent
appearance, as the duck tub is large and heavy and
is to be filled with water. A heavy stand is necessary
to support the weight.

CHINESE RICE BOWLS

THIS is a trick which Houdini obtained for his own program. It was shown to him by Carl Brema of Philadelphia. The author was present at the time. Brema had obtained the trick from a Chinese magician. It is a genuine Chinese routine to be used with the well-known rice trick. Houdini's notes state that "this is the Chinese misdirection and the best ever used in the bowl trick."

The effect of the rice bowls is known to every magician. Two small bowls are used. One is shown empty. It is filled with rice. The second bowl is inverted upon the first. When the uppermost bowl is lifted, the rice has doubled in quantity. The rice is leveled. The bowls are placed together. When they are separated, the rice has changed to water.

One bowl is unprepared. The other is filled with water. The mouth of the bowl is covered with a flat disk of transparent celluloid. The disk has a small projection, enabling the performer to remove it. The empty bowl is filled with rice. The bowl with the water is placed mouth downward upon it. The celluloid retains the water. The fact that the bowl is upside down leads people to believe that it is empty. The bowls are turned over. The upper one is removed. The rice rests upon the celluloid disk and appears to have doubled in quantity. The celluloid disk is removed when the rice is leveled. The result is water instead of rice.

In actual practice, the rice bowls give difficulty. The removal of the celluloid disk is often a problem. The Chinese method solves all difficulties and enables the performer to show the trick at close range.

Besides the bowls, the magician uses a large napkin. This is folded in thirds. It is laid lengthwise on the tray upon which the bowls are set. The napkin's length is more than double the diameter of a bowl. The water-filled bowl is inverted on the tray. It rests upon grains of rice, to prevent close contact between the celluloid disk and the tray. The ordinary bowl is inverted upon the prepared bowl.

Incidentally, the filling of the water bowl is important. The rim should be moistened, so that the disk will adhere. When the disk is in place it should be pressed in the center to force out all air.

In performing, the magician shows the empty bowl. He fills it with rice. He smooths the rice with a stick that is decorated with Chinese characters. He picks up the bowl of water and places it mouth downward upon the bowl of rice. He raises the two bowls by picking them up between the hands, fingers toward the body, thumbs outward. The act of raising the hands to their normal position inverts the bowls. The magician rocks the bowls to and fro. He replaces them on the tray. He picks up the Chinese stick and strikes the upper bowl. He lifts it and sets it on the tray. The lower bowl appears to have double the quantity of rice.

Now comes the clever portion of the routine. The magician smooths off most of the rice with the stick, leaving just enough to obscure the celluloid disk. He picks up the folded napkin and shows that it is merely a piece of cloth. He draws the napkin slowly across the bowl, lengthwise from front to back. When he reaches the projecting flange of the celluloid disk, he grips it between his thumb and fingers and draws it along beneath the napkin. By the time the front half of the napkin is upon the bowl, the disk is clear of the bowl. The magician lets the disk fall upon the rice that lies on the tray and without hesitation, he folds the back half of the napkin forward upon the front. Thus the bowl of water is completely covered by the cloth. The whole movement appears to be a simple doubling of the napkin. It disposes of the disk without the slightest chance of detection.

The empty bowl is immediately placed upside down upon the bowl that is covered by the napkin. The right hand raises the upper bowl the fraction of an inch; the left hand whisks away the napkin. The left hand picks up the stick and strikes the upper bowl. While the clang is still resounding, the two bowls are lifted; they are separated and the water is poured from one to the other.

Brass bowls of Oriental design are best in this routine. Houdini also suggests the use of a Ching Ling Foo water vase. This is a tall metal vase with a dividing partition, open at the bottom, closed at the top. When water is poured into the vase, it does not emerge when the vase is inverted, as it runs into the hidden compartment.

If the Ching Ling Foo vase is used, it is brought into the routine after the upper bowl has been set upon the folded napkin. The napkin is pulled away and the bowls are left together. A glass of water is poured into the Ching Ling Foo vase. The vase is struck with the stick and the hand is waved toward the rice bowls. The vase is inverted. The water has gone. The vase is laid aside. The magician goes to the rice bowls, strikes the upper one with the stick, and produces the water to conclude the trick.

PART EIGHT.

A SECOND-SIGHT ACT

THIS section is devoted to the explanation of a series of unusual tests which compose a complete act in themselves. It is one of the most interesting portions of the book and has been revised from original typewritten instructions that were with Houdini's notes.

A SECOND-SIGHT ACT

THE following material constitutes one of the most important items among Houdini's notes. It consists of a series of telepathic effects that enable two persons to present a most baffling entertainment. While the principles are not new and some of the actual effects have been shown as individual items, the complete routine with all of its variations forms a complete act in itself. Smoothly and carefully presented, the effect will prove phenomenal.

The usual second-sight act involves the transmission of thoughts from one person to another. The performers are usually a man and a woman, the man passing through the audience and receiving articles which the woman names while seated on the stage. Such acts are learned only after long and patient practice.

The second-sight act about to be discussed is of a different nature. It is of the type known to the profession as a "test," namely, a concentrated exhibition performed before a small and discriminating audience. It was designed as a routine to follow the usual second-sight act, but there is no reason why it should not be presented as an act in itself. This is particularly true because the act is not difficult. It does require keenness and practice; but two intelligent persons should be able to perform it with every variation after two or three preliminary trials.

Readers versed in magic will recognize the underlying principles of this act because most of them have seen effects in which a magician names the time on a watch or tells the denomination of a playing-card after such objects have been laid on the table during his absence. But few have ever seen an act of this sort worked up to a high-class state, involving so many tests that no repetition of one effect is necessary, and embellished with such unusual details that it carries all the effectiveness of a second-sight performance. This act does all that.

The performer, in introducing the act, discourses on the subject of telepathy. He states that he and his assistant can perform all the most remarkable tests that involve figures, cards, and blackboard writing while they are in separate rooms and not within hearing distance of one another. One committee conducts the woman from the room, while the man prepares to transmit the thoughts of those who remain.

A watch is set at any hour and minute. It is laid

face down on the table. A number is written on a card, which is sealed in a small envelope and placed upon the table. A line is selected from the page of a book. Initials are written between two hinged slates, which are then locked and placed upon the table.

The woman returns. It is best to have a blackboard available. She stands before the blackboard and writes answers to everything, performing the most complicated tests with ease and precision. The act is highly effective for platform performers and when it is done as a conclusion to a short second-sight act, its effect is naturally increased.

EXPLANATION OF THE PRINCIPLE

The basis of the trick depends upon a mental arrangement in which the table is divided into imaginary sections. This system is known to both the performer and his assistant. The table should measure about two by three feet, although a square card table may be used. Upon the table is an ornamental mat, with curved edges. This is shown on page 172. The mat should measure about twelve by sixteen inches. Laid crosswise, the mat is easily divided into twelve mentally noted squares, each four inches square. While the mat is useful, it is not absolutely essential after the system has been thoroughly understood.

Any rectangular mat will do; marks on the table will suffice; or, in the most advanced form, the mat itself may be visualized without actually being used. However, an ordinary mat will not arouse suspicion, since it appears to be a mere ornament.

The twelve squares are numbered, four to a row. When both performers can recognize any field instantly, they are ready to proceed with their preliminary tests. These will be described individually, with all the necessary modifications of the fundamental principle.

THE WATCH TEST

THIS test is not difficult to learn. Yet it is performed with such exactitude—even to the very minute indicated by the hands of the watch—that it will prove puzzling to the wisest observers.

When the watch has been set at a definite time and the performer has pretended to transmit that time to his assistant, the performer lays the watch upon the table, face down, but in a manner that indicates the exact time registered.

The hour is shown by means of the mat. There are twelve imaginary numbered squares. The performer puts the watch in the square that corresponds to the hour. Square one indicates one o'clock, and so on. The stem of the watch is the indicator that gives the position of the minute hand in reference to the numbers that appear upon the face of the watch. For instance, taking the top of the mat as twelve o'clock, the performer can indicate the number two (ten minutes after the hour) by pointing the stem toward the spot where number two would appear if the watch itself were surrounded by a dial. There is no difficulty whatever in indicating these imaginary numbers. If the time on the watch should be thirty minutes after two, the watch would be placed in number two square on the mat, with the stem of the watch pointing straight down toward the spot where the number six would be on the imaginary dial.

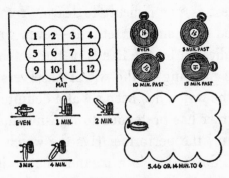

SHOWING TWELVE IMAGINARY PORTIONS OF THE MAT. ALSO POSITIONS OF WATCH, STEM AND PLACEMENT ON MAT.

The committee usually chooses some minute in between the fives and the performer is ready for this. Suppose the time is 5:18. He sets it to indicate 5:15, ignoring the three extra minutes for the moment; but he then indicates those additional minutes by a ring which surrounds the stem of the watch. To indicate one additional minute, he points the ring upward at right angles to the stem of the watch. To indicate two additional minutes, he bends the ring back so that it lies flat against the upper side of the stem. To show three additional minutes, he bends the ring so that it points downward at right angles to the stem. For four additional minutes, the ring is bent all the way beneath the stem. If the ring projects straight outward in its normal position, no minutes are added.

Thus for 5:15 the ring would be straight out; for 5:16, straight up; for 5:17, back against the upper side of the stem; for 5:18, straight down; for 5:19, back beneath the stem.

Once the system is understood, the performer can handle the watch without clumsiness. Upon receiving the watch, he notes the time and immediately decides the square upon which it belongs, the position to which the stem must point, and how the ring should be set. While looking at the watch, he observes his location, puts the ring in its correct position and immediately sets the watch face down upon the table.

This may be done with any pocket watch that may be offered by the committee, although it is a good idea to use a watch that is not running, for the time will remain constant and can be checked after the test.

The various positions are clearly shown in the accompanying diagrams, hence there is no need for lengthy examples. A study of the illustrations will make everything plain.

Presented as a single test, the watch trick is too apt to excite the close attention of the audience. It is merely one step in the entire series of tests that follow. After laying the watch on the table in a matter-of-fact manner, the performer calls for the next impression that he intends to transmit to his assistant.

It must be understood, of course, that the performer does not use the particular time that happens to be registered by a watch. He allows the spectators to set the watch at any time they may choose. It is quite natural for him to take the watch and look at it for a considerable number of seconds, since he is supposed to be engaged in concentration.

THE FIGURE TEST TO 10,000

IN THIS test, the performer invites the committee to choose any number up to 10,000. For instance, the number 3,862 is selected. This number is written on a card. The performer looks at the card and studies the number. He may either lay the card face down on the table or he may place it in an envelope and seal it there. That is a matter of choice. The essential details are the indication of the number.

There are four figures to be considered. In the instance given, those figures are 3, 8, 6, and 2. The performer indicates the first figure (3) by the square on which he lays the card (or envelope). He indicates the second figure (8) by the pointing of the card. This involves an imaginary dial surrounding the card, and corresponding to the numbers on the face of a clock. If the card is used alone, it should be a business card, with the number written on the blank side. Hence the name on the card serves as a pointer when read in its proper manner. If the envelope is used, one end is slightly marked so that the assistant will recognize it. In this way the envelope is useful. The performer has it ready in case some one chooses to use a blank card instead of a business card.

Having put the card on the table, the performer is through with the pencil for the time, so he lays it on

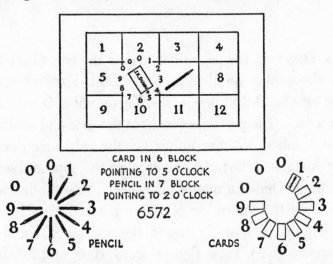

CARD IN 6 BLOCK
POINTING TO 5 O'CLOCK
PENCIL IN 7 BLOCK
POINTING TO 2 O'CLOCK
6572

PENCIL　　　　CARDS

FIGURES INDICATED BY CARD PLACEMENT, CARD POINTING, PENCIL PLACEMENT, AND PENCIL POINTING.

the table also. In this manner he indicates the third and fourth figures. The square on which he lays the pencil indicates the third figure (6) and the spot on the imaginary dial to which the pencil points tells the fourth figure (2).

In using the figure test, number ten serves as the figure 0. The spaces or pointers eleven and twelve are not utilized. Thus it is possible to indicate such

numbers as 53 by simply placing the card to show
0 and pointing it to show 0. The performer can also
extend this test, allowing any number up to 12,000.
He does this by utilizing the ten and eleven squares on
the mat. The twelve square indicates the figure 0 in
this instance. This plan must be prearranged beforehand with the assistant.

The diagrams show the working of this test; it is
an easy matter to indicate other numbers once the
principle is recognized. As in the watch test, the performer should avoid all hesitancy, placing the card
and pencil upon the table in an indifferent manner.

THE PLAYING-CARD TEST

ANOTHER test is performed with a pack of cards. This is best when two selected cards are used. The spectators choose two cards from the pack and show them to the performer. He places the two cards together and sets them on the table. He also replaces the pack of cards upon the table. The fact that the two chosen cards are squared together is a subtle touch. They indicate the name of but one card. It is the pack itself, so carelessly replaced, that declares the second chosen card.

The rule for indicating cards is simply numerical, running from one to twelve. Ace is one, then the cards go in rotation, jack being eleven and queen twelve. The squares on the mat are used as indicators. If a king is chosen, the pack is laid on the table near a corner—not on the mat at all.

An alternate plan to indicate a king is to lay the cards on any square but to spread them slightly; with two cards, they overlap a bit; with the entire pack, the cards are slightly fanned. This is not so good as the corner placement.

To indicate suit as well as value, the performer sets the cards in one of four positions. For clubs, the pack is laid so it points straight up and down. For spades, the pack points across. Hearts is indicated by a position of upper right to lower left, diagonally. In in-

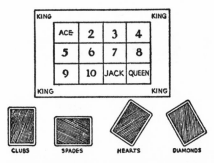

DIVISIONS OF MAT AND TABLE FOR PLAYING-CARD TEST. ALSO
POINTING POSITIONS OF CARDS.

dicating diamonds, the pack should point diagonally from upper left to lower right.

The joker is eliminated. It is preferable to use a borrowed pack; the two selected cards may be placed in an envelope, if desired, to prove indirectly that there are no marks on the chosen cards, though this possibility should not be mentioned in the performer's talk. It is also possible to indicate a third chosen card in a subtle manner by having the pack of cards in a case before the demonstration. To select three cards, the pack is taken from the case; the three cards are drawn, noted by the performer, and laid together or inserted in an envelope. To save time, the pack is not replaced in the case; the cards, the pack, and the case are placed on the table; and the position of the case tells the third selected card.

THE SLATE TEST

IN ITS most effective form, the slate test is performed with a pair of slates that are fitted with a lock. A person writes his initials between the slates. Then the slates are locked.

Here we have letters instead of figures, hence another system must be employed; but it is easy to remember, as it is based on the numbered squares of the mat.

The performer merely counts through the alphabet. The twelve letters, A, B, C, D, E, F, G, H, I, J, K, L, correspond to the numbers from one to twelve. Continuing, the letters M, N, O, P, Q, R, S, T, U, V, W, X also correspond to the numbers from one to twelve. The slates are placed on the correct square to indicate the first initial. If the letter is in the first set, the slates are pointed up and down. If it is in the second set, the slates are pointed across.

The second initial is indicated with the chalk. The performer puts it in the proper square; first set of letters, chalk pointing upward; second set, pointing across. The third initial is indicated by the key to the locked slates. It is placed and pointed like the chalk. Should there be no third initial, the performer gives the key to a spectator to hold. In case the letters Y or Z appear, they are indicated by placing the slates, chalk, or key to the left or right of the mat. Left indicates Y; right indicates Z.

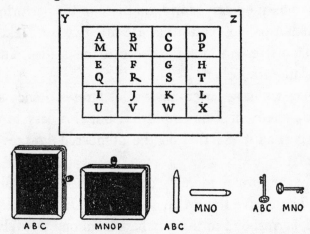

DOUBLE LETTER SYSTEM USED IN SLATE TEST. NOTE SLATES, CHALK, AND KEY.

The slates should be quite small. If the performer wishes to restrict himself to two initials, he can use a single slate, placing it with the writing downward. The slate tells one initial, the chalk the other.

In lieu of locked slates, two ordinary slates may be used and bound together by heavy rubber bands, one in each direction. A third rubber band is available in case one should break. This band is used instead of the key to indicate the third initial.

THE BOOK TEST

THIS is the most advanced of all the tests. The performer uses a small, thick book. The committee opens the book and selects a line or word on any page. The performer notes the line or word, closes the book, and puts it on the table. The assistant, entering, picks up the book later on and opens it to find the line or word. A word is preferable to a line if a dictionary is used.

Here we have the mat divided into tens; not units. Square 1 is 10; square 2, 20; and so on. After 120, the tens continue around the table outside of the mat. 130 lies directly above the mat; 140, upper right corner; 150, right of the mat; 160, lower right corner, etc. Thus 200 is the upper left corner of the table.

Beginning again, the squares of the mat have the values 210, 220, and so on; the points that lie outside the mat run 330, 340, up to 400. The book that is used should have less than four hundred pages. Hence the upper left corner of the table is not needed as a 400 indicator. Instead, it is given the value of 0.

To indicate any ten below two hundred, the book is placed on the correct spot, with its title side in view. To indicate any ten above two hundred, the book is placed with its title downward. Inasmuch as the chosen page will probably be a unit, the book is

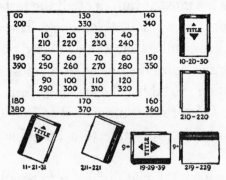

NUMERICAL INDICATIONS USED IN BOOK TEST.

turned to indicate the units, by utilizing the plan of the imaginary clock dial surrounding the book. If the top of the book points to one o'clock, the page number ends in one. Two o'clock, two; three o'clock, three; ten o'clock, zero.

When the assistant enters, she notes the book and in coming to the test, picks up the book, opens to the correct page and finds the line. The performer uses a simple system to indicate the line. In reading the line (or word) to himself, he marks it with his thumbnail. If the whole line is used, he makes the mark beside it. If a single word is used, he marks beneath it. With a dictionary, the performer simply marks at the side of the word.

THE COLORED-PENCIL TEST

THIS is a very ingenious test that may be used in addition to the others or which may replace the ordinary figure test. In order to understand it, refer first to the figure test and its method of indicating numbers of two figures by means of a card or a pencil.

The performer uses three colored pencils: red, blue, and green The committee is told to write two numbers of four figures each, one above the other. These are to be added below a line. The addition is done on the back of a calling-card. The first number is written in one color, the second in another, the third in another; and the committee has absolute choice of the order in which the colors are to be used, for example, green for the first number, red for the second, blue for the total.

There are also three pieces of chalk that correspond in color to the pencils used. The assistant writes with the chalk on the blackboard and duplicates both selected numbers as well as the total in the exact colors of the writing on the card.

The three pencils and the card are used to indicate

the numbers alone. The red pencil shows the first two figures of the first number; the green pencil shows the last two figures of the first number. The blue pencil shows the first two figures of the second number; the card shows the last two figures of the second number. The total is not indicated. The assistant simply adds

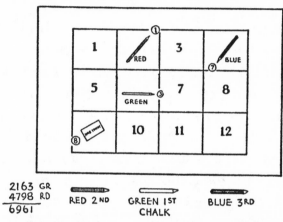

2163 GR
4798 RD
————
6961

RED 2ND   GREEN 1ST   BLUE 3RD
                 CHALK

TWO FOUR-FIGURE NUMBERS ARE INDICATED ON THE MAT. THE CHALK POSITIONS SHOW THE ORDER OF COLORS.

that after writing the two numbers on the blackboard. The order of the colors is indicated by the pieces of chalk. The three pieces are laid in a row, either on the edge of the table or on the base of the blackboard. The center chalk (green, for instance) represents the first number; the chalk on the left (red), the second number; the chalk on the right (blue), the total.

This is merely an elaboration of the figure test and the accompanying illustrations give examples.

PRESENTATION OF THE ACT

THE act may be varied to suit the particular occasion, but the following presentation covers many important points that will make it most effective. The articles that are to be used are lying on the table. After the assistant has left the room, the performer begins the tests. He should start with the slates and the book, utilizing the smaller articles later. This is because both the slates and the book are large objects. They completely cover any square upon which they are placed. Should the cards or pencils require the same square as the slates or the book, the small articles may be placed upon the large ones.

The blackboard is standing beside the table. The assistant, upon entering, immediately observes an article such as the watch, and going to the blackboard, draws a picture of a large clock dial, upon which she registers the time exactly. She asks if that is correct and the watch is turned up so that she can have proof that she was right. That gives her the opportunity to detect the next item—the playing-cards, for instance.

She pretends to be undergoing great concentration and spends most of her time working at the blackboard.

With the book test, she picks up the book and runs through the pages in a thoughtful manner. She stops at different pages and still keeps on a meditative search after she has discovered the marked word. She lays the book on the table and after thinking at the blackboard, writes the chosen word.

The performer either retires or goes to the background as soon as his assistant enters the room. The impression is that he has sent certain thoughts to the woman, but that she is also depending upon the helpful concentration of the committee. After each test, she replaces any article that she has picked up, putting it on the table in the same careless manner adopted by the performer.

Without the blackboard, the woman can name certain thoughts aloud. She can also use a large slate for her writing. The vital part of this performance is effective presentation. The idea of two minds thinking as one must be stressed to the utmost.

Some performers may choose to do the simpler tests only, considering the entire table as divided into twelve squares. This is a good plan in first presenting the act, as it simplifies the work and makes a short, effective routine. But the more involved tests should not be neglected, as they surpass the simpler ones and will bewilder persons who think they have an inkling of the method.

There are certain impromptu tests that can be shown very effectively. The performer may ask for a match box, a cigarette case, a card case, or some similar object. Receiving a match box, he counts the number of matches it contains, closes the box with the matches in it, and lays the box on the table. The woman sees the box and notes that it has been put in simple numerical position, its square indicating the first figure, the way it points, the second figure. She names the number of matches in the box as an addition to her regular routine.

While the routine given here—with the additional impromptu tests—is a wonderful act in itself, many additions and variations will occur to individuals after they have performed the act themselves. They will discover methods of increasing the effectiveness of the act and should not hesitate to make any improvement which they feel sure is of value.

The author recommends this entire act as an excellent and practical demonstration of mental magic. It is one of those deceptions that can be learned and performed by two persons previously unversed in magical methods.

PART NINE.

STAGE ILLUSIONS

HERE is the magic of the illusionist. In building his large magical
show, Houdini constantly added
new illusions and made plans to
build even larger mysteries. The
items in this section include illusions that were built and used and
also those that were planned for
future construction.

DUNNINGER'S SIX CHICKS

THIS stage illusion was originated and designed by Dunninger, from whom Houdini obtained the illusion for stage presentation. A description of the apparatus was among Houdini's notes, crediting the illusion to Dunninger, who has consented to its inclusion in this volume.

A large cabinet is used in the illusion. It is mounted on a high platform and the sides consist of colored slats, the top being solid. Thus the cabinet bears a resemblance to a huge cage, through which the audience can clearly see.

The magician speaks as follows:

"Having presented a series of experiments in which I have made use of a variety of animals, I take pleasure in offering an effect with a number of chickens. I direct your attention to the cabinet, elevated high above the stage; I likewise draw your attention to the simplicity of its construction. With your very kind permission, I will present my six little chicks."

The orchestra plays fast music and six girls hop

upon the stage, wearing chicken costumes. They stand three at a side, with their hands in back of them.

The cabinet and platform are wheeled around to show all sides. The slatted front opens like a door and assistants enter to draw down blinds within the other three sides. This makes the cabinet a solid box with an open front.

The six chicks hop into the cabinet at the magician's command. The slatted door is closed. The girls are plainly visible through the bars. Directly in front of the cabinet is a small stand which contains flash powder. The magician fires several quick shots with a revolver. At the same instant, the charge of powder is ignited. There is a dazzling flash. The cabinet is seen to be empty.

While the spectators stare in bewilderment, the magician orders the dissection of the cabinet. His uniformed assistants proceed with this work. They take down the slatted front and carry it from the stage. They lift off the top. They raise the blind on one side and remove the side. They do the same with the other side. They finally raise the blind at the back and take down the back. Nothing remains but the thin platform, which is wheeled off the stage with various portions of the cabinet upon it. It is a complete disappearance, leaving no clue for the audience.

In considering the construction of this cabinet. it

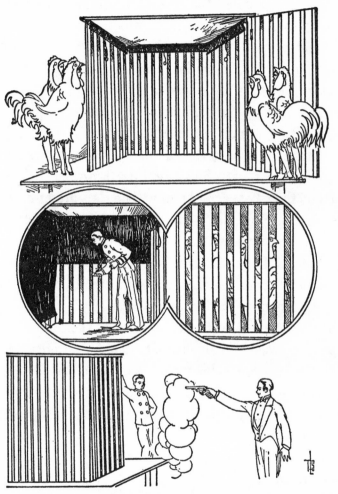

THE "CHICKS" ENTER THE SLATTED CABINET. BLINDS ARE DRAWN.
GIRLS SEEN THROUGH FRONT SLATS. THEY DISAPPEAR.

must first be noted that the platform is considerably larger than the space that forms the bottom of the cabinet proper. There is a ledge all the way around, outside the slatted walls. The blinds that pull down inside the walls are black in color.

The back of the cabinet has a door that opens inward. This is not noticeable. It is well constructed and appears to be part of an ordinary slatted wall.

It is the front of the cabinet, however, that demands the most careful study. The slats are of double thickness. Each slat is wider than the space between it and the next slat. The back portions of the slats are moveable. They slide sideways, in grooves. All moveable portions of the slats are connected by rods at the top and bottom of the frame. Thus, by a simple mechanical operation at the front side of the cabinet, the space between the front slats can be automatically filled by the moveable portions of the slats.

The facings of these moveable portions are painted black. When the spaces between the slats are closed, the cabinet appears to be empty, because the inner blinds are also black and form a dark box when they are drawn down.

The girls, with their light-colored costumes, form a striking contrast when inside the cabinet. They are plainly seen by the audience. The flash powder is the cue for an assistant at the front side of the cabinet.

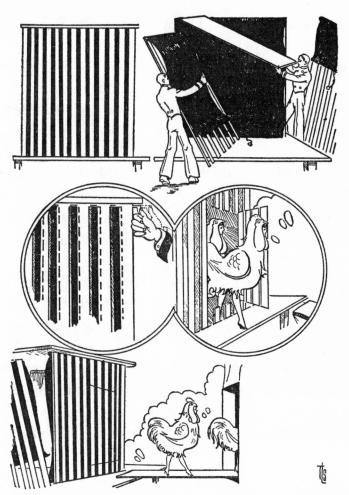

Top, CABINET BEING DISSECTED (ALL CURTAINS RAISED). *Left Center*, SPECIAL "FILL IN" SLATS AT FRONT. *Right Center*, GIRLS STEPPING TO BACK OF CABINET. *Bottom*, PASSING FROM CABINET THROUGH BACK DROP.

He closes the openings between the slats. The movement of the black sections cannot be seen because of the dazzling flash. The shots from the magician's pistol cover the noise of the apparatus.

The magician allows some time for the audience to appreciate the fact that the cabinet is apparently empty. During this interval, the girls are busy. They raise the blind at the back of the cabinet. They open the secret door. They step out and line themselves along the ledge at the rear. They close the door behind them and draw down the blind by reaching between the slats.

When the magician gets the cue that all is ready, he orders the dissection of the cabinet. Just as the back blind was unnecessary while the front slats were closed, so is the closed front unnecessary now. The assistant operates the slides so that the spaces between the slats are reopened. On this occasion, he performs the operation slowly and any slight noise is drowned by the playing of the orchestra. The inside of the cabinet is jet-black—the chicks being gone— and the movement of the sliding portions of the slats cannot be detected.

The front of the cabinet is removed; then the top and the sides. This is not a rapid operation. The cabinet is set near the back of the stage and while the dissection is going on, a trap or panel opens in the

scenery behind the cabinet. The bottom of this opening is above the platform of the cabinet. A board is
pushed through and its end rests on the ledge where
the girls are standing. One by one, the six chicks walk
the plank and stoop as they pass through the open
panel. The board is drawn after them. The panel
closes. By the time the assistants have begun to take
down the back of the cabinet, the last of the six vanished girls is safely away back stage.

FRAME AND CABINET

THE cabinet used in this illusion is a very small one—so small in fact that it can scarcely hold a human being. The cabinet has thin, solid sides and a curtained back. It is mounted on a wheeled platform. The front of the cabinet is a frame covered with thick paper.

When the magician introduces the cabinet, the frame is on the front. The cabinet is wheeled around to show all sides. Then the frame is removed to exhibit the interior. To convince the audience completely that the cabinet is quite empty, the magician lays the frame against the front of the cabinet, to one side. He steps into the cabinet and parts the rear curtain, allowing a view clear through. He closes the curtains, replaces the frame, and awaits results. In a few seconds, the paper bursts and a young lady steps from the cabinet.

This illusion depends upon quick, well-timed presentation. It may be handled by one person—the performer. The girl is in the cabinet when it is

DIAGRAMS SHOW IMPORTANT STAGES OF THE ILLUSION. NOTE GIRL
BEHIND FRAME WHEN CURTAINS ARE SHOWN EMPTY. ALSO
THE POSITION SHE TAKES BEHIND CURTAINS.

wheeled around at the center of the stage. While the magician is removing the frame—a task that requires several seconds, the girl parts the curtains and goes to the back of the platform. She closes the curtains in front of her, so that she is not seen when the frame is removed.

After exhibiting the frame, the illusionist sets it carelessly against the front post of the cabinet, on the right side. This is necessary so that he may enter the cabinet and spread the curtains. While the magician is stepping into the cabinet, the girl takes the cue and steps off the back to the stage, making a long step so that her feet will not be seen beneath the platform. She virtually comes around to the side of the cabinet when she performs this action. As a result, the girl is out of view, being hidden behind the frame that projects from the cabinet.

As the magician closes the rear curtains, the girl again steps on the platform and makes her way to the back. She is safely there before the magician picks up the frame. When the frame is in position, the girl spreads the curtains and enters the cabinet. Another wheeling of the cabinet would be superfluous. All is ready for the appearance of the girl, which takes place when the magician gives the cue.

The notes suggest a lithograph showing the picture of the girl. This would make an excellent front for the frame, although a sheet of white paper is quite effective and does not give a direct suggestion of the appearance which is due to follow.

THE CASK ILLUSION

THIS is a very bold illusion, as it is performed while a committee is upon the stage. The method is quite unusual. The magician invites several persons to come on the stage to examine a large cask, which is more than twice the size of an ordinary barrel. The cask is in the center of the stage and it proves to be quite empty. Attention is called to a skeleton platform. The committee examines all parts of the platform. When all are satisfied that the cask and the cabinet are empty, the assistants invert the heavy cask by means of metal handles on the sides. The magician lets a committee member pound the sides and the bottom of the cask, proving its solidity.

The people on the stage take chairs at the sides. The assistants lift the cask and carry it to the platform, turning it so it is upright. The magician approaches with a sheet of paper, which he places over the top of the cask. A metal hoop is put upon the paper. It is hammered into place so that the top of the cask is covered with a drumhead. A pistol shot follows. The paper bursts and a man emerges from the cask.

The occupant of the cask makes his entry through a trap in the stage. The whole procedure is designed to mislead the committee as well as the audience. Those who might suspect a trap would naturally suspect the bottom of the cask also. But the person does not come through the bottom of the cask. The actual entry is made when the cask is inverted.

There is one peculiarity about the interior of the cask. That is the presence of short metal rods near the bottom. They are scarcely noticeable and appear to be there to reinforce the construction. But their purpose is different. The cask is on the trap at the beginning, when the committee comes upon the stage. The case completely covers the trap. When the cask is inverted, its mouth comes over the trap, which opens while the bottom is being hammered. This covers all noise made by the man who comes up through the trap. He seizes the bars at the bottom of the cask and hangs by them while the trap closes.

The assistants lift the cask and carry it in its inverted position. This substantiates the idea that the cask is still empty. In setting the cask top up, it is turned away from the audience, so that no one gains a view of the interior. The concealed man hangs close to the bottom. He cannot be seen, because the cask is large inside.

CASK SHOWN EMPTY. BOTTOM STRUCK TO SHOW SOLIDITY.

The rest of the illusion is a matter of routine. The paper is affixed to the top of the cask while it is isolated on the platform and the man within makes his appearance as soon as the magician fires the revolver.

CASK LIFTED TO PLATFORM AND TOPPED WITH PAPER. MAN AP-
PEARS. *Bottom*, ASSISTANT ENTERING INVERTED CASK THROUGH
STAGE TRAP.

A VANISH IN MID-AIR

THE notes concerning this illusion state that the idea was described to Houdini by the famous magician, Chung Ling Soo, an American who gained great success in the guise of a Chinese wizard. Soo was none other than Billy Robinson, formerly stage manager for Herrmann the Great. He was the creator of many startling effects in magic. This mid-air vanish is typical of his ingenuity.

A board is resting on the stage or upon a raised platform. The magician introduces his assistant, who is placed upon the board and fastened to it by straps. The board is carried to the back of the stage, where it is placed upon a metal framework or trestle, which is specially designed to receive it. The board rests firmly in the metal frame, which is tilted forward at an angle of forty-five degrees, so that the entire audience can see the assistant.

The framework is within an open-fronted cabinet. It is well away from the sides, back, and top of the cabinet, which are made of plain cloth. There is no

ASSISTANT STRAPPED TO BOARD, WHICH IS PLACED IN FRAME
WITHIN CABINET.

opportunity for the assistant to make a quick get-away. The magician stands at one side of the stage and aims a pistol at the cabinet. He fires a shot; there is a puff of smoke from the front of the cabinet. In a flash, the board falls to the stage. The man is gone. The skeleton framework is unoccupied. The board is picked up and carried forward. It is merely a thin slab of wood, its straps hanging loose. The assistant has escaped and disappeared—performing both wonders in the fraction of a second!

The explanation lies in both the board and the frame, while the cabinet plays a certain part in the mystery. The board is double. It is actually two boards, held together by metal catches. The top board has straps that do not pass completely through it. Its under side is a thin, highly polished metal mirror. The lower board is a thin one, which is fitted with straps on its bottom surface. The double board is not exhibited closely before the vanish. The assistant is strapped to it. It is immediately tilted forward and carried to the framework. No one sees the bottom of the board.

The framework is a mechanical device. It is supported between two pivot rods—one at each end. These are arranged so that the operation of a simple releasing device will cause the entire frame to make a semirevolution, turning away from the audience.

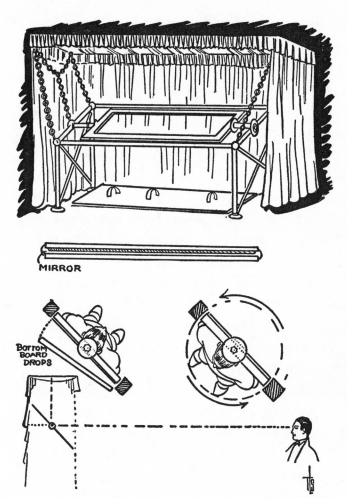

MIRROR

Top, BOARD DROPS. ASSISTANT VANISHES. *Center,* DOUBLE BOARD.
LOWER PORTION DROPS WHEN CATCH IS RELEASED. *Bottom,*
LOWER BOARD FALLING. ASSISTANT BENEATH REVOLVING UPPER
BOARD. NOTE THE SPECTATOR'S LINE OF VISION. MIRROR RE-
FLECTS TOP OF CABINET.

The same operation causes the loose lower board to fall from the upper one, which is securely in the frame.

When the magician fires his pistol, the machinery is set in motion. Coincident with the half-turn of the frame comes a puff of smoke and bright light from the front of the cabinet. This prevents the spectators from observing exactly what happens. The most that can be seen is a slight motion of the frame. The lower board drops as the frame revolves. It strikes the stage. The upper board stops with its mirrored side upward. The polished surface reflects the top of the cabinet, which is identical in appearance to the back. The spectators can apparently see through the framework. It looks absolutely empty. The dropping of the dummy board is the subtle touch that renders the deception perfect.

The boards that are used should be wide and long. This prevents any view of the man beneath the mirrored board. The forty-five-degree angle is sufficient to keep him completely out of sight. The depth and height of the cabinet are properly arranged so that the reflection of the top will appear to be the background. The dummy straps on the lower board appear to be the actual straps which held the vanished man.

As the board is brought forward, a curtain falls, ob-

scuring the presumably empty cabinet. This enables
assistants to remove the mirrored board from the
frame and to release the hidden man. The illusion
should be presented on full stage, as the concluding
number of a magical act. It is an excellent trick, since
the mechanical operation can be made simple and
sure. With proper construction, this illusion should
work with perfect precision and its action is so fast
that there is no chance of the spectators' realizing
what takes place.

SAWING A WOMAN INTO TWINS

HOUDINI had many ideas for improvements of old illusions. One of the most sensational of modern stage tricks was the illusion of "sawing a woman in half," which was exhibited by many magicians with many variations. When Houdini started out with his full evening show, the sawing trick was no longer a novelty. He did not use it in his program. Nevertheless he, like many other magicians, gave considerable thought to the possibilities of presenting the illusion in a new guise.

His notes contain the details of a new variation of the sawing trick. This material gives the basic principles of the idea, with many suggestions for actual working. The following description and explanation have been developed from the notes.

The illusion begins with the exhibition of a long oblong box, which is resting on a large square platform. The platform is turned around to exhibit all sides of the box. The box has two doors in front and

SAWING A WOMAN INTO TWINS. CUTTING THE CABINET.

two doors on top. These are opened before the box is turned around.

A large woman comes on the stage and takes a reclining position in the oblong box. The illusionist closes the doors and the assistants carry in two sawhorses, which are set in front of the platform. Each front door of the box has sectional divisions and these are equipped with small curtains. The magician raises a curtain near one end to speak to the woman. This proves to be the foot end of the box, so he lifts the curtain near the other end, revealing the woman's head as well as her feet. This is done as the assistants pick up the box and place it upon the sawhorses.

The woman gives her consent to the performance. The illusionist closes the curtains and calls for a huge saw. He and an assistant saw the box in half. The two sections are turned so that the cut ends are away from the spectators and the halves are taken completely apart. A woman has apparently been cut in half.

Now comes the surprising conclusion. Instead of restoring the woman—as in the old sawing trick—the magician has the boxes turned so that the open ends are toward the audience. As the boxes turn, their half-lids open and each box is seen to contain a small girl, dressed to resemble the woman who originally appeared. The woman has been sawed into twins!

The explanation is found chiefly in the platform

on which the box is first exhibited. The platform is nearly square. There is considerable space behind the box. In the platform is a compartment, which starts from beneath the box and continues to the back. When the front doors and the top of the box are opened, the two little girls, who are concealed in the platform, open lids above their hiding-place and take their positions behind the box. All this is concealed by the box and its doors. The action does not take place until after the platform had been turned around.

When the girls are safely behind the box, the doors and lid are closed. The bottom of the box is released. It goes downward at the back of the box, being hinged at the front. The platform beneath it acts in a similar manner. This enables the large woman to enter the platform. She moves out to the back; the bottom of the box and the top of the platform come back into their normal places, actuated by springs. These portions lock securely.

The back panels of the box are really secret doors. The small girls open them inward and one enters each section of the box. They close the secret doors behind them. The girl at the head end of the box lies with her knees doubled up; the girl at the foot end takes a sitting position with her feet extended.

By this time, the sawhorses are on the stage. Assistants raise the box. It is placed on the horses. The illusionist opens the curtains. He reveals the head of one girl and the feet of the other. This leads the audience to believe that the woman is still in the box. After the curtains are lowered, the sawing commences. The saw follows a regular path. In fact, the box is really two separate sections, which are temporarily joined by thin boards. There is no danger to the girls, as the saw goes between them.

When the sawing is completed, the open ends of the box are turned away so that each girl can be ready in a normal sitting position. Then the open ends are turned toward the audience. Acting on this cue, the girls raise the lids and make their appearance. They come front and do a dance while the sections of the box are shown by the assistants, placed on the platform, and wheeled away.

This illusion has excellent possibilities. It adds an element of comedy to the trick. The finish is surprising. It requires considerable speed in the changing of positions in order to produce its full effectiveness.

The box—as has been mentioned—is really two sections temporarily joined. This means that the box is not destroyed with each performance. It can be easily repaired by using new strips of wood between the sections.

Houdini's notes suggest means of bringing the girls behind the box from the wings instead of the plat-

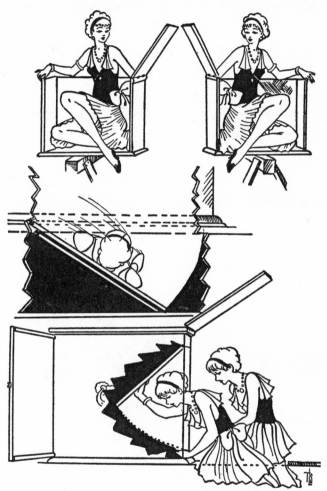

Top, THE TWINS APPEAR FROM THE SEPARATED BOXES. *Below*, ESCAPE OF WOMAN INTO PLATFORM. TWINS COME FROM PLATFORM AND ENTER THROUGH THE BACK.

form, but such a plan would not be as practicable as the use of the special platform with the girls concealed at the outset. The only quick way to dispose of the large woman is in the platform; and since the platform is to be utilized for that purpose, the concealment of the small girls there is the better plan.

SARDINES IN OIL

THIS is a very novel stage illusion. The principal object on the stage is a huge flat can of sardines. The mammoth container rests upon a skeleton platform, which is wheeled around by the magician's assistants, so that all sides may be observed.

The illusionist steps up on the platform. An assistant brings him a giant can-opener. He runs around the edges of the tin can, opening the front and the sides. The assistants slide back the lid and the performer steps into the tin can to prove that it is entirely empty. The front of the can is lifted upward on hinges so that the spectators can see into the interior.

The lid is pushed back in place. A net is stretched in front of the platform, running to a metal rod, supported on two upright legs. The front of the can rises of its own accord. Out flaps a human sardine—an assistant garbed in fish costume. This is repeated. One by one six giant "sardines" arrive upon the scene. They scramble from the net and stand in a line on the stage.

GIANT SARDINE CAN SHOWN EMPTY. THE "SARDINES" APPEAR.

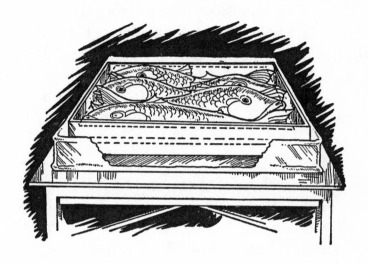

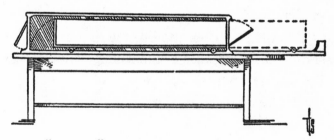

HOW THE "SARDINES" ARE PACKED. NOTE HOW INNER CONTAINER
SLIDES BACK ON TRACK WHEN TOP IS DRAWN OPEN.

This large sardine can is of double construction. It has an inner section which is really a drawer, permanently attached to the lid. The drawer has a hinged flap in front. This is closed. The human sardines lie packed in the inner drawer. The back of the drawer is the back of the can. It has hinges at the bottom so it can be opened from the outside to enable the "sardines" to pack themselves before the trick.

After the platform is revolved, the assistants step to the back while the illusionist is at work with the can-opener. He merely cuts a silver paper binding that makes the top of the can appear to be tightly shut. After completing the front and sides, he concludes his work. Meanwhile the assistants have pulled out two tracks that extend backward from the platform. The inner drawer is mounted on rollers. When the assistants pull back the lid, the drawer goes with it, sliding easily because of the rollers. The flap front of the drawer appears as the back of the interior of the can. The lid conceals the drawer and its contents.

When the lid is slid back over the can, the drawer moves into place. The assistants push the tracks into the platform. Everything is ready for the appearance of the human sardines, who roll into view, one by one.

The accompanying illustrations show the effect of the illusion as the audience sees it, while the diagrams explain the details of the apparatus.

THE TRANSFORMATION CABINET

THE purpose of this illusion is to cause the transformation of the performer, who changes into another person while isolated in an open-front cabinet six feet above the stage. The cabinet is simply a box, with no opportunity for concealment, as it is hardly large enough to contain the performer.

The magician climbs a ladder and sits in the cabinet, facing the audience. The assistants arrange two ladders, one on each side of the cabinet. They bring on a large cloth and spread it on the stage. Each takes a corner of the cloth as it lies directly below the cabinet. They mount the ladder step by step until the bottom of the cloth is above the stage. The magician is concealed from view but there is no chance of his escape. The spectators can see above, below, and on all sides. The pole on which the cabinet is mounted is by far too small to accommodate a living person.

After a few moments, the assistants slowly descend the ladders. The top of the cabinet comes in view, then the front. Instead of the performer, another person is seen—in the illustration, a girl. The assistants reach the stage. They spread out the cloth. The ladder is put in front of the cabinet and the new arrival descends to the stage.

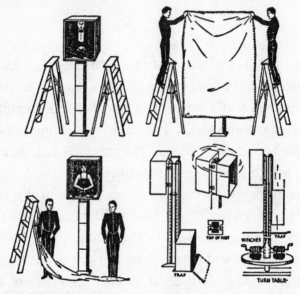

THE ILLUSTRATIONS SHOW THE CHANGE OF THE PERFORMER FOR AN ASSISTANT. THE DIAGRAMS GIVE THE CONSTRUCTION OF THE POST AND MECHANISM BENEATH STAGE.

The secret of this illusion involves various mechanical details, which are illustrated in the diagrams. It should first be noted that the cabinet is not mounted on the top of the pole. It is suspended from the front of the pole. The audience does not know exactly what holds it there. The pole is hollow and a cable comes up from beneath the stage and out of the top of the pole. It holds the cabinet.

There is also a second cabinet—a replica of the first. This is beneath the stage. It is attached to the bottom of the pole, which runs beneath the stage, the base that the audience sees being merely a dummy. A second cable runs up through the center of the hollow pole, over the top, and down the back through the stage. It connects with the second cabinet.

As soon as the assistants spread the large cloth and prepare to ascend the ladders, a trap door opens behind the pole and the man below stage turns a winch that raises the duplicate cabinet. It comes up behind the cloth, traveling at the same rate of speed as the assistants. When the cloth has covered the cabinet that contains the magician, the duplicate cabinet is in place behind the original.

We must now consider the construction of the pole. It is nothing but a hollow shell below the cabinet. Inside it is a round metal pole, also hollow. The cables pass through this pole. The top part of the square pole—that is, the portion behind the cabinet —is also metal and is permanently attached to the round pole. The round pole is mounted on a turntable below stage. On this table are the winches that control the pulleys.

As soon as the rear cabinet is in place, the table is

turned. The inner round pole and the upper portion of the square pole revolve as one piece, bringing the duplicate cabinet to the rear and the original cabinet to the front.

The assistants are then ready to lower the cloth. The winch that controls the performer's cabinet is released. His cabinet travels downward behind the cloth. The trap door was closed as soon as the duplicate cabinet had cleared it. Now it opens, when the cloth touches the stage. The magician and his cabinet pass through the trap; the trap closes and the work is done.

The back of the shell pole and both the front and the back of the revolving square portion are grooved. Behind each cabinet are little wheels that fit into the grooves. These enable the cabinets to run smoothly up and down the pole. The turntable is located some five feet below the level of the stage so as to allow room for the cabinet and the operators who work below stage.

Each cabinet should be fronted with a thin gauze blind. This is pulled down by the performer after he is in place. When the second cabinet is revealed, the blind is not raised until the assistants have lowered the cloth. The purpose of the blind is to keep the spectators from seeing exactly who is in the cabinet, although a form is visible through the gauze. This keeps attention on the cabinet, particularly at the conclusion of the illusion. If the girl should be fully revealed the instant that the cloth came below the cabinet, people would be searching for clues before the trick was completed.

The illustrations show the effect as well as the explanation. The gauze curtains are not illustrated. They must be considered as an additional item that adds to the effect. The pole is marked into ornamental sections so that no suspicion will be attached to the actual break which is necessary just below the level of the cabinet.

DE KOLTA'S ILLUSION

BUATIER DE KOLTA was one of the outstanding geniuses of magic. He invented many remarkable illusions and utilized principles which have since been adopted by many magicians. Among Houdini's notes was a description of an illusion performed by De Kolta which has never, to the auther's knowledge, been described in print. Houdini's notation bears the date January 13, 1905—less than three years after the death of De Kolta. It states that the illusion was successful at a private showing and was later presented on the stage of the Winter Garden in Berlin.

The illusion is the disappearance of a woman. She stands at the center of the stage and is covered with a large flag, held by the performer. The magician commands her to walk forward. She advances slowly toward the footlights. The magician fires a pistol. The flag collapses. The woman is gone.

The trick is accomplished by means of a wire frame which is worn by the woman. The frame is collapsible. Two strong threads—or thin wires—are attached to

it. One thread starts from the head of the frame. It
passes through a hook overhead toward the front of

A GIRL DISAPPEARS INSTANTANEOUSLY FROM BENEATH A CLOTH.

the stage. Then it travels to the rear. There is an extension of this thread that leads off backward from

the frame, so the thread virtually forms a loop which may be controlled by the performer or a hidden assistant.

The other thread is attached to the bottom of the frame. It passes forward along the stage, through a hook, and back to the controller. The woman enters wearing the frame; the threads are pulled taut as the magician drapes her with the flag. He takes care to conceal the frame entirely beneath the cloth.

While the adjustment is being made, the woman slips away from the frame and enters a large table at the back of the stage. This is close behind the spot where the performer is standing. The magician steps away and tells the woman to step forward. The threads are drawn and the form gives the appearance of the woman slowly advancing. The correct manipulation of the bottom thread produces the semblance of a walk.

When the form reaches the desired spot, the magician fires a pistol. The upper thread is released. The form collapses and the flag drops upon it.

An illusion of this type requires careful handling and proper adjustments in order to be effective. Lighting is an important factor. Simple though the explanation proves to be, it is this type of illusion that creates the greatest impression when properly performed. It is a typical De Kolta illusion.

There are optional methods whereby the woman

Top, FRAME IN CLOTH. HOW THREATS OPERATE THE FLIMSY DUMMY. *Bottom,* GIRL ESCAPING INTO TABLE BEHIND CLOTH. NOTE COLLAPSE OF FRAME.

could make her getaway. A stage trap or an opening in the scene close behind would dispense with the use of the table.

THE FLIGHT OF VENUS

THIS illusion is of special interest, as it is one which Houdini planned for many years: the vanishing of a girl placed on a sheet of plate glass. Houdini mentioned this effect to the author on several occasions. An illusion involving a sheet of plate glass and a girl was described in a magical publication which appeared shortly after Houdini's death, but it was not the illusion to which Houdini referred. He specified that in his illusion, no stage traps were necessary; and the trick that was published required a trap.

The author was pleased to find a description of the plate-glass illusion, with its explanation, among Houdini's notes. There is no certainty, however, that this was the final form to which Houdini had developed the idea. The illusion, as explained, is certainly unique. Its practicability could only be demonstrated by actual experiment. Houdini spoke of the illusion as though it were completely designed and merely awaiting actual construction. It is probable

Top, THE GIRL IS PLACED ON A SHEET OF GLASS. *Bottom*, THE GIRL
IS COVERED WITH A CLOTH.

that he made further plans for it after writing the brief explanation which appears in his notes. Yet there is no proof that he departed from the fundamental principle that he originally decided to use.

As the audience sees it, two Hindu assistants are standing on the stage when the curtain rises. They are facing the side of the stage. Between them they hold a sheet of plate glass. The magician introduces a girl clad in a scanty costume. She assumes a reclining position upon the sheet of plate glass. The magician and an assistant cover her with a large cloth. While the cloth completely hides the girl and the glass, it at no time touches the stage. There is absolutely no opportunity for the girl to escape by means of a trap. The men are standing well forward and there are no wings near by.

A few moments after the cloth has been placed upon the girl, the magician whisks it away. The girl has vanished. The sheet of glass is transparent. She has apparently disappeared into thin air. The assistants carry the glass from the stage.

Now for the explanation. The foremost Hindu is a dummy figure. The figure is hollow and is considerably larger than the girl. As soon as the girl is covered by the cloth, she moves forward and enters the dummy figure. The form has no back. The opening is covered by a coat which is cut down the middle and

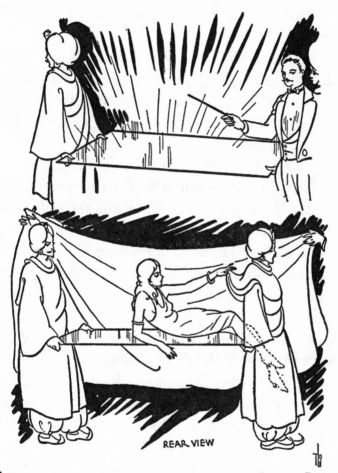

REAR VIEW

Top, THE GIRL DISAPPEARS WHEN CLOTH IS REMOVED. *Bottom,*
HOW THE GIRL ENTERS THE DUMMY FIGURE.

held taut with strips of elastic. The girl's tight-fitting costume enables her to enter the figure without difficulty.

When the cloth is removed, the girl is gone. She walks off inside the figure, carrying the front end of the glass. In doing so, she turns toward the back of the stage, to keep the spectators from observing the figure too closely.

There are certain important details which must be considered in connection with the illusion. As described, with two assistants, it is doubtful whether the dummy figure could remain upright and support the end of the glass. The illusion has been described and illustrated with two assistants—one a dummy—in order to clarify the idea. The notes, however, suggest the use of four assistants dressed as Hindus. The advantages of such an arrangement are obvious. With one man at each of the three corners of a large sheet of glass, the dummy figure could be stationed at the far corner at the front. A man would be between the figure and the audience, obscuring a close view of the dummy. Furthermore, the man at the front of the glass could support all the weight so that the dummy figure would bear none of the strain and would actually be supported by the glass itself. This arrangement greatly increases the practical possibilities of the idea. With four men holding the glass, there would be less suspicion on the part of keen observers.

To make the illusion most effective, the cloth should contain a wire frame resembling the form of the woman. Her entrance into the dummy figure is effected while the cloth is being held in front of the glass. With the wire frame, the cloth can be placed upon the glass and left there, apparently covering the girl. In the vanish, the cloth is swept away and crushed, the light frame collapsing within it. There is no possibility of the girl's being in the cloth. The clear glass, well above the stage, alone remains.

Correct construction of the dummy figure, proper lighting conditions, and precise routine are essential factors in this illusion. Much of its success depends upon the ability of the performer who presents it.

THE GIANT BALL OF WOOL

CERTAIN successful stage illusions have been adapted from smaller tricks, while on some occasions, the principles of stage illusions have been applied to a smaller scale. This illusion is an outgrowth of a famous old trick—the production of a missing article in the center of a ball of wool.

In this instance, the missing article is a girl who has vanished in some mysterious way. Suspended on a trapeze is a solid ball of heavy wool. The end of the wool is attached to a huge reel. An assistant unwinds the wool, the ball revolving as he does so.

When the wool is nearly unwound, the lady makes her appearance. She pushes aside the remaining strands and emerges from the ball of wool, dropping to the stage to receive the applause of the audience.

This effect is obtained by very simple means. The girl is in the ball of wool from the outset. She is made up as the double of the girl who previously disappeared. The diagrams show the construction of the apparatus. There are two spheres connected to the

THE HUGE BALL OF WOOL IS UNWOUND. A GIRL APPEARS FROM ITS
COILS.

trapeze, both attached to pivot rods. The outer sphere is made of thin wire which is covered with the wool. This sphere revolves when the wool is unwound.

The inner sphere does not revolve. Each pivot rod is hollow and contains a central axis which is stationary. The inner sphere is a strong framework of metal, open at the front. It is covered with a thin layer of wool. It has a platform at the bottom, upon which the lady rests.

She is put in this place before the presentation of the illusion. The strands at the back of the ball of wool are parted to allow the woman to obtain air. When the time arrives to unwind the ball of wool, she closes the loose strands in the back.

The ball is unrolled. When it reaches the thin wire sphere, the assistant stops and the woman spreads the strands in both the inner and the outer sphere, thus making her way into view of the audience. It is unnecessary to unwind the ball of wool after the woman appears. Hence the illusion is concluded before either the thin wire frame or the center sphere has been completely revealed.

This illusion offers a highly effective conclusion to a series of disappearances, as the ball of wool can be on the stage for some time before it is used. The trick will prove of interest to the audience and it has sufficient elements of mystery to make it worthy of presentation.

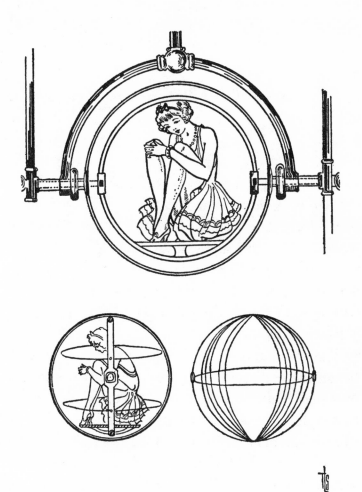

CONSTRUCTION OF APPARATUS, SHOWING INNER BALL WHICH DOES NOT REVOLVE. NOTE WIRE COVERING THAT HOLDS WOOL, THROUGH WHICH GIRL FORCES HER WAY.

A VANISH FROM A LADDER

THE disappearance of a girl from the top of a ladder is not a new idea in stage illusions; but in the form described in Houdini's notes, it includes certain details that add greatly to the effectiveness of the trick. The ladder that is used is broad and heavy, with large rungs. It is held upright by two assistants, who support it near the rear of the stage, in front of a low, ornamental picket fence.

The girl climbs the ladder and sits on the top rung, facing the audience. She raises a cloth and drapes it over her head and shoulders. Then the ladder begins to topple. The assistants have trouble holding it. They lift it and carry it toward the front of the stage. The cloth falls to the floor. There is a scream—the girl is gone! The assistants carry the ladder to the footlights and take it from the stage.

The secret lies partly in the construction of the ladder and partly in the ornamental picket fence. Along the back of the fence is a cloth that matches the background of the stage setting. There is a space between the fence and the back curtain. The ladder has a special rung, which is the same distance above the stage as the top of the picket fence. This rung is merely a shell, open in the back. It contains a roller blind, the same color as the back drop. The end of the blind has projecting rods which extend to the sides of the ladder.

When the girl climbs the ladder, she naturally places her hands upon the sides. In this manner, she draws up the blind as she climbs. The blind stretches from the special rung to the top rung, where the girl hooks the loose end to two special catches behind the back of the ladder. The movement of the blind is hidden by the girl's body. When she seats herself upon the top rung, the spectators still believe that they see between the upper rungs of the ladder.

With the cloth in front of her, the girl draws two sets of wire rods from the posts of the ladder. These are fitted with springs and they form a mechanical holder for the cloth. The girl is free to slip from behind the cloth. She drops in back of the ladder, behind the picket fence. The roller blind and the cloth behind the pickets hide her departure.

When the girl is safely away, the assistants begin to let the ladder sway. They grip the ladder near the top and release the catch which holds the blind. It springs down behind the rung as the ladder is carried

THE GIRL CLIMBS A LADDER. SHE RAISES A CLOTH.

THE CLOTH FALLS. THE GIRL IS GONE! EXPLANATORY DIAGRAMS
SHOW "GETAWAY." NOTE ARRANGEMENT OF PROJECTING WIRES
FROM TOP OF POST. THESE HOLD THE CLOTH. ALSO OPERATION
OF BLIND THAT MATCHES THE SCENERY.

forward. Another release on the part of the assistants causes strong springs to draw the telescopic rods into the legs of the ladder. The cloth falls to the floor. The girl screams from behind the picket fence. She is gone and the evanishment seems unexplainable.

The ladder may be shown near the footlights before and after the exhibition, which gives this illusion a most convincing effect.

PART TEN.

SPECIAL STAGE EFFECTS

THESE are mysteries of the illusion type which are different from the usual items that compose a magician's program. They have been placed in a separate section to distinguish them from general stage illusions.

LIVING-HEAD ILLUSION

THIS is an improvement on the old stage and side-show illusion of the "living head," which was introduced in its original form some seventy years ago and which has appeared in many varied forms.

An upright box is set in the center of the stage. It is a cabinet about six feet in height, somewhat like an oversized victrola. There are doors in the center. These are opened to reveal a narrow cross-shelf on which rests the living head of a woman. The head speaks and proves conclusively that it is alive.

The spectators can see below and above the head. They observe two closed doors at the rear of the cabinet. The magician closes the front doors, hiding the head from view. Then he opens all four doors so that people can see directly through the cabinet to the scene behind it. The head rests upon the shelf during the entire exhibition, after which the doors are closed and the cabinet is wheeled away.

The first part of the illusion is entirely an old principle. The space in which the head appears is cubical in shape. A mirror runs at an angle of forty-five degrees from the lower front of the opening to the upper rear. The mirror is actually in two sections—the narrow shelf forming the division. There is a hole in the

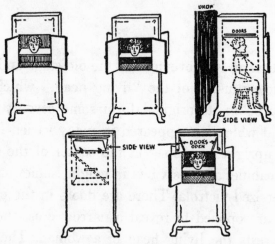

CONSTRUCTION OF CABINET FOR THE LIVING HEAD. NOTE ARRANGEMENT OF MIRROR. DOORS OPENING ABOVE THE HEAD SHOW TOP OF CABINET, WHICH MATCHES BACK DROP, GIVING ILLUSION OF "CLEAR THROUGH" VISION.

shelf. The woman sits in the lower part of the cabinet with her head through the opening in the shelf.

The mirror reflects the upper portion of the cabinet. In the usual version, the reflected surface would simply be covered with a light-colored cloth. It appears to be the back of the cabinet. Houdini's improvement, however, involves the opening of doors in the rear. Hence the surface above the woman's head is patterned in the form of two doors. Those who look into the cabinet see the head on the shelf and the doors apparently behind the head.

The magician then closes the front doors. In opening all the doors of the cabinet, he opens the back doors first. This operation causes the dummy doors to open upward. This is due to a mechanical connection. At the very top of the cabinet is an interior lining which matches the screenlike scene behind the cabinet. Hence when the front doors are opened, the spectators apparently see through the open rear doors to the scene in back. In reality they are observing the reflection of the inner surface at the top of the cabinet.

The cabinet must be in its exact position to make this illusion effective. The distance from the shelf to the top of the cabinet must be exactly the same as the distance from the shelf to the screen behind. The same applies to the positions of the fake doors above the head and the real doors at the back of the cabinet. Those in the audience never see the inside of the back doors, but they do see the latter project when opened from in back. Hence they expect to see through and believe they do see through.

ART AND NATURE

MAGICIANS frequently make use of mechanical transformations or stage effects which cannot be classed as actual mysteries. This idea, entitled "Art and Nature," is a surprising effect of a semi-magical nature. It begins with a large pedestal in the center of the stage. The pedestal suddenly becomes a farmer seated in front of a tree stump, with a wheelbarrow before him.

The diagrams give a very definite explanation of the transformation. The secret lies entirely in the pedestal. It is hollow. The farmer is inside it. The pedestal springs open when released. It is divided into five sections. The rear section is stationary. There is a break directly in front of the farmer and the sections spread out to represent a tree trunk. There are spring hinges at each connection. This is illustrated in the diagram, which shows the view from above.

The sectional view of the pedestal shows the farmer and also the position of the catch that holds the front

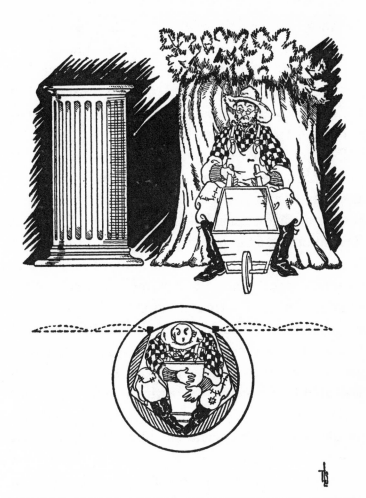

A PEDESTAL BECOMES A FARMER WITH WHEELBARROW, IN FRONT
OF A STUMP. THE DIAGRAM GIVES A TOP VIEW OF THE PEDES-
TAL, SHOWING HOW IT OPENS.

together. The catch is on the top of the pedestal. The farmer releases it. The front springs straight upward. Its lower side is covered with the artificial foliage that represents the leaves on top of the tree trunk. The spring foliage is packed inside the top of the pedestal, above the farmer's head.

The collapsible wheelbarrow is represented in all the explanatory diagrams. The drawings that show the operation of the pedestal indicate the position of the wheelbarrow when held by the farmer. The wheel lies flat on the axle, bringing it flush with the barrow frame. When the pedestal opens, the wheel is free to swing at right angles to the frame, actuated by a weight when the barrow is lowered. The sides and ends of the wheelbarrow are collapsed flat upon the frame. They spring up when released. The handle and the legs of the barrow pull out of the frame, the weighted legs dropping on a swing pivot.

The transformation is accomplished very quickly, as all the necessary operations blend, following each other automatically. The construction of the apparatus is very ingenious and the change of the pedestal is certain to prove a surprise to the audience. This trick would be suitable for a revue as well as for a magical entertainment.

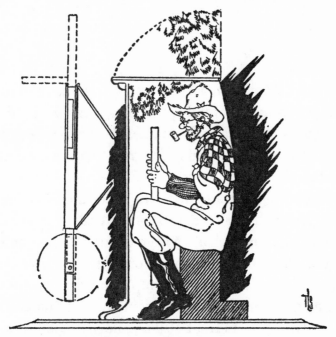

DETAILS IN CONSTRUCTION OF UNFOLDING WHEELBARROW. ALSO
OPERATION OF THE PEDESTAL.

THE DECAPITATION ACT

THE decapitation act is a complete scene in itself. It involves several principles, and while the routine is comparatively simple, the performance is filled with surprises and is designed to make a strong effect upon the witnesses.

The rising curtain discloses a torture chamber. The scenery is painted to represent the interior of a prison. The magician is a grim inquisitor who stands in the center of this dismal room. At the left of the stage is a flat, raised platform. At the right stands a sturdy guillotine. It is set at right angles to the audience. To its left, in front of the knife blade, is a small basket. In the foreground is a much longer basket, which has a hinged cover.

Two jailers enter. Between them they are conducting a helpless prisoner. He is brought before the inquisitor, who points silently to the guillotine. The prisoner turns and gazes despairingly toward the stone archways at the back of the stage. He pleads with the magician, but to no avail. In desperation, he breaks loose from his captors and flees for safety. He is caught and brought back to the inquisitor, who sentences him to instant death. He is laid upon the guillotine, a framework high above the stage. His head projects from the front of the guillotine. The magician releases the blade. The prisoner's head is severed from his body. It drops into the small basket which awaits it. The assistants lift the body and drop it into the long basket in front of the guillotine. They close the lid of the basket while the magician exhibits the head of the victim.

He brings a cloth from the basket and uses it to cover the gruesome object. He looks about him for a place to put this trophy of the execution. Spying the table at the opposite side of the stage, he goes there and carefully sets the head upon it. He carefully lifts the cloth and again reveals the head. It rests motionless for a moment. Then, the head turns. The lips move. Gradually, the head shows absolute signs of life. It speaks accusingly to the magician and demands that it be restored to its body. The magician covers the head with the cloth, to free his mind of this menace. The head still speaks in muffled tones. The magician calls for the basket which contains the body of the guillotined prisoner. Lifting the head beneath the cloth, he puts it in the basket. The lid is closed; a moment later it opens of its own accord to reveal the prisoner restored to life, his head safely upon his shoulders.

The act is performed with the aid of three persons, all of whom represent the prisoner. One—a double of the prisoner—is concealed in the large table at the left of the stage. The other is a short man. He wears a cloak over his head and upon it is a dummy head that resembles the prisoner. This man is concealed at the back of the stage. He stands behind the pillar between the two archways. When the original prisoner escapes from the jailers, he runs through the arch at the right and apparently reappears through the arch at the left. In reality, he goes through an opening in the back drop directly behind the pillar. It is the false-headed assistant who emerges and comes back upon the stage.

The action is now very rapid. Constantly struggling, the prisoner is carried to the guillotine. The axe, which has no sharp edge, is released and it strikes off the dummy head. This is carefully rehearsed so that the man on the frame runs no risk—in fact a papier-mâché axe is sufficient to create the illusion. The body—apparently headless—is dropped into the long basket. The dummy head is carried across stage and placed upon the table. It is covered with a cloth that contains a wire form to retain the shape of the head. The man in the table reaches through a trap in

THE DECAPITATION SCENE. THE LARGE DIAGRAM SHOWS HIDDEN
ASSISTANTS—ONE BEHIND POST; THE OTHER IN TABLE AT
LEFT. THE LOWER DIAGRAMS SHOW THE OPERATION OF TRAP
IN TABLE. ALSO THE DUMMY HEAD AND HOW ASSISTANT WEARS
IT. THE ESCAPE AND RETURN OF ASSISTANT FROM LONG BASKET
IS ALSO EXPLAINED.

the top of the table and draws in the false head. He thrusts his own head through in its place. The trap is designed to open and close in the shape of an enlarging circle, so that it finally fits tightly around the neck of the real man.

It is this head which performs various actions and accuses the magician. When his head is covered with the cloth, the man goes back into the table. The cloth retains the shape of the head. In the meantime, the "decapitated" assistant has escaped from the basket. The basket rests directly in front of a stage trap. The back of the basket falls flat and the man rolls through and goes down the trap. The original prisoner comes up through the trap and takes his place.

The basket is lifted by the assistants. It is turned so that the cover opens toward the audience. While the assistants hold the basket, the magician opens it and thrusts the cloth inside, stowing it at the end of the basket. He has apparently placed the head with the body. The basket may be set on the stage or rested upon the table at the left; in either event, it opens immediately and the original prisoner makes his appearance, safe and sound.

There are suggested variations to this routine that are worthy of consideration. The table at the left may be constructed on the bellows principle—namely, a table with a double top, the lower part dropping when released and retained by the upper with the aid of heavy straps or strong cloth.

With a table of this type, the third prisoner is not needed. After the guillotining, the magician goes to the table and removes the large cloth that covers it, to show that the table has a comparatively thin top. In covering the table with its large cloth, the magician drapes the cloth from the front, letting the cloth cover the space between the stage and the table. The original prisoner comes up through a trap and releases the bellows, taking his place within the table. Then the cloth is carefully arranged on the table. The cloth has a slit portion that goes over the trap in the table top.

It is still necessary for the original assistant to get into the basket which contained the body. The most convenient plan is to bring the basket over to the table, empty. When it is set on the table, a trap opens in the table top behind the basket and the original prisoner takes his place in the basket.

Another plan is to have the table fitted with mirrors or a cloth that matches the scenery behind it. This enables the prisoner to come and go through the trap as he pleases. He puts his head up through the table. When he withdraws his head, he drops through the trap and comes up through the trap by the guillotine, before the basket is lifted by the jailers.

In the author's opinion, the original routine given in this description is the best, as it avoids complications. Since a dummy head must pass for the real head of the victim, the stage cannot be fully lighted; and the head of a third person can easily be made up to pass for that of the original prisoner. The dramatic sequence of the act is intriguing and helps to create the necessary illusions.

THE TORTURE PILLORY

THE torture pillory is an excellent escape trick, which may be recommended for its ease of operation as well as for its effectiveness. The plans for this apparatus were given to Houdini and were contained in his notes.

The pillory is mounted on an upright rod or pedestal. It consists of three frames joined together. Each frame opens on a hinge. The escape artist places his wrists in the end holes and his neck in the center. The upper sections are closed. They are locked with padlocks, which may be supplied by the audience.

Despite the fact that the pillory has stood a brief examination by a committee from the audience, the escapist leaves it very quickly after it has been covered by a cabinet. The pillory is shown again, with all the locks in place and no trace of any trickery.

The diagrams reveal the secret of the pillory. Each frame opens two ways—either by the hinges, as the spectators know, or by sliding upward. The brass strips at the side of each frame are really grooves into which the upper portions fit. The brass strips at the top are not connected with the strips at the sides, although they fit so closely that they appear to be tightly joined.

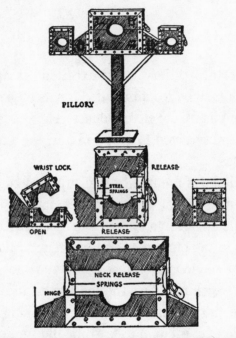

PILLORY

WRIST LOCK

RELEASE

STEEL SPRINGS

OPEN

RELEASE

RELEASE

NECK RELEASE

SPRINGS

HINGE

THE PILLORY AND DETAILS OF ITS CONSTRUCTION.

In order that the pillory may stand a reasonable amount of inspection, the grooves at the sides of the frame are fitted with curved springs. The upper portions of the frames press against the springs and virtually lock in place. The escape artist effects his release by exerting pressure in an upward direction.

He is in an excellent position to raise his head and force out the frame which binds his neck. He then attends to the frames that hold his wrists. Following his escape, he pushes the frames back into position, so that they are clamped between the springs.

This is an excellent pillory escape, as it is sure and simple in operation. Most escapes of this type depend upon some trickery in the locks or the hinges. Those are the parts that the committee is sure to examine. The very ingenuity of this device is the important point that prevents the examiners from discovering the secret.

A MILK-BOTTLE ESCAPE

THE milk bottle used in this mystery is an unusual one. It is of huge size, large enough to contain the magician, with room to spare. A committee from the audience inspects the bottle. No trickery is discovered. A glass top with a glass flange is also examined. Like the bottle, this shows no trick. The bottle has four holes in the collar and there are corresponding holes in the flange of the cover; but these stand minute inspection.

Their purpose becomes evident when the magician enters the bottle. The cover is placed in position and two glass rods are thrust through the holes. These rods are solid glass; like the bottle and its cover, they have been subjected to close examination. There are holes in the ends of the rods, into which padlocks are inserted by the committee. This imprisons the performer in the glass bottle. He has no way of reaching the padlocks.

The customary cabinet used in escape work is now placed over the bottle. The audience waits for a few

THE PERFORMER ESCAPES FROM THE GIANT MILK BOTTLE BY
BREAKING THE GLASS RODS AND REPLACING THEM WITH NEW ONES.

minutes. The magician appears from the cabinet. The
curtains are raised and the bottle is found intact, with
the locks still attached to the ends of the glass rods.

This is a very effective escape, since the all-glass construction of the apparatus precludes any traps or mechanical arrangements. It also enables the committee to make a quick examination before and after the demonstration, while the fact that the magician is visible when confined also impresses the audience.

The secret is a simple one—another point in favor of the escape. There is little chance of the magician's encountering difficulty. The glass rods are obviously unfaked, although each is scored with ornamental rings, or circles, cut in its surface. These excite no suspicion, as it would be impossible to unscrew a glass rod in the center. Nevertheless, the rings aid the magician. As soon as the cabinet is lowered, he strikes the glass rods with a solid object and they obligingly break in half.

The broken rods are pushed from the holes. The stage is covered with a thick cloth to prevent the broken rods from shattering. The magician lifts the lid of the bottle. He emerges and replaces the cover. The padlocks on the broken rods have been supplied by the magician. He unlocks them with duplicate keys. He produces two duplicate rods, which are concealed under his coat or in the curtains of the cabinet. He puts these through the holes and locks them with the padlocks. Then he hides the broken glass rods and opens the curtains to make his bow to the audience.

PART ELEVEN.

ANTISPIRITUALISTIC EFFECTS

HOUDINI, in his campaign against fraudulent mediums, designed a number of large tricks that would enable him to duplicate the feats of ghost-makers on the stage. They are patterned after the so-called wonders of spookdom, but are planned for presentation in a spectacular way.

A SPIRIT CABINET

THIS is a very mysterious act. It is a duplication of the celebrated séances in which spirit mediums cause articles to materialize. It is produced on the stage under the most exacting conditions.

First, the performer is searched. He is tied and taken to a cabinet. The cabinet is of the simplest construction. It is nothing but a floor with solid, upright posts. It has curtains, which are thoroughly examined. A committee surrounds the cabinet while the performer is seated on a chair within. The curtains are closed. Then manifestations take place. Faces and hands appear through the cabinet curtains. Finally flowers are thrust forth. They come in increasing quantities. When the curtains are opened, the performer is sitting in the chair, still bound.

Most of these manifestations can be performed without the necessity of escaping from the ropes. There are, however, many ways of loosening ropes and getting back into them, if this plan is deemed necessary. The real mystery, however, is the appearance of the faces and other spooky forms, while the production of the flowers is most amazing.

Yet the answer to these manifestations is a simple one. The cabinet has one peculiarity of construction that will invariably escape notice. Its platform is mounted on four round, metal legs. These elevate the platform from the stage. One of the legs is hollow. It appears to be solid because it has a metal core which fits very tightly. These legs are within the range of the curtains. As soon as the curtains are closed, an assistant below stage pulls down the core of the hollow leg. This leaves an opening through which the required objects are pushed up for the performer's use.

The spirit hands and faces—even complete spirit forms—are simply articles made of silk or rubber that can be inflated. They are covered with luminous paint. They are supplied as needed; when the performer is through with them, he sends them back through the leg of the platform. The flowers are pushed up while the performer is going through various manifestations. He ends his demonstration by pushing the flowers into view. The quantity of the flowers is limited only by the time which the performer intends to give to the manifestations.

When the cabinet is opened and the performer is released, a complete inspection can be made in con-

FLOWERS THAT MATERIALIZE IN AN EMPTY CABINET ARE PUSHED
UP THROUGH A HOLLOW TABLE LEG, FROM BENEATH STAGE.

clusion. The assistant under the stage has pushed the metal core back into the hollow leg. All the legs appear to be quite solid and they are the one part of the cabinet which the average committee will ignore. This is an excellent spirit trick, as it reproduces various phenomena which many mediums claim they produce by psychic means.

THE SPIRIT KNOTS

ONE type of physical phenomena frequently demonstrated by fraudulent mediums is the production of knots in the center of a cord or other pliable object. It was a test of this type that convinced Professor Zoellner that Slade, the medium, had fourth-dimensional powers. Knot-tying tricks are always effective; and when they seem to be accomplished by a spirit force, they are doubly perplexing.

This knot trick is intended for use in connection with cabinet manifestations—the magician demonstrating that he can duplicate the most remarkable feats of mediums. It can also be done without the cabinet by plunging the stage into absolute darkness. The second plan should prove more workable, as the trick is accomplished very quickly when there is plenty of space available.

The magician uses a piece of clothes-line about twenty-five feet in length. It is stretched out; then the center is loosely coiled so that the ends will be close together. Two assistants stand near each other and one end of the rope is tied to the wrists of the first man, the other end to the wrists of the second man. The investigating committee is satisfied that all is fair. The knots on the wrists can be sealed if desired.

Then comes darkness. If the men are in a large cabinet, the curtain is drawn; if they are on the stage, the lights are extinguished. In either case, strange results occur. When the men are again seen, a few moments later, they are instructed to walk apart, and to the amazement of every one, the rope between the men is tied in several genuine knots! This has been accomplished without any disconnection of the ends of the rope from the men's wrists. The seals are unbroken. The single knots along the rope can be thoroughly examined. Everything stands close examination.

The method is a good one. It will be recalled that the magician coils the center of the rope. There is absolutely no trickery about that action; in fact, the coils can be made after the men are tied to the ends of the rope. But when he wants knots, the magician simply lifts the coils all together, gives them a twist and drops them over the head and shoulders of one of the men. When the coils reach the floor, the man is told to step forward. When the men move apart, the coils become knots.

If the performer's own assistant is at one end of the rope, this can be done quickly, with no chance of detection. The assistant steps out of the coils as soon as they strike the floor. The trick can be performed with a volunteer, but it will require bold and artful work on the part of the magician. He must be sure that the coils are large. In dropping them over the man's head, he must pretend to be simply gripping the man's shoulders while he instructs him to move a little further away.

The trained assistant is better, as he will respond quickly and will be sure to step free of the coils. He can come on the stage as a member of the committee. Any one may tie the knots on his wrists and thus the committee will be convinced that all is fair. The man at the other end of the rope has no chance of discovering what is taking place.

THE VANISHING CHAIR

THIS is a comedy trick that may be used as a pseudopsychic trick. The outcome is both surprising and laughable. The magician shows a small platform with a tent hung above it. He calls attention to the cloth-covered chair that is on the platform. He states that he will seat himself in the chair and produce some strange results while a member of the audience is with him.

Having procured a volunteer, the performer allows his hands to be tied behind his back with a length of cord behind them. He stands in front of the chair and the volunteer stands beside him. The performer is just sitting down in the chair when an assistant lowers the tent. Immediately a loud argument begins within the tent. Finally the performer demands that the tent be raised. He is standing, still bound, beside the committeeman; but the chair is no longer on the platform. The magician accuses his companion of having purloined the chair. The man denies any such action. the tent is shaken and searched. The magician looks everywhere. Yet he can find no trace of the missing chair.

The reason is that the chair is not nearly so solid an object as it appears to be. It is nothing more than four narrow boards; two long ones and two short ones. The long ones are set at the rear to represent the back. The short ones are at the front. The cloth covering gives the semblance of a solid chair. The

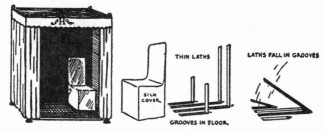

DETAILS OF THE VANISHING CHAIR.

magician does not actually sit in the chair at any time.

The boards of which the chair is formed are portions of the floor of the cabinet. They are hinged and weighted to drop flat on the floor, filling empty spaces. The magician removes the cloth cover by stepping to the back of the chair after the tent has been lowered. His hands are behind his back; he stuffs the cloth cover under the back of his coat. The cloth is quite light and flimsy; it is tucked away very quickly. The release of the cloth causes the upright boards to drop into place. In a very few seconds, the magician gets rid of the supposed chair while he keeps up a running fire of loud argument with his companion.

When the tent is raised, the volunteer is more surprised than the audience to see that the chair is missing. He is unable to answer the magician's accusations and this adds to the fun. It is a very effective spook demonstration.

This trick gives the performer an excellent opportunity to produce all sorts of articles from the volunteer's coat. This leads to further comedy. The magician can accuse the man of having the chair hidden somewhere. He demands the right to search his companion and takes that opportunity to "load" various articles into the man's pockets. This is a familiar form of comedy magic and it is made doubly effective as an aftereffect to the surprising vanish of a chair.

SPIRIT PHOTOGRAPHY

S PIRIT photography has caused much interest in psychic circles. Many trick methods of obtain‧ing spirit photographs have been exposed. A spirit photograph is one in which the person's picture is surrounded by dim, hazy faces, which are termed "extras."

This is a stage demonstration of spirit photography. The person presenting the act agrees to produce a spirit photograph, using a subject from the audience. Any volunteer is used. The picture will be taken and developed on the stage.

A committee of six comes to the stage. Three are seated in chairs on each side. On the right is a powerful light above the center chair. The man whose picture is to be taken is seated in that chair. The camera is set up. The photograph is snapped.

The plate is taken into a cabinet at the left of the stage. The cabinet is provided with a developing bench and a pan that contains the necessary bath for the plate. The performer has requested a photographer to join the committee. This man goes into the cabinet. The plate is laid upon a shelf at the front of the developing bench. Other committee members are invited to enter the cabinet to assist in the development of the photograph. The curtain is closed.

Meanwhile the performer shows various cards which bear the printed names of famous persons. These are laid face down on a tray. Members of the committee decide upon one of the cards. They take it from the tray and read the name aloud.

During the interim while the photograph is being developed, the performer presents other phenomena in a cabinet on the center of the stage. This can be a spirit cabinet of the type described in this section of the book. After the manifestations, the committee members emerge from the developing cabinet bringing with them the finished photograph. Upon the picture appears the dim face of the famous person selected. The spirit form is gazing over the shoulder of the man in the photograph.

The subject who is photographed is a confederate of the performer. He is the only "plant" in the committee. He is one of the first to come upon the stage. The performer naturally selects him as a good subject. From then on, he plays a passive part. He simply poses for a direct picture from the camera.

His picture has been taken beforehand, on a plate

Top, SETTING FOR THE SPIRIT PHOTOGRAPHY ACT. THE LOWER
DIAGRAMS SHOW THE GIRL CONCEALED IN THE PHOTO CABI-
NET; ALSO HOW SHE SWITCHES THE PLATES. THE TRAY FOR
CHANGING THE CARDS IS ILLUSTRATED. NOTE ITS SLIDING FLAP.

prepared with the ghostly image of some famous person. The developing cabinet has a secret compartment in the side. This compartment tapers from the front. Its presence is not suspected. At its widest point —near the back—a small girl is concealed. She has the prepared plate in her possession.

When the performer enters the cabinet, he lays the unprepared plate upon the shelf in front of the developing bench. He stands in front of it momentarily while he calls for the people who are to develop the plate. The girl reaches through the curtained side of the cabinet and substitutes the prepared plate for the unprepared one. This exchange can be made later, if desired. The plate may be put on the shelf and the curtain drawn part way just as the committee is about to enter. This will hide the exchange. In either case, the innocent appearance of the cabinet is of great advantage and the exchange can be accomplished without detection.

The name of a famous person is forced upon the committee. In order to accomplish this, the performer utilizes a special tray. The tray is covered with a loose cloth, which may be drawn to one end. Under the double folds of the cloth are cards that bear only one name—that of the famous person whose dim picture is on the prepared plate. The genuine cards, which are examined by the committee, are placed on the tray. They are pushed to the end away from the hidden cards. The performer carries the tray across the stage and takes that opportunity to move the slide from one end of the tray to the other. This draws the loose cloth over the varied cards and exposes the set of cards that are all alike. No matter which card is selected, the desired name will be the one read. That name, incidentally, is not among the varied cards, which have too many names to be remembered. So the performer can draw back the slide to expose the original cards and then deliver the cards from the tray into the hands of the committee. This allows examination before and after the choice of the name.

The working of the tray is illustrated in the drawings which accompany the diagrams of the stage setting and the developing cabinet.

A MATERIALIZING CABINET

THIS idea of Houdini's involves a small cabinet in which mysterious manifestations can be produced. It is intended as a stage effect of pseudopsychic nature.

The cabinet is mounted on legs and forms a three-walled box. In place of an ordinary door or curtain, it has a front that slides up and down, so that at any time the interior of the cabinet can be revealed.

The slide—to which Houdini refers as a "half-door"—is removed when the cabinet is shown. The slide is exhibited on both sides. It is put back in place. The cabinet is turned around to reveal all sides.

Then the usual manifestations take place. Bells ring; objects are thrown through the open top of the cabinet. The slide is raised and a chair falls out. Any object placed in the cabinet seems to come into the power of unseen hands. It is also possible to "materialize" a ghostlike form within the cabinet.

The manifestations are performed by a boy concealed within the cabinet. The sliding front has a

THE DOOR IS TAKEN FROM THE SMALL CURTAINED CABINET. WHEN IT IS REPLACED, MANIFESTATIONS FOLLOW. NOTE HOW THE BOY ENTERS FROM BEHIND THE CURTAINS. HE RISES WITH THE DOOR, THANKS TO THE SPECIAL LEDGE WHICH HE RELEASES. NOTE THE WEIGHTS FOR RAISING AND LOWERING THE DOOR WITHOUT SUSPICION.

folding shelf, which is not observable when the door is exhibited by itself. At the outset, the boy is behind the cabinet on a projecting ledge. When the front is put in position, the boy enters through the rear of the cabinet. He pulls down the shelf and takes his position behind the sliding front.

The performer releases the front and raises it. This is very deceptive, as the slide is controlled by a counterweight which offsets the weight of the boy. It goes up and down without great effort on the part of the performer. After showing the inside clear, the performer lowers the slide. The cabinet can be wheeled around if desired.

The boy takes care of any objects that are placed in the cabinet. He beats tambourines and rings bells. He sets a chair against the front so that it will topple when the slide is raised. He may don a luminous costume and appear as a ghost through the top of the cabinet or in the cabinet itself while the slide is raised and the stage is in semidarkness.

After each series of manifestations, the slide is quickly raised in an effort to catch the pretended ghosts; and on each occasion the cabinet is seen to be quite empty.

Houdini classed this cabinet as a practical method for duplicating the phenomena of pretended mediums, on a lighted stage.

SOME MEDIUMISTIC EFFECTS

THESE are brief notations of tricks which can be worked in connection with a séance, by a magician who is producing psychic effects to prove that spirit phenomena can be demonstrated by natural means.

One is a small luminous light which floats about in a most mysterious fashion while the magician's hands are securely held. This is simply a large-headed thumb tack, which is coated with luminous paint and previously placed on the sole of the shoe. The foot is raised and moved about so that the light can be seen.

The second is a development of the same idea. In this instance, a small face appears and moves about among the surprised sitters. The performer uses a sock which is pink in color. It is coated with luminous paint and made to represent a face. The performer simply slips his foot from his shoe and moves it about, replacing the foot in the loose shoe after the "materialization."

The third effect is that of spirit hands that surprise the sitters with their cold and clammy touch. In this trick, the performer must free his hands. He has a rubber bag available; the bag is filled with ice. By putting his hands in it, the performer makes them cold and they are capable of producing a weird sensation when they touch the faces of the sitters.

A GREAT CABINET ACT

THIS routine is performed with an ordinary cabinet of the simplest construction. It is built up on the stage and is surrounded by a committee. The person who plays the part of the medium is searched in the cabinet. Nevertheless, unusual manifestations take place under the direction of the performer, who is on the stage. These particular manifestations can be best described by explaining them.

When the medium is seated in the cabinet, he appears to be in a trance. The performer waits until the medium has gained this condition, aided by a few supposedly hypnotic passes on the part of the performer. Then the performer closes the curtain. At this point, the medium secretly obtains a small bundle from beneath the performer's coat. The bundle contains a long piece of rope, a red silk handkerchief, a plain white handkerchief, and a quantity of envelopes.

The passing of the bundle is by no means difficult. The performer can close the curtain from the inside of the cabinet, keeping constantly in view at the edge of the curtain and stepping out just before he completes the closing of the curtain. With this procedure, the medium simply takes the bundle from the back of the performer's coat, under cover of the curtain. Another method is to close the curtain from the outside of the cabinet. The performer stops at the end to hook the corner of the curtain carefully on the horizontal rod of the cabinet.

This gives the medium ample opportunity to reach around the edge of the curtain and steal the bundle from the front of the performer's coat. The performer is naturally facing the cabinet and he takes care to be right against the curtain. Whichever method is employed, the result is the same. The medium is supplied with the articles that are needed.

Now the performer exhibits a rope that is a duplicate of the one smuggled to the medium. He instructs the committee to tie it in a certain number of knots. The performer supervises this operation. Meanwhile the medium is busy tying himself with the duplicate rope. The performer takes the rope which the committee has tied and holds it above the cabinet. He drops in the rope. The medium catches it coiled and thrusts it under his coat. The performer immediately throws open the curtain. The medium is seen to be tied in the knots on the rope—apparently the very knots made by the committee!

The committee examines the medium and makes sure that he has been securely bound by "spirit" aid. If desired, the knots can be tightened. The curtain is closed. Horns and tambourines are dropped in the cabinet. The horns are blown, the tambourines are drummed. The curtains are opened to show the medium still tied. This is due to the fact that the medium is tied by any one of the many rope ties which permit quick release and reëntry into the knots. Ties of this type are too well known to warrant extensive description, as the real novelties of this act are to follow.

The performer closes the curtain and shows the red silk handkerchief. He reaches through the curtain and holds the handkerchief within the cabinet for about one second. He brings out the handkerchief. It is tied in knots. This is because the medium has released himself and has tied the duplicate red silk in knots. He simply takes the original silk from the performer's hand and places the duplicate there.

Now comes a very clever test. The performer borrows an ordinary white handkerchief. Various members of the committee identify it. The performer starts to place it in the cabinet. The instant his hand is within the curtain, the medium substitutes the duplicate handkerchief, which appears to be the same. The performer quickly withdraws his hand, holding the handkerchief, and requests the committee to decide upon an exact number of knots. This is settled. While the performer talks about the remarkable things that will occur, the medium quickly ties the original handkerchief in the required number of knots. The performer puts the duplicate handkerchief into the cabinet, immediately receives the original, brings it out, and gives it to the owner.

Now the performer borrows a business card and inserts it in a large envelope. He seals the envelope and starts to place it in the cabinet. He withdraws it to show that it is really sealed and he asks the committee to name any number of envelopes up to a certain number—say ten. The performer then carries the envelope to the cabinet and inserts it. A few seconds later he brings it out. It is opened by the committee. Another envelope is discovered within. Still another envelope and so on, until, when the required number of envelopes have been discovered, the card is found in the last one.

This is due to quick work on the part of the medium. The envelopes which he took from the performer early in the séance are nested. He also has a duplicate large envelope, sealed with a card inside. As the envelope with the borrowed card comes through the curtain, the medium substitutes the duplicate. He tears open the original envelope. He hears the number of envelopes called for and arranges the nest accordingly, by removing any center envelopes that are not required. The performer takes his time outside the cabinet while the medium seals the card in the number of envelopes desired. Then comes another switch while the envelope in the performer's hand is held inside the curtain.

The act may be concluded by any further manifestations, such as the release of the medium. The notes suggest the use of a committeeman in the cabinet, this member of the audience emerging with his face blackened and his coat turned inside out. It is preferable to have a confederate in the committee for this type of work. All articles dropped into the cabinet are concealed by the medium, either beneath his coat or somewhere in the curtains of the cabinet.

PART TWELVE.

NOTES ON KELLAR

THE material in this section has been selected from Houdini's notes that were direct references to the methods and experiences of Harry Kellar, who for years was recognized as America's greatest magician.

NOTES ON KELLAR

HOUDINI's notes on Kellar were compiled in 1916 and 1917. They were based on conversations between Houdini and Kellar and they are, accordingly, of unusual interest. They are given here very much as Houdini prepared them. In the notes, the comments appeared in typewritten form. Certain observations have been omitted, as they were obviously private statements that were not intended for publication. These were chiefly remarks concerning Kellar's experiences in connection with magic.

KELLAR'S ROPE TIE

Readers will be interested in Houdini's verbatim description of Kellar's performance of his famous "rope tie" as witnessed by Houdini. It is dated November 12, 1917, and reads as follows:

"Having been honored by Harry Kellar to assist him on his farewell appearance before the public and as he had instructed me in his rope tie, it was my great fortune to watch him in real action.

"In his start he has two men tie his left hand, slowly and deliberately. The knot is on the front of the wrist and is tied way down into the flesh, so tight that the cord is on a level with the flesh. Kellar stands there a few seconds, slowly calling attention to the knots which he has had two men tie; then asks two more to help and the way they yank each other around creates a good-natured impression. I think his idea is to get the committee good-natured, which they actually become.

"In fact, he slowly walks to the men and says: 'Put your fingers on the rope and you will see that the rope is way into the flesh.' He goes to all of them; then, when he places his hands behind his back, he does the rope steal behind his palms. The psychology is to work slowly and deliberately, as open and above board as possible.

"Kellar stood in the center for a moment, his tied left hand extended showing the knots. Then he slowly says, 'I will want the right hand tied behind my back, right up against the knot, in this fashion.' He places the right wrist on top of the knot, showing just how it will look. While he is turning around, he places his hands behind his back, gets the proper position and slack and has two men tie same.

"They tie a number of knots and in his hands I never saw a better manipulation, nor do I believe any man ever lived who could do the knots as well."

In another note, Houdini gives this description of the method used in the Kellar rope tie:

"The idea is to have the rope fastened, so that when you help tie the knot or when the committee pulls the ropes, one end is actually pulled in the palm of your hand. In this way your fingers steal enough slack so that when the second hand is tied, it rests against the wrist and enables you to keep the slack until required."

This bears out the recognized principle of the Kellar rope tie, which many magicians have imitated. The rope is first tied about the left wrist. Slack is gained while the back of the right wrist is pressed against the knots on the front of the left wrist. This action takes place while the hands are going behind the performer's back. The slack must be retained while the ends of the rope are tied in front of the right wrist. It requires considerable strength. Kellar was so successful with this trick that he could release his right hand and replace it almost instantly, showing the hands still firmly tied.

THE CABINET TIE

Here are Houdini's instructions for the rope tie in connection with a cabinet. They are marked: "Harry

Kellar's Instructions, September 1, 1916." They are recorded with slight changes:

"First you call for a committee. You are tied. The Kellar rope tie. There are three chairs in the cabinet. The middle chair faces the audience; the other two chairs face each other. Bells and tambourines are on a chair. The ends of the rope are put through holes in the chair, about five inches apart in the back part of the seat. Kellar is tied at the left side of audience, right side of cabinet. The assistant takes a large silk handkerchief which is several sizes too large for Kellar. He poises it on Kellar's head so it will not fall. A committee-man is asked to close the door in front of Kellar and to fasten the little hook on the bottom. There is no hook. While he looks for it, Kellar jams the hat over the committee-man's eyes.

"The door is immediately opened; next time it starts to close, Kellar grabs the tambourine and throws it up in the air. The door is immediately opened. Kellar is seen tied. Both doors are closed. The opposite door is opened and quickly closed to show Kellar; then the first door is opened quickly to show Kellar still tied.[1]

"The doors are closed. Bells ring. Spirit hands appear (through an opening in the upper portion of

---

[1] This and subsequent effects show that Kellar used a complete release of both wrists. The slack obtained by the removal of the right hand naturally made it possible to release the left.

the door). A brass ring is handed through the window (in the door) and the door is opened. The brass ring has gone up Kellar's right arm. He is still tied. The doors are closed after Kellar states he will perform the feat of releasing himself which the Davenport Brothers claimed was done by spirits. He comes from the cabinet with the rope in his hand. Kellar walks down with the rope coiled in his hand and says that he will now perform the Davenport feat of retying himself. He enters the cabinet and does a 'self tie.' He is examined to see that all is well.

"When doors close, Kellar cries 'Door' and the door is thrown open as Kellar's coat comes flying out. Kellar's hands are examined and found still tied. A gentleman's coat is placed in the cabinet. The door is closed. Almost instantly the door is opened and Kellar is found with committee-man's coat on his back, with hands still tied.

"Kellar's coat is on the chair, the committee-man's coat is on Kellar's back. Kellar says he will hand the coat through the door and challenges the committee-man to put on the coat before Kellar puts on his own coat—after he has taken committee-man's coat off. The door is closed. Almost instantly the committee-man's coat flies through the door. One sleeve is turned inside out. Before he can realize the condition, the door is again opened and Kellar is found with his own on; he is tied in the same manner as when first examined.

"The committee-man is now asked to go into the cabinet with Kellar. He takes a seat on the chair facing Kellar. He is requested to put his hands on Kellar's knees to see that he does not move. The doors are closed and instantly great commotion takes place. The doors fly open. The committee-man rushes out with hair disarranged and rushes to his seat in an excited manner. The doors close. Instantly Kellar walks out to the center of the stage with the rope uncoiled and bows."

While this description is somewhat lacking in certain details, it gives a good idea of the numerous possibilities of the rope-tie act as performed with the cabinet. The cabinet is patterned after the one used by the famous Davenport brothers, who claimed spirit aid in their performances. The curtained windows in the center of each door aid in the ejection of various articles.

Houdini's notes add: "Kellar takes the committee-man in his confidence. He tells him to run around the cabinet yelling, etc. He has never had a man refuse to assist him."

He also states: "Kellar would have all kinds and thicknesses of rope, so when any stranger would bring rope, he would be prepared to cut same and his assistant would bring a tambourine in which would be the duplicate rope. I suppose it would be a good idea to have a double tambourine, with a skin on both sides to hide the duplicate rope.

"Kellar's hands and wrists are very powerful and he can do this trick with great dexterity. He has performed it forty-seven years."

KELLAR'S COMMITTEE CABINET

Among notations given him by Kellar, Houdini gives a brief description of a special spirit cabinet which Kellar designed for test seances and used on certain occasions. A committee was brought on the stage and an examined cloth was laid in the center of the stage. A walled cabinet was then constructed and the committee formed a circle about it.

After the stage was plunged in darkness, manifestations commenced. The stage was occasionally lighted dimly, so that objects could be seen as they were tossed from the top of the cabinet; but for the materialization of ghostly forms, complete darkness was used. After the seance, the cabinet was taken to pieces and a second examination revealed no traces of the cause of the manifestations.

As in other forms of the cabinet trick, a concealed assistant was used to produce the pretended phenomena. The entrance and exit of the assistant was accomplished by a simple artifice. He was concealed in the flies—the scenery above the stage—and as soon as the lights were extinguished, the assistant was lowered by a cable into the open-topped cabinet. He brought with him the articles necessary for the materializations. The assistant was drawn up to his hiding place while the stage was again darkened and the examination of the cabinet took place shortly afterward, after the performer had called for lights.

NOTES ON SUSPENSION

A note dated October 29, 1917, is very interesting. It reads as follows:

"Harry Kellar told me last night and, I remember, he has often related to me that Maskelyne laughed at De Kolta because of a suspension trick that De Kolta had in mind. Yet I believe that it was through this that Maskelyne eventually invented his suspension.

"De Kolta was going to get thousands of long human hairs, knot them together and tie small weights to the ends; then put them over the branches of a tree in Central Park and perform a suspension in mid-air in the open."

Houdini also mentions a suspension trick which Kellar said was sold to him by the originator. The man performed the trick on a small scale. He raised a dummy figure in the air and walked all around it. The secret was a very thin piece of glass which extended straight upward. The figure was set upon the glass and the glass was so thin that the edges could not be seen. The secret proved to be of no value to Kellar, as it was impractical for the levitation of a human being.

A KELLAR REMINISCENCE

The following story was told by Kellar to Houdini; it was Kellar's account of an experience that he had in the year 1879. Houdini wrote a brief description of it, dated September, 1916. The story is remarkably interesting as an important event in Kellar's early career. It also is typical of the many anecdotes related by one great magician to another, when they talked of their past adventures.

During Christmas week in 1879, Kellar was appearing in Edinburgh, Scotland. He had hired the Waverly Theatre from the owner, Baillie Cranston. Kellar was booked to play in Dundee the week following. He had encountered a series of misfortunes and these reached a climax in Edinburgh. His principal assistant was taken ill and Kellar had no one to fill the man's place.

He explained matters to Baillie Cranston and the theater-owner asked if his son Robert would do as an assistant. This pleased Kellar immensely, as he was not anxious to hire a stranger in his work. He knew that young Cranston would keep secret anything he learned; so he instructed Robert in the work required and the young man proved to be a capable assistant.

Business was bad that week. On Saturday, Kellar went to see Baillie Cranston. He owed the theater-owner forty pounds and mentioned the fact. Baillie Cranston had not forgotten it. He expected the money.

"Well," said Kellar, "I wish you would trust me with that forty pounds, Mr. Cranston. Furthermore, I would also appreciate it if you would let me have forty pounds in addition, so that I may take my company to Dundee, where I have a certain engagement with Cook's Circus."

Baillie Cranston was too dumfounded to reply. He had expected Kellar to pay the money that was owing; this proposal that he should double the debt was something he had not anticipated. He made no effort to restrain his astonishment. He finally turned to his son, who was present, and said:

"Robert, what nerve this man has! He owes me forty pounds and instead of paying it, he has the impudence to ask me for another forty!"

"Well, father," replied Robert, "if I had the

money, I would be willing to lend Mr. Kellar one hundred pounds. I am sure he would pay it back."

The theater-owner was even more astonished at his son's statement.

"You seem to know Mr. Kellar very well," he said to his son.

"I have known him only during this engagement," returned Robert Cranston. "Nevertheless, Mr. Kellar does not appear to me to be a man who would not repay a friend."

Baillie Cranston was thoughtful. He was impressed by his son's confidence in Kellar.

"Very well," he said, "if you would trust him with one hundred pounds, I'll trust him with eighty. You can have forty pounds, Mr. Kellar, and pay it back to me with the other money that you already owe."

Kellar received the forty pounds. The next day was Sunday. In the morning, Kellar went to the railway station. He bought tickets for his entire company and checked all the baggage to Dundee. All the members of his company gave up their rooms. Everything was packed and ready for the trip. While returning from the station, Kellar encountered Robert Cranston and told the young man that he was leaving for Dundee on the next train. Robert Cranston looked at him steadily and said:

"Mr. Kellar, my father has been very kind to you

and I feel that you should appreciate his kindness."

"I do appreciate it!" exclaimed Kellar. "I have promised to repay my debt to him as soon as possible—"

"It is not a matter of money," interrupted the young man. "It would greatly displease my father if he knew that you were traveling on the Sabbath. If you really want to please him, I would advise vou to remain until the morning."

It was Kellar's turn to be astonished. He expostulated with young Cranston. He explained that he needed to get to Dundee as soon as possible and added that he had bought all the tickets and had checked the baggage. Nevertheless, Robert remained firm in his opinion. At last Kellar realized that it was his duty to please the theater-owner who had loaned him the money. Even though he did not agree with Baillie Cranston's scruples in regard to traveling on Sunday, it would be an act of courtesy and appreciation to conform to his benefactor's ideas.

Robert Cranston said that he would fix everything. He went to the station and made all the necessary arrangements. He had the tickets changed to the next day. He gave orders to hold the baggage until Monday. The members of the company arrived just after these matters had been completed. They registered a complaint to Kellar. They were packed and had given up their rooms. They saw no reason for remaining in Edinburgh. But Kellar had now become as obdurate as Robert Cranston. The company was forced to find new lodgings. Robert Cranston invited Kellar to spend the evening at his home, which Kellar did. Baillie Cranston was pleased because Kellar had made the decision not to travel on the Sabbath.

The next morning, Kellar overslept. When he arose, he went to breakfast, and while he was eating read a newspaper. Large headlines told of a terrible tragedy. The bridge over the Tay River had weakened during the height of a great gale. The central section had given away while a train was passing over it. The train and all its passengers had been precipitated into the waters below and not a single person had survived. It was on that very train that Kellar and his company had arranged their passage to Dundee.

Robert Cranston eventually became Lord Cranston. Some years later, when Kellar was performing in his Egyptian Hall in Philadelphia, Cranston visited him and reminded him that he was the man who had saved Kellar's life.

CONCLUSION

IN SUMMARIZING this collection of Houdini's notes on magic, the author wishes to remind the reader that every item in the book has been taken directly from Houdini's own material. The tricks and illusions explained in this volume represent merely a selected portion of those which Houdini planned for publication.

Houdini used, built, and described various tricks which were not contained in his notes; but it is an evident fact that the only secrets of magic which can be authentically presented in connection with Houdini's name are those which formed a part of his own collection of original notes.

The subject of magic is so broad that it would not require great ingenuity to prepare a book on magic that included some of Houdini's methods and label it with Houdini's name. Articles have appeared in various magazines and other publications that have purported to be exposés of Houdini's actual secrets. Except for those which are gleanings from books which Houdini himself wrote, such articles cannot be accepted as genuine Houdini material.

The author alone has had access to Houdini's own notes, and he has chosen to base all his writings on that material. Houdini himself collected and prepared every item which has appeared in these pages, as well as those which appeared in the author's previous book, *Houdini's Escapes*. They have been taken from the only authentic source of information. The author has considered it a privilege to take up the work which Houdini himself intended some day to perform. Hence he has adhered to the actual thoughts that were expressed in the material to which he had access. The original notes remain available. Nothing more need be said.